SELECTED WORKS OF PEARL
JEPHCOTT: SOCIAL ISSUES
AND SOCIAL RESEARCH

Volume 1

THE SOCIAL
BACKGROUND OF
DELINQUENCY

THE SOCIAL BACKGROUND OF DELINQUENCY

University of Nottingham
Rockefeller Research 1952–54

PEARL JEPHCOTT

with
MICHAEL P. CARTER

LONDON AND NEW YORK

This edition first published in 2023
by Routledge
4 Park Square, Milton Park, Abingdon, Oxon OX14 4RN

and by Routledge
605 Third Avenue, New York, NY 10158

Routledge is an imprint of the Taylor & Francis Group, an informa business

© 2023 Josephine Koch

All rights reserved. No part of this book may be reprinted or reproduced or utilised in any form or by any electronic, mechanical, or other means, now known or hereafter invented, including photocopying and recording, or in any information storage or retrieval system, without permission in writing from the publishers.

Trademark notice: Product or corporate names may be trademarks or registered trademarks, and are used only for identification and explanation without intent to infringe.

British Library Cataloguing in Publication Data
A catalogue record for this book is available from the British Library

ISBN: 978-1-032-33020-4 (Set)
ISBN: 978-1-032-37556-4 (Volume 1) (hbk)
ISBN: 978-1-032-37563-2 (Volume 1) (pbk)
ISBN: 978-1-003-34080-5 (Volume 1) (ebk)

DOI: 10.4324/9781003340805

Disclaimer
The publisher has made every effort to trace copyright holders and would welcome correspondence from those they have been unable to trace.

The Social Background of Delinquency
University of Nottingham
Rockefeller Research 1952–54

Director:
Professor W.J.H. Sprott, M.A.

RESEARCH WORKERS

MISS A.P. JEPHCOTT, M.A.

MR. M.P. CARTER, B.A.

DEPARTMENT OF PHILOSOPHY

LONDON AND NEW YORK

Contents

Foreword for 2023	v
Foreword	vii
Introduction	1
I The Object of the Research	2
II The Selected Town – Radby	12
III The Field of Study	52
A Method	52
B Facts relating to the five Delinquency Areas	72
C Pilot Survey	78
D Dyke Street and Gladstone Road – A Comparison	86
E Carnation Street Area and the Knoll Estate. Introduction to the 5-point Scale Range	110
F The 5-point Scale Range of Households	124
IV Conclusions	195
V Appendices	215
A Childrens's Paintings and Writings	216
B Interviewing Schedule	220
C Map of Radby	224

New Foreword

For the last twenty years, I have been championing a return to the work of the sociologist Pearl Jephcott (1900–1980). Despite my not knowing about Jephcott's work before a random encounter with an oblique reference to one of her books, since rediscovering her work, Pearl Jephcott has changed my orientation towards sociology and sociological practice. What started as a side interest transformed, for me, into an academic obsession to uncover as much about Pearl's life and work and a desire to share my findings with others so that they may also benefit from her writings. Born in Alcester, Warwickshire, UK, and following a career in 'girls clubs' after graduation from Aberystwyth University in 1921, Jephcott undertook ground-breaking and innovative, impactful research in the areas of childhood, youth, community, class and gender. It's not only what she wrote, but also how she researched that has become so instructive in highlighting the creative and imaginative possibilities for sociological research work. An originator and an early adopter of many research methods, Pearl Jephcott deserves to be rediscovered and for us all to be more 'like Pearl'.

Following completion of her master's degree, one of the first studies Jephcott worked on was *The Social Background of Delinquency* (1954) at the University of Nottingham. In collaboration with Michael Carter and Professor W. J. H. Sprott, Jephcott wanted to test the hypothesis that within specific working-class areas, different behavioural standards are upheld. As such, delinquency occurs where behaviours differ from 'normally expected standards' (Jephcott and Carter 1954:26). Funded by the US Rockefeller Foundation via a grant of $7,200, the fieldwork was undertaken in 'Radby' (Hucknall, a former mining town in Sutton-in-Ashfield, Nottinghamshire).

Yet why should we read a book from the mid-1950s or revisit the core themes or the arguments that it presents? For me, there are three main reasons. First, *The Social Background of Delinquency* is a lost 'classic'.

vi *New Foreword*

In many respects, it is an unusual book in that only two hundred copies were initially printed and distributed in the UK. It is unclear why the decision was taken to produce the work in this format or who it was that decided to only send the bound volume to a limited number of social science and sociology departments. However, despite the origins of the book and the decisions taken, this approach meant that an essential piece of research examining the social location of delinquency remained hidden from many and limited the potential impact that this work could have had. Second, at the time of 'publication', considering the social location of delinquency, as opposed to the dangerous pathological individual or 'bad seeds', was something of an innovation. Indeed, this research pre-dates the work of many social psychologists in this area, such as Stanley Milgram and Philip Zimbardo. It also appears ahead of similar texts, such as Elias and Scotson's *The Established in the Outsiders*. Yet to peer beyond the official statistics and received commentaries of the time, Pearl Jephcott drew upon the rich tradition of community-based studies where people are understood as being 'dynamically bonded' together, necessitating analysis of whole situations rather than individual circumstances. Third, to achieve this, Pearl Jephcott and Michael Carter immersed themselves in the locale. Not content with a mere survey, the research design was multifaceted and included ethnographic observations, key informant interviews, personal history analyses and 'the playroom method' explicitly designed to ascertain children's views. *The Social Background of Delinquency* is more than a simple study of delinquency. It is a rich, detailed study of a diachronic whole that deserves recognition.

By her death in 1980, Pearl Jephcott had spent considerable time immersed in the field, observing, recording, and reflecting upon what she saw in the social world around her. The result is a legacy of richly detailed, keenly observed social studies that give voice to her respondents and continue speaking to many contemporary debates.

John Goodwin
University of Leicester
October 2022

Foreword

This research project had its inception, in the discussions which took place among the members of a Research sub-committee which had been set up by the Central County Committee for the Prevention of Juvenile Delinquency. The county in question is the one in which "Radby" is situated. Our first idea was to make some case-history studies of boys on probation, but obvious difficulties arose when we reflected on the nature of the relationship between the probation officer and his client. We then turned our minds to what has always seemed to me to be a much more fruitful field of enquiry: the social climate from which so many of our delinquent population come. I had for a long time felt that a disproportionate amount of attention had been paid to what one might call the "pathological aspect" of delinquency. My own delinquent and near-delinquent friends displayed no pathological symptoms whatever; on the contrary they were radiantly "normal". Their standards, however, were in many ways different from my own, and yet seemed quite "natural" in them. We came from different worlds. Would it be possible, I wondered, to get a clearer picture of these different worlds? We had noted, on our delinquency maps, that some areas in the neighbouring towns were more delinquescent than others. Would it be possible by studying such areas, to portray the way of life of their inhabitants? Through the generous aid of the Rockefeller Foundation we were enabled to make an attempt.

I secured the services of Miss Pearl Jephcott, who had already done distinguished research into the activities of adolescents, and Mr. M.P. Carter, a graduate of the University of Nottingham. Their report is entirely their own work. In it they describe how the focus of the research shifted from a comparative study of contrasting streets to a typology of family standards. I need not re-write what they have written, but one point may, perhaps, be made. It is often said of delinquency that "it is all a matter of the family", and in a sense the results of this

viii *Foreword*

research may be held to support such a view, The point I wish to make, however, is that we have been concerned, not so much with the happy or unhappy relations within the family circle, as with the culture of the family, and more particularly with the culture which develops when families of the same type live side by side in the same area. Of course "it is all a matter of the family" because a child is inducted with a culture in the family circle, and the culture he will receive will be determined by the type of family in which he is brought up.

We hope that such pioneer research as this will be followed up by further investigations, more particularly from the delinquent point of view. Our contention is that delinquency from one of our "black" streets is likely to have a different psychological import from that of delinquency in a "white" street, and that "treatment" must differ accordingly if it is to be effective. This can only be verified by a study of the social background of a large number of delinquents, in order to see whether it is true, as we suggest, that some delinquents are so because they have standards which differ from those officially accepted, while other delinquents go astray because of some unusual temperamental characteristics.

In conclusion, we should like to express our gratitude to the Officers of Local Authorities who have helped us, particularly those connected with the Local Education Authorities, the County Planning Department and the County Probation Service, to the Ministers of Religion in "Radby", to the warden and officers of the "Knoll" Community Centre, and to those families in "Radby" who co-operated with us in our enquiry into their way of life.

W.J.H. SPROTT

Introduction

The Research deals with the social climate in which juvenile delinquency crops up time after time. It is not concerned with the kind of delinquency that springs from psychological trouble, nor does it extend its investigation to the criminal underworlds. What it does deal with is "bad" behaviour among people who could be classed as normal members of ordinary English society. In other words, it attempts to explore certain aspects of the sub-cultures within respectable society which appear to breed behaviour that is officially classed as delinquent.

The Research is based on "Radby" (pop. 23,000), a working class town in the Midlands which has a high proportion of miners. A description of Radby is given in Section II. The methods adopted for the Research are stated in Section III. They were based on house to-house interviewing and on participant observation. In Radby it had been noticed (before it was chosen for the Research) that delinquency was concentrated in five, relatively small, areas. These areas are described in Section IIIB. Within each of these areas the Research set out to study a pair of streets, These looked much alike. The people were in similar types of occupation and were of about the same economic level. But while one of the pair was "white" i.e., had almost a delinquency-free record, the other had such a long-standing history of trouble that Radby itself classified it as a "black" street.

A Pilot Survey was undertaken in the first of the five areas (Section IIIC). In the second of the areas a straight comparison was made between one of its black, and one of its white, streets (Section IIID). Then, for reasons given in the text, the comparison between streets was replaced by a comparison between individual households living within the streets of the five chosen areas. Each household was "placed" on a 5-point Scale (Section IIIF). The conclusions drawn from these various comparisons, and their possible bearing on juvenile delinquency in normal, working class areas, are presented in Section IV.

1 The Object of the Research

The belief that juvenile delinquency is an "individual" matter, caused by some psychological idiosyncracy or maladjustment in a particular offender, has been widely held ever since the subject has had serious study. It has come to be accepted that a large number of cases of delinquency can be attributed to such maladjustments. Those postulated by Stott[1] are a case in point. But it is also believed that juvenile delinquency is a subject to which disciplines other than psychology and medicine can make some contribution.

Comprehensive studies such as that of the Gluecks[2] have emphasised the need for an eclectic approach – an approach which recognises the complexity of the problem. Such an approach seeks to analyse delinquency with reference to a comprehensive assessment of various influences such as physical and mental retardment, broken homes, inadequate facilities for leisure-time activities, and so on. Such approaches recognise that various "social factors" – such as overcrowded living conditions – may be operative.

In addition there may be distinguished investigations into the causes of delinquency which place emphasis upon the broad sociological background[3] – such as "the aftermath of war", or, still more broadly, the conditions which the capitalist system embodies.[4] For example, it may be stated that the son of a businessman is trained in the art of becoming a businessman: the object is to gain money, which in

---

1 D.H. Stott : <u>Delinquency and Human Nature,</u> Dunfermline, 1950.
2 S. & E. Glueck : <u>Unraveling Juvenile Delinquency,</u> The Common–wealth Fund, New York, 1950.
3 cf. Durkheim : Chagne Etat de Civilization a sa criminalite propre. <u>Regles de la Methode Sociologique.</u>
4 cf. R.K. Merton : <u>Social Theory and Social Structure,</u> The Free Press, U.S.A., 2nd Printing, Oct. 1951.

The Object of the Research 3

turn secures for him (within the framework of the capitalist system) a sought-after position in society. But a similar path of progress is not open to the "working class man", although the desire to assume a comparable position in society may well be present and encouraged. If the desire to rise is sufficiently strong, an alternative method of gaining money may be resorted to, namely theft. An allied theory is that delinquency has the characteristics of the class in which it arises.[1] For example, the ways in which a middle class man contravenes the law of the land will bear the middle class stamp, and will in that way differ from the ways of the common thief.

The variations in patterns of behaviour from one culture to another are a commonplace to the sociologist: the works of Ruth Benedict and Margaret Mead in particular, suggest that it is reasonable to assume that not only will different acts be regarded as "criminal" by different societies, but also that the reasons for these criminal acts being committed at all will vary in different societies. Following on from this, it would seem reasonable to infer that factors operating to cause delinquency, or to create a situation in which it has a greater or lesser chance of occurring, are likely to vary between sub-cultures. Spinley[2] has recently investigated the varying weaning habits in two subcultural groups, and has detected various factors within these groups which tend to produce two contrasting ways of life. Presumably, therefore, a study seeking to discover the causes of delinquency would find different causes operative within these two groups: or may find causes operative in one group and absent in the other.

There are, then, two main points to be emphasised. The first is that there may be delinquency arising out of environmental or cultural circumstances in addition to delinquency arising out of psychological or pathological disorder. In this connection Mays[3] has pointed out that it is necessary to "make a broad distinction between environmental delinquents and chronic offenders". Mays says that "the two groups overlap, and disharmony in the parent-child relationship and environmental affection will occur in both groups". He goes on to say that "the attrition of ethical standards and the general deterioration of social attitudes may have more far reaching consequences than the occasional dramatic descent of one individual into confirmed criminality". May's

---

1 Sutherland : <u>White Collar Criminality</u>, Am. Soc. Review V, 1940
2 B.M. Spinley : <u>The Deprived and the Privileged</u>, London, 1953. International Library of Sociology and Social Reconstruction.
3 J.B. Mays : <u>The Study of a Delinquent Community</u>, British Journal of Delinquency, July, 1952, Vol. III, No. 1.

4   The Object of the Research

thesis is that the "environmental offenders" pass through a phase of lawlessness, which may be of a duration of only a few years. This thesis is open to argument. The main point for the present discussion, however, is that he considers the distinction essential to any interpretation of juvenile delinquency, and whether or not the environmental delinquent is less likely to be a chronic offender than is the victim of an inadequate parent-child relationship is a question which need not concern us at the moment.

The second point to be made is that environmental factors vary in accordance with sub-cultural groups, and in so far as environmental factors are of causal significance in the occurrence of delinquency, so will such causes vary as between sub-cultures.

Pearce,[1] in his recent book on the medical aspects of juvenile delinquency, writes :

> "A child who has grown up in a society of thieves may have a character which would make a community of puritans shudder. Nevertheless, this child in his way is just as mature as any other".

In other words psychological adjustment or maladjustment is not an absolute, but is understandable only when considered in relation to the environment of which the individual is a part.

Pearce also says that,

> "With the ordinary run of juvenile delinquents the child's internal policeman is often very lax and may even disapprove more of the fact of having let himself be apprehended than of the actual misbehaviour".

The significance of the latter statement to the present research has been pointed out by Professor Sprott in a review[2] of Pearce's book :

> "In some sections of the community this does not point to a peculiarity of the delinquent: it is, as one might say, the generally accepted opinion. If you are brought up in a social environment in which delinquent conduct is condemned, it may require a peculiar temperament or specially unhappy circumstances, to bring you before the court. If, on the other hand, you have been brought

---

1 J.D.W. Pearce : Juvenile Delinquency, Cassell & Co. Ltd., 1952.
2 The Listener, April 9th, 1953.

The Object of the Research 5

up in a world in which delinquent conduct is merely <u>risky</u> conduct, the predisposing factors to overt delinquency need not be so 'pathological'· No one will dispute the importance of the study of individual cases – indeed, every case is 'individual'. No one will dispute the significance of the factors discussed by Dr. Pearce – unhappiness, instability, precocious sexuality and so on. But his book needs supplementing by a comparative study of moral climates, and of the variety of techniques adopted for the socialisation of children: the middle class conscience is very different from fear of the cops."

Mack has also indicated the need for research into the "social climates" in which delinquency occurs. In a review[1] of Ferguson's recent book[2] Mack writes :

"although the study professes to concentrate on the social setting, it is so contrived as to miss the main social facts: types of group relationships, modes of group activity, social and moral climates of different neighbourhoods, and so on, It is not possible to get at these facts by totting up differences between series of individuals, To return to the comparison between slum and slum clearance areas in Glasgow, it looks as if both alike might be 'delinquent neighbourhoods', distinguished from other neighbourhoods by their non–acceptance of the moral standards of the greater part of the city. But to observe the special kinds of relationship and the standards of private and public behaviour prevailing in such neighbourhoods would involve a method of direct and participant group study quite different from the mixture of documentary and family – case work hero employed, The Gluecks faced the same issue explicitly (see <u>Unraveling Juvenile Delinquency</u>, p.19) and firmly put it aside. If they had studied the neighbourhood as an entity they would have had to discard the highly doveloped tech unique they had developed for the observation and assessment of series of individuals. But they preferred to shape their problem to the modal required by their instruments – like the car, nose and throat surgeons of yesterday. The same kind of decision is implicit in this study. It is to be hoped that the endemic failures of the

---

1 J.A. Mack : Review in the <u>British Journal of Delinquency</u>. Vol. III, No. 4, April, 1953.
2 T. Ferguson : The Young Delinquent in his Social Setting. London : Oxford University Press, 1952.

6   The Object of the Research

technique of series comparison to yield anything but historical information may stimulate investigators to undertake the partici- pant and even experimental study of social behaviour, normal and aberrant, in its natural setting, the living body of society·"

Shaw, too, in 1929, pointed out the significance of the "moral climate" in which delinquency arises :[1]

"It is clear than in the study of juvenile delinquent behaviour it is necessary to understand the culture – the more general so- cial norms, the local community, the family, the gang, and other groups in terms of the traditions, sentiments and attitudes of each group and the relationship in which the person stands in each·"

And,

"It has been quite common in discussions of delinquency to attrib- ute causal significance to such conditions as poor housing, over- crowding, low living standards, low educational standards, etc. But these conditions themselves probably reflect a type of commu- nity life. By treating them one treats only symptoms of more basic processes. Even the disorganised family and the delinquent gang, which are often thought of as the main factors in delinquency, probably reflect community situations."

Page has touched upon the same sort of conception :[2]

"In any inquiry into juvenile offences knowledge of material con- ditions – the degree of poverty or want in the home of the offender, for example – is of importance. But it is of secondary significance in comparison with knowledge of moral and spiritual values – such matters as the relations of a child with its parents, the tone of the home, the bearing of different members of the family towards one another and so on."

The importance of the sociological approach has also been remarked upon by Chess,[3] who has emphasised the necessity of "understanding

---

1 C. Shaw : Delinquency Areas, Nov. 1929.
2 Leo Page : Crime and the Community, Faber and Faber, Ltd., London, 1937.
3 Stella Chess : in "Psychodynamics of Child Delinquency", American Journal of Orthopsychiatry, Vol. XXIII, No. 1, Jan, 1953.

The Object of the Research 7

the individual child and the meaning of his behaviour at the particular time and place",
and,

> "it must be known whether the behaviour is in agreement with the dominant mores of child society of his social group, or divergent from these mores. It must be known, too, whether parental attitudes accept the mores of the neighbourhood or are in conflict with them."

Later Chess writes :

> "the problem of delinquency as a whole is not likely to be answered by individual psychotherapy. It requires epidemiological and sociological approaches. Under such circumstances it becomes of crucial importance to distinguish between delinquency in children who present personality disturbances which can be helped psychotherapeutically, and delinquency which is purely a sociological problem. In those children who in addition to delinquent behaviour also showed phycological disturbance, one must be keenly aware that delinquency is not ipso facto neurotic or psychopathic, and the delinquencies a may or may not be the portion of the behaviour that represents psychological disturbance."

These points are precisely relevant to the present Research. The Chairman of the symposium at which Chess made her remarks, Dr. Karpman, pointed out that Chess's analysis left unanswered "the same question and the same problem that has been asked of C. Shaw, and it has never been adequately answered". Namely, "why is it that in the slum areas only certain boys become delinquent and others do not?" – all the children of a particular neighbourhood are presumably influenced by it, why, there – fore, do some become delinquent and others remain untainted? Two comments on this point may be made. The first is that the large volume of crime which remains undiscovered or which is not reported to the police, or which is reported and not solved, may well account for an appreciable number of the offenders which one might anticipate finding in such "slum cultures", but which are not reflected in criminal statistics. In this connection May's study is again of interest. For this study the general hypothesis was that

> "the rate of delinquent behaviour in such an area (which lies along the south end docks of Liverpool, forming a compact though

8   The Object of the Research

heterogeneous zone of about 10,000 people) is very high and that delinquency is an accepted part of the pattern of juvenile conduct handed down by tradition and maintained by the familiar system of gang allegiance".

On the basis of his interviews with 62 members of a Settlement Club, Mays estimated the total delinquency for the group as a whole as "a little over 82 percent", and he says that "it is reasonable to suppose that this enormous percentage might at some time or another have been hauled before the magistrates", Further, "it is more then likely, too, that some of the 18 percent who denied any delinquent activity were lying". Mays points out that "it is not to be assumed on the basis of this brief investigation that delinquency even within this particular area is widespread and universal. One important fact, however, does emerge: that in neighbourhoods such as the one under review most boys at one time or another are open to strong delinquent infection and the majority for a shorter or longer period manifest active symptoms. Such behaviour would appear to be an integral part of the pattern to which boys in the area conform".

The second comment is as follows : in any society or culture, individual members adhere only more or less to the pattern of the community. There are variations within cultures just as there are variations between cultures. The point which the sociological approach must emphasise is that in certain sub-cultures it would appear that some of the dominant mores are conducive to delinquent behaviour. This is a different matter from saying that all members of certain cultures are delinquent. The fact that a cat may look at a King does not imply that all cats always look at Kings.

Finally, Taft[1] has summed up the compass of the sociological approach, which

"deals with social relations. It asks how far delinquent behaviour is a product of group patterning ... it does not confine its attention to the family, but is concerned with the influence of other primary and secondary groups, such as clubs, gangs, neighbourhoods and communities." It is "concerned with the particularly social world of the delinquent" ... the "status of the delinquent in his family, of his family in its neighbourhood, of his neighbourhood in the

---

1 D.R. Taft : Sociological Research in Criminology in the U.S.A., The Journal of Criminal Science, Vol. I.

The Object of the Research 9

larger community, etc." "Sociological criminology is concerned with the moral standards of the law as darling crime, but more concerned with varying groups moral norms as influencing the delinquent to depart from legal behaviour as defined by the law."

The necessity of the sociological approach to the problem of delinquency has been outlined above. It would be appropriate at this point to give a few examples of the sort of findings which such an approach is likely to produce. Some of the ways in which environmental factors operate to cause delinquency – or to create the conditions in which it may well occur – are discussed by Mays in the study referred to above. Mannheim has indicated that in certain localities there exists an attitude which accepts some kinds of theft which are in no way condemned:

> "Stealing coal occupies an important place in adolescent delinquency of the coal–mining districts, and it becomes clear from the Records that activities of this kind, according to the verdict of large sections of the local population, are not regarded as comparable to ordinary thefts. The children sometimes seem to concentrate exclusively on this type of offence, which strongly confirms the view that they do not regard it as morally wrong."[1]

And Robb[2] has referred to the same sort of situation in the London area in which he based his research. Robb says that if the chance of not being caught is thought to be a good chance, then it is likely that a person from this area will satisfy his immediate desire at the expense of the law. Robb emphasises that he is not suggesting that all the citizens are hardened criminals, but says that nevertheless many crimes are accepted, or at any rate are not disapproved of. A person who has served a sentence of imprisonment may be regarded as unfortunate rather than bad, especially if the offence of which he has been found guilty is an offence against the public authorities.

In a recent newspaper article reference has been made to a "dangerous minority" who are responsible for juvenile offences:

> "The hallmark of this dangerous minority is their utter aimlessness. They live for the present: desires of the moment must be

---

1 H. Mannhcim : <u>Social Aspects of Crime in England between the Wars,</u> Geo. Allen & Unwin Ltd, London, 1947.
2 J.H. Robb : <u>A Study of Anti–Semitism in a Working Class Area,</u> Ph.D. Thesis, London, 1952 (Unpublished).

10 *The Object of the Research*

instantly gratified" ... "these youngsters have no morals, no standards of behaviour. Though vaguely aware that certain acts may precipitate police action, they do not really understand why. As a Borstal governor put it : 'My hardest task is to persuade them that they have done anything wrong'".[1]

In <u>A Comparative Study of Deprivation in Jamaica and Liverpool</u>,[2] it is stated that in an area of Liverpool "a different code of ethics is hold towards people in the outgroup. It is not stealing to do a little shoplifting in the big stores, but a really terrible crime to pinch anything from the Mum". Finally, it should be noted that the works of Shaw and McKay abound in examples of the characteristics of delinquency areas in large cities.

There is, then, a relationship between the distribution of delinquents and the prevalence of social values and standards other than those uphold in the community at large, as reflected in the law of the country, and as uphold by the majority, or by law–abiding citizens, Thus

"a boy may be found guilty of delinquency in the court, which represents the values of the larger society, for an act which has at least tacit approval in the community in which he lives".[3]

The above quotations and references indicate that many people have suggested that in order to study delinquency it is necessary to consider the social background in which it arises. It is the purpose of this Research to study a specific social background, and to compare it with similar areas which present no cases of delinquency, or delinquency to a much smaller extent. As has been said above, this Research is not concerned with what may be termed "psychological delinquents". Nor does it deal with a criminal social background – with a society whose very organisation is directed towards illegal activity, and whose life is dominated by anti-social intent. This Research is directed towards a "normal" social setting, which is not in itself criminal in the pathological sense, but which appears to be conducive to delinquent behaviour. The emphasis of the Research is therefore upon different types of cultural background rather than upon individual delinquents. "Black"

---

1 B. Faithfull–Davies : Youth in Trouble, <u>The Observer</u>. Jan 10th, 1954.

2 Madeline Kerr : Department of Social Science, Liverpool University. Unpublished paper.

3 C. Shaw & H. McKay : <u>Juvenile Delinquency and Urban Areas</u> University of Chicago Press, 1942.

The Object of the Research 11

streets,[1] containing a relatively large number of delinquents have been compared with "white" streets which are similar to the "black" streets with regard to economic level, standards of housing and so on, but which may not produce delinquency at all, and certainly do not produce it to such a marked extent as the "black" streets. The aim is to discover whether there are factors present in the "black" streets which might be considered as conducive to delinquency, but which are absent in the "white" streets; and, conversely, whether factors present in the "white" streets which are likely to operate against the development of delinquency, are absent in the "black" streets. Such cultural backgrounds as those being studied in this Research, since they are normal, as distinct from pathological backgrounds, might be expected to include large numbers of households which do not, in fact, produce delinquents. Such backgrounds are far removed from the worlds in which it is common for people to make a calculated endeavour to secure a living by means of criminal activity.

Thus it is that the number of known delinquents who are resident in the areas in which this Research was centred is small. But what we hope to show is that the bulk of the delinquents come from certain localities and types of households which present traits which are conducive to delinquency, and traits which are social rather then psychological. If it can be shown that the social background is of significance in the particular ways which will be described, then some contribution will have been made to the problem of delinquency.

The basis of the Research is the concept that "the behaviour which the community defines as delinquent is socially conditioned, and arises out of a process of social interaction and imitation, precisely as does behaviour that is not defined as delinquent".[2]

The hypothesis of the present Research is that within working class areas different standards are upheld, and that the differences between the norms of behaviour contribute to the differential rates of delinquency distribution.[3]

---

1 The use of the terms "white" and "black" is not intended to indicate any moral appraisal on the part of the Research workers. The terms are used merely to differentiate between areas in which there is little or no official delinquency, and areas in which delinquency is marked.

2 E.L. Hooker: From The Sociology of Urban Life Smith & McKahan.

3 For the purpose of this Research, "Delinquent behaviour" is behaviour which is illegal according to the law of the land. A "dclinquent" is one who has performed an act which contravenes the laws and regularions upheld in the Criminal Law Courts.

II The Selected Town – Radby

Unlike much of the Research referred to carrier, this present study seeks to assess the social background in which delinquency occurs in a comparatively small town. The Research consists of an intensive, rather than an extensive, survey into the social values upheld in small, well-defined areas of the town. Before describing the specific areas it is necessary to consider some aspects of the town of "Radby" as a whole.

Radby is a small town (23, 000 pop.) situated 7 miles from a large Midland city. The centre of the town, the Market Place, is approximately four miles from the nearest extremity of the City's boundary. A good 'bus service connects Radby with the City, and with surrounding villages. A river flows on the east side of the town and from its valley the ground rises gently to high ground on the west. The proximity of the City means that 750, 000 people live within ten miles of the centre of Radby, and movement to and from the town for work is on a fairly large scale (see p. 15).

History[1]

The Domesday Survey shows that in 1086 Radby was a small cluster of dwellings with a population of sixty. It remained an agricultural village throughout the Middle Ages. In 1769 there were still only two hundred houses. It was about this time that the town began to develop: there was much building to accommodate the influx of people occasioned by the rapidly rising hosiery industry. Within a century the number of houses was more than doubled, and by 1843 Radby had more than 2, 680 inhabitants. Two years later, over 750 machines were being worked. The

---

1 Much of the information contained in this and the following section is taken from the County Planning Department, in particular the Report of the District Factual Survey (Assn. of Planning and Regional Research, 1948).

The Selected Town – Radby 13

bulk of the inhabitants were employed in framework knitting, warp and bobbin lace making. A colliery (No. 1) was sunk in 1861, and as the mining population increased, so the town spread until it become a "sprawling, shabby area of mixed development". By 1901 Radby "had assumed many of the characteristics of a mining town".[1] The extent of the expansion is indicated by the fact that by the end of the century the population had increased fivefold since 1861.

Population Growth (National Census figure):

Radby U. D. C.

1801	1821	1841	1861	1881	1901	1921	1931	1939
1,497	1,940	2,680	2,836	10,023	15,250	16,834	17,839	20,760

By the end of the nineteenth century, however, the period of rapid expansion had passed its peak. It was succeeded by a period of relatively gentle growth and in 1951 the population was 23, 213.

Although the town's main expansion, owing to the development of mining, was completed by the beginning of the century, its population is still decidedly young and masculine. A 1947 comparison of Radby figures with the national ones showed that (a) the number of women between 15 and 34 was 2% greater than the national average, (b) the number of children under 15 was 11% greater, (c) the number of men between 15 and 64 was 5% greater. On the other hand the numbers of women over 40 and of men over 65 were well below the national average.[2]

Layout and Housing

The colliery owners did not build more than about 100 house for their employees. But private builders coped with the situation, and provided almost all of the accommodation necessary for the rapidly growing population in the latter half of the nineteenth century· Thus a large proportion of the houses in Radby arc still either owner-occupied or rented from private owners. The town developed within clearly defined bounds – railway lines in the east and west, the Railway Bridge in the north and Station Hill in the south. It is only since the end of the first World War that development has extended beyond these bounds. The

---

1 Report of the <u>District Factual Survey</u>
2 <u>Report on the Draft Development Plan for the Urban District</u>, County Director of Planning – Revised 1951.

14 *The Selected Town – Radby*

19th century housing development radiated from the Market Place and Main Street, which remain the nerve centres of the town, and, to a lesser extent, along Colliery Road. As the town's collieries developed, communities sprang up in the area to the north of the Market Place, in the Colliery Road area, and also at Station Hill in the south. Until 1935 the Urban District Boundary ran close to the centre of the town in the east, and industrial development "gravitated naturally to the west",[1] so that Radby has tended to spread in recent years to the west and southwest. Expansion has been limited in the north by the tipping area of No. 3 Colliery, and in the south by valuable smallholdings.

The two periods during which the bulk of present-day Radby was built, pre-1900 and post-1918, have a material bearing on the character of the houses. Only a few back-to-back houses were constructed, and those which did exist have been converted or demolished.

After the first World War there was a considerable shortage of houses in the town, but private builders were not very active until 1928. The local authority built about 370 houses (1919 Act) and by 1939 had put up 146 houses (1936 Act). Since 1946 the local authority has built more than 215 houses, and extensive building is still taking place. Between 1928 and 1938, private builders created 1,200 houses. Although many new houses have been built since the war, there is still a shortage of ac-comodation, and many houses are "overcrowded". In July 1953, 1,200 applicants were on the Council's waiting list for houses and bungalows.

Until the turn of the century Radby was a comparatively compact entity, although it "lacked variety and cohesion".[2] The housing development was based on the minimum requirements of the public Health Act of 1875, and the usual pattern was long rows of terraced housing separated by narrrow streets, with common yards in which a row of W.C.s was situated. These houses have deteriorated and now present an atmosphere of "squalor and social congestion".[3] Today Radby suffers from scattered and unconnected development. In particular the areas to the west of the older part of the town tend to be isolated. This is especially true of the private development areas, which include the Knoll Estate and part of the West Estate. However, the opening of a new primary school between these two estates, and the tendency for the new Council building on the estates to breach the gap, is rendering them less isolated from each other, although jointly they remain comparatively isolated from the old part of the town.

1 Report of District Factual Survey
2 Report of District Factual Survey

The Selected Town – Radby   15

Employment and Industry, and their Social Implications

Coalmining is the town's dominant interest. Nearly 3,000 miners are resident in Radby: at least a third of all the residents depend on mining for a livelihood. There are 3 mines, but not all the miners living in the town work at these collieries.

Conversely, miners dwelling outside the town are employed in the Radby pits. Many men are employed at a large engineering works, and in other factories (of. p. 31) and an appreciable number are employed by the Building and Distributive trades. About one half of the employed women and girls work in hosiery and textile factories.

A "Journey to Work Survey" of 1948[1] shows that on balance the town is an exporter of labour.

		M.	F.	Total
a	Persons living and working in Radby	2575	828	3403
b	Persons living in Radby and working outside	2111	426	2537
c	Persons living outside and working in Radby	1328	325	1653

Coalmining still attracts over a quarter of the youths leaving school each year, and hosiery and textiles account for 70% of the girls. The following table gives an analysis of the first employment taken up by boys and girls on leaving school. The figures relate to the Radby and District Area of the Youth Employment Service, but are a fair indication of the position as relating to Radby alone.

First Employment. Year ending 31st July, 1950

Boys	%	Girls	%
Coalmining	27	Hosiery	54.5
Building	11.5	Textile, Clothing, Cotton	17
Hosiery	9	Distributive	14.5
Engineering	7	Other	14
Distributive	8.5		
Other	37		

The local newspaper, the <u>Radby Weekly Gazette,</u> shows that the first years of peace following the 1914–18 war brought with them growing

---

1 Figures supplied by the Ministry of Town and Country Planning to the County Planning Department.

16   *The Selected Town – Radby*

industrial unrest, and that there was great distress in the district. In October, 1920 there was a miners' strike, followed by an uneasy settlement which terminated in another strike in the April of the following year. This time the strike was of 3 months, duration. A distress fund was organised, and soup kitchens provided over 100,000 meals. The great strikes of 1926 were even more disastrous for the townspeople, and are still talked of with bitterness. Even when the coal strike ended in December there was no employment for many, and the quota system caused short time for those who were set on again. As the <u>Radby Gazette</u> reports, "over Radby hung the black shadow of widespread unemployment, the 'dole', and the means test". In 1929 a general world depression "intensified the distress in this district".

Figures supplied by the Ministry of Labour and National Service indicate that the national slump in the 1920s was reflected in Radby by a large amount of unemployment. The only available official figures refer to the Radby Employment Exchange Area, and therefore include four small parishes in addition to Radby. However, the overall picture given is a good indication of the position in Radby.

In 1929 there were approximately 7,000 men and women employed in the Radby Area, whilst 1,000 were registered as unemployed, of whom 800 were men. In 1935, there were 969 men unemployed and 915 on short time. By 1938 there were about 12,000 insured employees in the Area, and 2,000 of these, one sixth, were unemployed, of 7,421 men who worked in the mines and quarries, 1,194 were unemployed.

The figures suggest that Radby, with so large a proportion of its population dependent on coal mining and the hosiery and textile industries, suffered as much during this depression period as most of the industrial towns in this country.

The depression affected miners and textile workers particularly. Economic deprivation was manifest. Contemporary reports in the local press of this period state that many families were poverty-stricken, and these reports are supported by information ascertained by the research workers in general conversation with the townspeople, and during their interviews in connection with the Research. Radby people had never been used to a large income, but during the depression many had no regular money coming in apart from Public relief payments, and the wage from an occasional day's work. Even when employment was obtained there was no guarantee of permanency, and the wages were low. Many families, too, were large, as is seen from the following analysis of the 4,390 "private" families in the Urban District.[1]

---

1 Census 1931 For Census purposes a Private Family is any person or group of persons included in a separate return as being in separate occupation of any premises or part of premises. Lodgers are so treated only where returned as boarding separately.

The Selected Town – Radby   17

No. in family	1	2	3	4	5	6	7 (cntd.)
No. of families	176	850	1034	986	606	349	198
No. in family (cntd,)	8	9	10	11	12	13	14
No. of families	15	47	29	14	3	1	2

Thus 738 families, or 16+%, had 6 or more members living in the same household. The possibility of having sufficient money to feed such families and to provide and furnish a reasonably comfortable home was remote. With the improvement of the country's economic position in the 1930s, however, and especially with the re-armament programme and the outbreak of war in 1939, the employment situation was improved. At the outbreak of war although many men were called away to the Services, the majority, being in essential occupations such as mining, remained in Radby.

No statistics are available for the exact number who served in the Forces, but the variation in the number of insured employees in the area, as shown in the following table, gives some indication of the effect of the call–up on the town.[1]

	Men 18 & over	Boys under 18	Women 18 & over	Girls under 18	Total
1939	8,904	667	1,577	601	11,749
1943	8,011	695	1,758	601	11,065
1944	8,287	652	1,615	545	11,099
1945	8,724	539	1,616	491	12,370
1946	9,474	534	1,658	424	12,090
1947	10,648	674	1,443	368	13,133

It is seen that the numbers of employed men and women in the area remained fairly constant throughout 1939–47, except for an increase of approximately 2,000 men aged 18+ during the years 1946–47. Even allowing for a substantial movement of labour in and out of the area during the war years, the figures would appear to support the contention that the great majority of Radby men remained in the town during this time. A report in the local newspaper states that "Radby's quota of men in the Fighting Services was not so great (as in the first World War) nor were the casualties so heavy, but the town made a

---

1 Information as provided by the Ministry of Labour and National Service.
  No figures are available for the years 1940–42, but 1943 is generally regarded as the peak year of mobilisation.

18 *The Selected Town – Radby*

great effort industrially". Work became regular and wages improved vastly. The "war effort" provided opportunity for overtime in the pits, at higher rates of pay. Many women worked in munition factories and in the hosiery and textiles factories, whose importance to the country in time of war was considerably increased. The women, too, earned good wages, supplemented by their overtime work. Women who were unable to go out to work took in piece-rate work from the various factories. Radby became very prosperous as compared with the pre-war years. As elsewhere, of course, the increase in the spending power was offset by the fact that fewer ways of spending money were available. But the public houses, cinemas and Dance Halls remained possible sources of enjoyment, and although Radby has a good record for the National Savings Efforts it would seem that much of the available money earned was spent as soon as it was earned.

The prosperity of the war years continued with the coming of peace. In July, 1953, the estimated number of insured employees in the Area was 13,880 – of whom 11,135 were males. The number of wholly unemployed persons registered was 48, of whom 30 were men: while there were 67 unfilled vacancies for men, 51 for women, and 20 for young persons. Prospects in the Coalmining and Hosiery industries were good: there was no danger of unemployment, at any rate in the immediate future.

The Miners

A distinction should be made between coal–face workers and other men employed in the mines. For all miners above the age of 21 a minimum wage of approximately £7 is paid, but many workers in the pits earn as much as 50/- per shift. The system in operation is that if a miner works five shifts in one week, he gets paid for six: in this way, he may earn £15 per week - and more if he actually works an extra shift. From this the National Insurance contribution of about 5/- must be deducted, and also Income Tax in accordance with family commitments. The wages of most of the miners therefore compare very favorably with those of other workmen, whether skilled or not. In addition, every miner is entitled to a monthly allowance of coal, which is more than adequate for the majority of miners. Instead of the coal, a minor may opt for a monetary allotment of about £2. 10s. per month.

The wages of youths in the mines compare very favourably with those obtainable in other employment. The minimum wage for five shifts at the age of fifteen (that is, the first post-school year) is £3. 3s. This is received during the 16 weeks course of training which each recruit to the industry now undergoes, and which includes theoretical as well as practical work. If a boy has successfully passed the course of training (and most do), and is working underground, he will then receive over £4 per week. At the age of twenty the minimum wage for a surface worker is £5. 5s. per week, whilst coal face workers get much more than this.

A youth employed in the mines is exempt from his two years National Service. Radby therefore has relatively more youths between the ages of 18 to 20 years than is usual in non-mining areas. This fact is emphasised when it is remembered that Radby's population is "still remarkably young and masculine".

It has been pointed out that of a total population of 23,000, 3,000 men in Radby are employed in the mines, and many families are primarily dependent on mining for their livelihood. For a large section of the population, therefore, there is no economic reason for "poverty": indeed many homes are comparatively prosperous. But it should be emphasised that this prosperity is a fairly recent phenomenon. In many cases the new situation has not led to any major change in the general pattern of expenditure for the family. If the proviso is made that many miners have purchased television sets, and put in more modern fire grates, even in rented houses, it would appear from interviews and observation, that in an appreciable number of cases no effort has been made to better the material conditions of the home· The standard of furniture, decorations, clothes and so on has not noticeably improved. Much of the increased income is expended on immediate pleasures, in particular in clubs and public houses. This tendency is strengthened where, as in many cases, the miner's wife is made a weekly allotment for housekeeping, out of which all such items as furniture and clothing for the family have to be purchased; improvements in wages are not normally passed on – even proportionately – to the housekeeping allowance. The hire-purchase and clothing club system also help to perpetuate the old standards for this system enables the housewife to obtain necessary goods which she would not otherwise be able to purchase, without asking for an increase in the weekly housekeeping allowance.

The above generalisations are subject to many qualifications. But this research is concerned with testing the hypothesis that within working class areas different standards are upheld, and with relating this to the distribution of delinquency. The thesis here being put forward is that there are standards evident which are at variance with the "normally accepted standards". From these one would expect a substantial and permanent increase in income to be followed by a noticeable

20   *The Selected Town – Radby*

improvement in the material conditions of the home.[1] The miners and their families have not been used to such relatively large wages, and are not therefore accustomed to spending them. This has resulted in what some may call foolish expenditure, e.g. a failure to meet such needs as good clothing and a more comfortable home. But it is not just the lack of practice in administering relatively large wages that accounts for the position. Many of the miners-and other people of Radby - appear to have a different scheme of priorities from that normally upheld. It is doubtful whether many of them would recognise or support the idea that a comfortable home is a basic necessity. This is illustrated by the fact that, even when a family has a television set, there are often no comfortable chairs from which to watch the programme. The things on which money is expended are those which lead to immediate satisfaction, and to a larger quantity of the known pleasures – three evenings at the pub, or club, or dance hall instead of two. Many Radby men are keenly interested in such things as fishing, the cultivation of allotment holdings, and the rearing of praise birds – interests which involve patience, expenditure and looking ahead. There has boon one radical change, the large number of Radby people who now go away for a summer holiday. The pite close down and a man may receive up to £40 holiday money. To this may be added "holiday savings" which have accumulated during the past year as well, of course, as the holiday pay of the other members of the family. The favourite resort is the seaside, that is, three or four coast towns within 80 miles of Radby that are the traditional holiday resorts of the Midlands. The following report appeared in the <u>Radby Gazette</u> in August 1953.

> "With the local collieries and most of the works and factories closed down for their annual holiday, the town has presented a semi-deserted appearance this week. Hundreds of people left the town at the weekend for the seaside and country, there being a great exodus by train and 'bus. For those that remained at home there has been no lack of variety in rail excursions during the week."

---

1 On this point, cf.F. Zweig : <u>The British Worker</u> Pelican Books, 1952.
  "The increase of wages in time raises the life of the whole communities, but as far as I can see these changes are very slow, and there is a considerable time-lag between the increase and the change. When a man earns more he rarely uses the surplus to change over to a different pattern of expenditure, but spends more in accordance with the same pattern"

The Selected Town – Radby 21

These points will be considered in more detail in the section dealing with the special areas being studied in this Research.

The fact that Radby is predominantly a mining town has other implications for this study.[1] The majority of the miners work on the shift system. This means that during the course of three weeks, a miner will be employed on three different shifts: 6 a.m. until 2 p.m., 2 p.m. until 10 p.m., and 10 p.m., until 6 a.m. The lives of all the members of the family are affected by this arrangement, and where there are many mining families living in the same streets whole neighbourhoods will be influenced. When the miner is "on nights" he requires a certain amount of sleep during the day, and this demands some quietness from his own and neighbours' children and from other adults of his household. Since it is often impossible to keep a young child quiet by telling him that his father requires sleep, the miner may well get insufficient sleep – with consequent ill-effects upon his health or temper or both. The child for his part has to be "persuaded" to keep quiet in a variety of ways, often resolving themselves into either a reward for ceasing to misbehave (as opposed to a reward for behaving well) or into physical punishment for the offender. The position is further complicated by the fact that, in two of the areas to be studied in detail below, the houses are very small and closely adjoin one another; the street in front is narrow, and there is a common yard behind. It is not strange, all these things considered, that the language used in these areas is sometimes strong ('pit grammar') or that the methods of child control (the word is used advisedly as opposed to "rearing") do not comply with the theoretical advice given in the nursing manuals. It is not only when the men are on night shift that special circumstances apply in the miner's home. If he starts work at 2 p.m., the mornings constitute his leisure-time. He often spends the morning in the public house, therefore, drinking and playing dominoes. If he is on morning shift, he expects his meal on arriving home sometime after 2 p.m., that is after the school children's dinner time, and he has to get up early to be at the pit by 6 a.m.

The implications of the shift system are many and diverse. The family is seldom all together, apart from at the weekend. Even if the practice – were conditions to permit of it – was for the family to sit down together for a meal, the opportunities for this in many miner's families are few. The position is still further complicated when more

---

1 For a fuller discussion of mining Communities cf. F. Zweig <u>Men in the Pits</u>, Victor Gollancz Ltd·, London, 1948.

22 *The Selected Town – Radby*

than one member of the household is employed on shift work. The ways in which parental influence applies to children thus vary necessarily from those which apply when, for example, the family are all at home together most evenings in each week, and where conversation and leisure–time activities are engaged in constantly within the family. With a miner's family, such a situation is frequently impossible, even were the desire to effect it present. On the other hand, the shift system permits miners to spend more time with their young children especially those not old enough for school, than is possible for many fathers. For example when a man is on afternoon shift he may take his child for a walk in the morning. If he were on ordinary day shift this opportunity would not present itself, and the child might well be in bed and asleep when he arrived home from work.

In most towns it is unusual to find the majority of the residents of a Street engaged in the same occupation; but in some streets in Radby most of the employed men are miners. In Dyke Street, one of the streets to be considered in more detail below, over 68. 5% of the chief men of the households are miners, and in addition to these many sons, brothers, lodgers, etc., are also employed in the pit. The same situation holds for other streets, where the frequent piles of coal (representing the monthly allowance) in the roadway proclaim how many of the household have a miner occupant. This seems to lead to a greater "common sentiment" prevailing in those particular streets, and this sentiment is emphasised when the hazards of underground work in the pits are considered. It is not unusual for a man to be injured – whether seriously or not – at work, and minor accidents frequently occur. There is an unstated but ever-present realisation of the possibility of fatal accident at work, of widowhood, of fatherless children and so on. Large scale tragedies in the mines have been less frequent in recent years, but they have been sufficient in number to make aware the miner of the dangers of his occupation. Accidents on a smaller scale, involving the deaths of one or two men, occur more frequently. It is a recognised phenomenon that during war years many people became more conscious of the possibility of sudden death, and go all out for immediate satisfactions and pleasures. The chances of death in the mines are more remote, but just as apparent, and it may be that they give rise to a similar outlook.

Before passing on from this general consideration of the Radby miners, one contrast in their outlook – reflecting a difference in their standards – should be pointed out. Many of them are proud of, or at any rate reasonably content with their work, and would like their sons to follow the same occupation. Some are anxious for then to do so because of the good wages, some because of the exemption from Military

Service, and some because it is a man's job. But other miners do not want their children to go into the pit, and give two main reasons, the danger, dirty and heavy nature of the work, and the wish that they should gain a white collar job.

The Factory Worker

In 1951 there were in the Radby Employment Exchange Area a total of 1,497 non employed in what may be termed "factory work", of whom it is estimated that approximately two thirds were semi-skilled or unskilled. The following account is based on Mr. Carter's period of participant observation in a Radby factory. The description applies specifically to the factory in which he was employed, but is thought to be applicable to most factories in Radby in its general content i. e. with regard to wages, hours and conditions. There is one exception, a large engineering factory which employs 610 men, of whom only 209 are classified as semi-skilled and unskilled. (Factories in which mostly women are employed will be considered separately): -

"For a period of four months I worked in a factory situated near the centre of the town. During this time I had to comply with the order of life with which the majority of working class men have to comply throughout the year – that is, the necessity of commencing work at a certain hour, of having a certain amount of time allowed for a mid-day meal, and of having a comparatively short period of leisure time in the evenings and at weekends. Work begins at 8 a.m. and continues until 5.15 p.m. On Saturdays work finishes at noon. Thus the basic working week is 45 hours. However, during most of the time while I was employed at the factory overtime was being worked by most of the employees. This involved starting at 7 a.m. and finishing at 6.15 p.m., and 2 p.m. on Saturdays. On Sundays there was a shift from 8 a.m. until noon. There are tea-breaks of 10 minutes in the morning and afternoon, and one hour is allowed for lunch. Leisure hours are thus severely curtailed.

Most of the men are semi-skilled or unskilled, about ten men operating capstan lathes and turners, and the remainder (about eighty in all) being engaged in the routine work of drilling sheet metal and machine parts, and in general laboring and assembling. No high degree of skill is required, and the constant plea of many employees, 'roll on 5.15' (time to 'clock off'), summarises adequately the attitude of many of the men to their work, although a few men avowed their liking for it.

The flat rate per hour for most of the men is 2/11d., but piece-work and bonus schemes operate and permit a rate of up to 3/6d. per hour.

24   *The Selected Town – Radby*

For a 45–hour week an employee would therefore receive approximately £8, less National Insurance and Tax. By working overtime he could earn about £12+ per week. The wives of several of the men are also in work, so that the net weekly incomes of some of the men's families are considerable. Some prefer to have more leisure and earn less through overtime, but most preferred to take advantage of the opportunity for working overtime, especially since the opportunity was less likely to occur to such an extent in the approaching winter months. The idea of the men who preferred to work overtime was not so much to earn sufficient to enable them to save, and spread their savings over the time of lower income in the winter, as merely to make as much money as possible whilst they could. Some did become satiated after several months of long hours of working, and would then go easy for a few days.

For non-skilled men in particular, factory work may be dull and routine and no great intelligence or ability required. For many work is a necessary evil, performed only in order to earn the wages to keep a home going and to enjoy what little time remains. On the other hand, the interests of many of the workers are limited in range, and their intelligence is not high. Some indeed state that they would rather be at work than not (even if they dislike the work), for what is the use of having time to spare if you have not sufficient money to go to the pub or club? This attitude is supported by what appears to be a form of self-deception imposed by some men upon themselves. Thus, men performing the simplest of repetitive jobs often endeavour to persuade themselves and others that it is in fact a difficult job, and one which few other people could attempt. This presumably enables them to continue at work quite happily, where otherwise they would dislike the job intensely. This example is illustrative of the fact that many of the workers, in spite of complaints, appear to be adjusted to factory work. What appears to the observer as an intolerable situation to sustain for one's whole life appears to them as the natural course of events. Of course, it would be nice to win the 'pools', and it is annoying to see people who work in offices getting more money for fewer hours of work but there it is, 'you've got to live'. You see your mates every day, and have your chat at tea-break. You can joke during working time if you wish, and there is always the weekend to look forward to, and the wage packet on Friday night.

Several of the men had previously been miners, but had come out of the pit because of disablement or unsuitability for the work. Amongst these (and others working at the factory) there are some who have the same tendency as many miners to take a day off from work if they

The Selected Town – Radby   25

don't feel like going or if there is something better to do at home. Absenteeism constitutes a recognised problem in the mining industry. The attitude of the men appears to be that in previous years the employers frequently told them there was no work on certain days. Why, therefore, should they not take a day off when they feel like it? They are earning sufficient money to be able to afford a day off. The Income Tax system often operates, especially when high wages are being earned, to reinforce this fact. A man may find that he is 'working' one day a week for the Government. The men who practice absenteeism fairly regularly recognise little responsibility to the concern which employs them, to the nation which exhorts them to further effort, or to the foreman whose production plans are disorganised. "

Women at Work

The 1948 "Journey to Work"[1] survey showed that there were 1,254 employed women and girls living in Radby, of whom 828 worked in the town. More women are employed in Textile and Clothing factories than in other occupations. In 1951 in the Radby area 1,098 women were employed in Textiles and 290 in the Clothing industry, out of a total <u>for the Area</u> of 2,480. In 1953 one or two hosiery firms agreed to a greater use of part-time workers, with the result that a larger number of married women who were available for a limited number of hours a day were placed in employment. The women factory workers work a 5–day week, 8 hours a day. Legislation restricts severly the number of hours of overtime which women are allowed to work. The work is mostly clean, and of a repetitive nature: the women are employed either on machines or checking the finished products. Wages are comparatively good in Textile and Hosiery factories, and girls may earn at least £2. 10s. to £3 when first starting work at the age of fifteen even during the training period which several factories insist upon, and the facilities for which are provided by the management. After the training period women may earn a minimum of £5 depending upon age and ability.[2] Bonus systems based on production operate in several factories, and the basic wages are thus frequently supplemented. At work the women

---

1 County Planning Department. Figures supplied to Department by Ministry of Town & Country Planning.

2 In one Radby clothing factory, employing 400+ women and girls, there is a Training Centre for women aged 18 to 35. Courses last up to four weeks. Normal wages of £4. 2s. per week are paid during training. After training about £2 por week bonus can be earned above normal wage.

26 The Selected Town – Radby

are mostly in the company of their own sex. Married women of all ages mix, of course, with the younger women. In her recent book "The Deprived and the Privileged" B.M. Spinley has suggested that Married Women's Clubs in a slum area of London are notable for the obscenity of their members' talk, and she remarks upon the general obscenity of married women from this area. The same trait is evident in some of the women of Radby, but it is not clear whether it is specially apparent in married women: but in any case the influence of such women upon the younger women with whom they work is of significance. The Staff Adviser of a Radby hosiery firm employing over 400 women stated that Radby employees did not appear to be as keen on production as were the employees at his firm's City factory. They did not desire so much to earn extra money through incentive schemes, for their fathers earned more, as miners, than the average city worker, and Radby – being a mining community – leads a more "casual life" than does a city. There is a much larger turnover in the Radby factory – 47% in 1953 as compared with 29% in the City.

Many of the larger factories have canteens, in which the employees have their mid-day meal; they are able to converse whilst working: and they sometimes meet in the evening at social activities organised by the factories' Social Clubs. It seems that those factory social clubs are not supported with general enthusiasm, however. The majority of the employees participate infrequently in social functions, and only a few are sufficiently interested to take any part in organising social activities. The large factories employ women Welfare Officers, who keep the employees under their general surveillance.

Some of the married women who work in factories do so in order to supplement the family income for the purpose of running the home. But the wages of many of the women (especially the single girls) appear to be expended chiefly on "board", dresses, cosmetics, dances and cinemas. The amount of pocket money available to such individuals obviously varies, but it may be said that the wages earned appear to be adequate to provide for a considerable amount of leisure-time expenditure, if cosmetics and clothes be included under this heading. Certainly it may be said that many unmarried girls in Radby have as much, if not considerably more, money for leisure-time expenditure in this sense than their fathers and mothers have. As with the area studied by Spinley, and indeed in accordance with the findings of various other researches in this field, and with common experience, the women on the whole appear to marry young and to continue in their employment after marriage, until such time as a child is born. When the child is sufficiently old to be left with friends or relatives the mother often

The Selected Town – Radby   27

resumes employment. A grievance amongst some mothers in Radby is the lack of a nursery for young children in the town.

There are two factors which may be of significance in the tendency to marriage at an early age, one peculiar to a mining town.

a   National Service means that young men are away from the town from the age of 18 to 20 years. Army pay for the National Serviceman is not particularly good, but a marriage allowance is payable. By marrying fairly early in the period of National Service, it is possible to save this marriage allowance while the young wife continues at work. This represents a saving which might otherwise not have been made were the man not to have been called away from the town for National Service.

b   In mining towns relatively fewer men of this age are away from the town: the figures for Radby are not available but this might be a factor contributing to the earlier marriage of some people – the fact that the opportunity for meeting local girls constantly remains open.

Of course, these factors are in a sense contradictory but there is no reason why the same factor making for early marriage should operate in each case of early marriage. It appears to be the normal thing to live with "in-laws". immediately after marriage. Often the newly married couple have not sufficient money to furnish a house, even were one to be available.

Public Health

The figures provided by the County Medical Officer show that the rates of illegitimate births per 1000 live births in Radby during the years 1948–52 do not vary considerably from those of the County: the rates tend on the whole to be slightly lower for Radby than for the County. The rates of infantile mortality have tended to be somewhat higher in Radby during the same period; whilst the rate for mental deficiency incidence in 1952 was the same as the rate for the County. It is not possible to compile statistics relating to the incidence of Venereal Disease in Radby. The Doctor who deals with the problem for the County authority does not feel able to give any definite opinion upon the relative incidence of the condition as between Radby and other comparable areas, but his general impression is that "it does not constitute a special problem in Radby".

The statistics show that Radby conforms fairly well to the general standards of health obtaining in the County. Nevertheless it is a fact

28   *The Selected Town – Radby*

that the School Clinic is attended by a relatively much larger number of children in Radby than is usual with clinics in other parts of the County. But this may be attributable solely to the fact that

a the School Nurse has worked for a long time in Radby, and is well known and liked,
b the Clinic is easily accessible from all parts of the town.

It should be mentioned that the comparatively frequent minor accidents at the pits lead to the temporary disablement of miners from time to time: and also that there are quite a lot of ex-miners living in Radby who have suffered permanent disablement, sometimes acute, through accidents in the pits. Those are new either retired or working in jobs other than mining.

It remains true that the overall picture presents no special problems with regard to the health of the population of Radby.

Education

Although Radby conforms fairly well to the general standards of health for the County, the same position does not hold with regard to standards of education: for Radby falls below the general standards of education in the County in several respects. This is revealed in the Annual Report on Examinations, 1951/2, of the County Education Committee. The Report states:

"With Radby the intelligence appears to be distinctly below the County average and the number of awards made (to Grammar Schools) is very markedly below....... The number of children of low ability is highest in Radby – rising at times to a quarter of the school population of examination age. In interpreting the figures it is reasonable to say that children whose IQ is below 73 are probably unable to road at all, or if they can read, can read only with extreme difficulty. For Radby approximately 5% of the children come into this category. It must be remembered however that group intelligence tests (the moray House intelligence Test was used) are not a very satisfactory measure of children with low ability, although on the other hand, the picture over the course of the last four years is reasonably consistent."

There is no Grammar School in Radby, and a child who wins a scholarship must travel to school each day, at least as far as the City. Thus in 1952 of 29 boys and girls who gained awards, 26 travelled to the City (7–10 miles) each day, and 3 to a town 20 miles distant. It is possible that parents may be deterred from encouraging their children

The Selected Town – Radby   29

Grammar School Awards, 11+ years

	Eligible Candidates	Awards	% of Eligible Candidates	% of Eligible Candidates for the County	Average I.Q.	Average I.Q. for the County
1949	353	37	10.4	13.3	96.9	98.9
1950	349	21	6.0	13.2	97.7	101.1
1951	340	32	9.4	13.4	97.1	100.3
1952	369	29	7.9	12.9	95.8	99.4

Secondary Technical School Awards at 11+

	Ellgible Candidates	Awards	% of Awards	Awards for County	% of Awards for County
1951	340	8	2.4	150	4.6
1952	369	9	2.4	150	4.6

Incidence of Illiteracy and children of Low Intelligence

	I.Q. below 73 Radby = %	I.Q. below 73 County = %	I.Q. 73–87 Radby = %	I.Q. 73–87 County = %
1949	3.4	3.4	26.6	18.3
1950	4.6	2.9	20.3	15.4
1951	5.9	4.1	16.2	14.6
1952	5.1	3.4	20.3	15.8

to work hard for an examination – or, if one is awarded, may not accept it – because of all this travelling. Whether this is so or not, the position of Radby as compared with the County as a whole is clear: the educational attainment of Radby schoolchildren is relatively low.

There are eight schools in Radby containing eleven departments.[1] Five of these (eight departments) are structurally old, and in need of reconstruction or demolition. It is recognised by the Authorities that new school provision is urgently needed. Before the opening of the new

---

1 An Evening Institute of Education functions during the winter months, and provides instruction in e.g. arithmetic, dressmaking, and cookery,

30   *The Selected Town – Radby*

Primary School in 1950 the most recent school building was opened in 1897. Although some of the older schools are well constructed, they are, to quote a local historian, "very dark and sadly lacking in amenities". This means that for a large number of Radby children the physical characteristics of school are not very different from those of home. Both are old, cramped in space, and have the minimum of toilet and washing facilities. For many of the children it is probably true to say that their only first-hand experience of modern building, with clean appearance and decent amenities is that gained by visits to the cinema.

The new Primary and Infants Schools are, however, modern buildings of pleasant design and abounding in amenities. They are clean and open, with adequate window space and ventilation. There is a large hall in which the schools may gather, and good apparatus for physical training. Toilet facilities are excellent.

There does not appear to be any one explanation to account for the comparatively low educational standards of the children.

Social Life and Amenties

There are about 20 churches and chapels, and most of these have Societies for children and adults attached to them, including Youth Clubs and Boy Scout Troops. There are two cinemas, and the films exhibited are changed twice a week. The Public Library, situated by the Market Place is managed by the Urban District Council. The services and quality of the Library would be likely to be improved were the Local Authority to permit the County Library to take over its administration. As it is, the Library premises remain much as they were when first presented to the town by a citizen in the 1870s – except that nowadays it appears dingy and unwelcoming. There is a fairly large stock of books, and any book can be obtained from the County Service on request.[1] Apart from the lending section there is a reading room in which the daily papers are kept, and also a room in which old and disabled men gather each day to smoke, converse, and play cards or dominoes. Opposite the Library is the Parish Church. In front of this is the Market Place, which stretches down to the main through road. During the daytime, old men occupy the seats which are placed alongside the wall of the Church, facing on to the Market Place. This stretch is not lighted at night, and after school hours until late at night it is

---

1 During the year 1952–3, 122, 240 books were borrowed, of which 97, 937 were fiction, 10, 202 non–fiction, and 14, 101 juvenile.

The Selected Town – Radby   31

a favourite meeting place for children and teenagers. Usually there is much screaming and laughing to be heard coming from this area after dark. Market Day is on Friday, and the Square – and the Cafe opposite – provide convenient meeting places for the exchange of news.

The various Church clubs and groups receive support not only from their members, but also from the general public who attend such things as whist drives. There are one or two dramatic clubs and choirs, and the Radby Rotary Club consists of local businessmen and professional men. Some of the ways in which the townspeople occupy their leisure time are described in some detail below. Cinemas, dances, "pubs" and clubs are popular. But it must be remembered that many people spend their leisure time, or much of it, at home sitting about, reading, practicing hobbies, listening to the radio or watching television, tending allotments, rabbits or pigeons. Some remain at home because a lack of money prevents them from going out for their enjoyment; others because they prefer to pass the time at home. Television is very popular in Radby. Many people have sets, and others are saving in order to purchase them. In January, 1954, approximately 1,900 television licences were held by residents in the Radby district. This amounts to two families with television sets in every five families, or one set for every twelve persons resident in the parish.[1] Television probably keeps at home some who would otherwise go out for the evening. The Warden of the Knoll Community Centre has remarked that an object of such a Centre is to encourage families to enjoy their leisure time together: it appears that television is succeeding in many cases where Community Centres have failed.

In considering the following account of some important features of social life in Radby, it is necessary to bear in mind the above remarks concerning the variety of ways in which different people spend their leisure time.

Dances are held at least twice weekly in the Co-operative Hall, and in the Church Hall. The following remarks are based upon observation of some of the Co-op. dances. The dances attract large numbers of toon-age girls and youths. The girls dress gaily, and mostly look smart, even if cosmetics tend to be applied to excess. The current fashions with regard to hair styles and dress are complied with by the majority. The youths exhibit strong convictions about dress.

---

1 For Great Britain, in January 1954, the corresponding figure is <u>approximately</u> one set for every twenty persons resident in the country, but is must be remembered that considerable sections of the population were at that time inadequately served by television services.

32 *The Selected Town – Radby*

"American–Style" suits, consisting of fairly narrow trousers and long "draped" jackets, are popular. These suits are usually in pastel shades of blue, brown or green, and are made of a smooth worsted material (they cost from £8. 8s.). Pastel-shaded shirts, or bold-coloured ones are favoured. Often the collar and part of the front of the shirt is a different colour from the rest. Bright ties, sometimes with painted or embroidered illustrations of, for example, pin-up girls or footballers are also popular, but some youths prefer the shirt buttoned to the top, unadorned by a tie. Hair styles of the youths vary, but many are variations on the general theme of long hair piled up on top and swept back, or long at the sides and a short crop on top. The complete picture represents an attempt at novely, or at any rate a conscious break with traditional standards of dress for the working class. "Jiving" or "Be-bop" (quick tempo dancing) or the more sultry "Creep" are enthusiastically supported, and often the orchestra is accompanied by the voices of the dancers. Lively tunes are popular, and also songs which deal with such matters as hearts, kisses, and sweet-hearts sending letters of goodbye. The singing of many of these songs involves slurring vowel sounds and syllables, and modifying them in order to give an American pronunciation.

In the interval some go out to a public house for a "lemon dash", or for more potent forms of liquor.

Many of the youths are miners, and it will be remembered that their weekly income is quite high for people of their age. The Dance represents an evening's enjoyment for them, and is looked forward to: they feel big to go into pubs, as the older men do, and their style of clothing makes them feel someone. They attempt to give an impression of indifference to the opposite sex; and, indeed, many who attend the dances actually dance very little.

There are 13 Public Houses, mostly concentrated in the areas of the Market Place, Main Street and Colliery Road, and 5 licensed clubs. The "pubs" are very popular amongst many men and women. The men play dominoes and darts during opening hours, in the day (10.30 – 2.30) and also in the evenings. At weekends, and sometimes in the week, their wives accompany them in the evenings, or come in for the last hour. Considerable amounts of liquor are consumed in a pub in the course of an evening, especially at weekends. The men usually drink pints of beer and the women half-pints. At weekends, and sometimes during the week, there is music and singing. Until recently the Radby licensees were not permitted to have music on Sunday evenings, but a joint appeal to the magistrates was successful. A basis for the appeal was that the weekend is the only opportunity which many

The Selected Town – Radby 33

miners on night shift have for leisure time; also, the customer's liking for music was such that he was leaving the town on Sunday evening to visit pubs in surrounding villages and towns where no similar prohibition exists. In the early part of an evening at weekends there is general and private discussion amongst the people in a pub, and games are played. At about 8 p.m. a pianist starts, and many of the customers join in the songs, some giving solo performances. By 10 p.m. (closing time) many are there or less under the influence of liquor. By then the singing is more raucous, and there is much cheerfulness and joie de vivre. Many of the people will be present again at dinner time on the following day, and again in the evening, when the same process takes place. But some go into the City at the weekends, to visit pubs. People of all ages frequent the pubs, but it is noticeable that a considerable number of customers are youths of 16+.

A popular feature of most of the pubs are the games – cards, dominoes and darts. In 1954 a "Knockout" competition to determine the individual dominoes champion of Radby was arranged. Most pubs house Men's and Ladies' Darts Clubs, which usually participate in local leagues. Fixtures are played during the week, when a usually crowded bar is made more so by the arrival by coach of an away team. There is much drinking, but the procedure for the evening is fairly strictly adhered to. Namely, before each Match is started, a committee member from the home team will shout "This time ladies and gentlemen, please". This is followed by a general shout of "Game on, quiet". Comparative silence ensues, punctuated only by the noise of the barman at work, and by excited shouts of "Good old Bill", etc., when a high score is made. Some of the domino players are inclined to grieve over the necessity for quietness which means that their game is temporarily interrupted. Conversations such as the following take place: A. "Its a bugger if you can't have a game of dominoes in your pub" B. "Well, its only once a week" A. "One evening too many" B. "Aw, fuckit then, if that's how you feel".

There is much excitement if the home team wins, and those who win their games are very popular. A good throw denotes skill, and reflects to the credit not only of the player but of the entire clientele of the pub. A low score is, of course, indicative of "bad luck". The Darts Clubs alternate from week to week with home and away fixtures. For the away games a coach is hired, and there is much singing and shouting, and probably a stop in order to purchase fish and chips.

Attention has been drawn to the dress-habits of the youths at dance halls. No such attempted elegance distinguishes many of the male customers of pubs, at any rate during the week. Some may put on their

34 *The Selected Town – Radby*

best suits at weekends. But the popular form of dress is simply the ordinary working clothes, with perhaps a knotted scarf around the neck. Often a cap is worn. A distinction can be drawn, however, between those men who like to dress up when they go out for an evening, and those who do not make any change from their working clothes, except upon rare occasions. Many of the middle-aged women make rather poor attempts at attractiveness with the aid of liberally applied cosmetics. But frequently lack of technique combined with old and poor quality clothing leads to notable failure in the attempts. Some of the women, of course, succeed in appearing smart, although the language employed by them frequently belies their appearance. Others dress well and speak well. Prostitutes – people who regularly approach men with the object of offering sexual intercourse in exchange for a cash payment – do not apparently flourish in Radby. On the other hand the town has its share of women of easy virtue, who or may not charge for their "co–operation", A few of the latter are true to type in so far as they dress in a gaudy fashion, and are of garish appearance.

There is a strong local feeling that Radby "knows how to enjoy itself". Certainly there is much cheerfulness in the pubs and clubs. And in the summer a large section of the town's population becomes holiday conscious, In a similar way, there is much favour exhibited by large numbers of citizens on occasions of national celebration. Months of careful preparation by the Coronation Street Party organisers, for example, bore fruition on the Great Day with much revelry, so that "although far removed from the pomp and pageantry of the central scene in London... the people of Radby... celebrated the occasion with enthusiasm and gaiety which the worst efforts of the weather could not impair".[1]

Values and Standards Upheld amongst the Working Class people of Radby

In the previous section a rather general introduction and description has been given of some aspects of Radby's social life and amenities. At this point we propose to change the focus and take a much closer view of some of the values and stardards which may be encountered in Radby. The information analysed and considered below is based on Mr. Carter's experience whilst employed at the factory referred to earlier in this Report, and is supported by subsequent observation in

---

1 From an article in local newspaper, june 1953·

public houses, clubs and cafes. The following, then, is an account of some of the values upheld by sections of the population of Radby. The analysis does not necessarily hold good in its entirety for any particular section or neighbourhood. The interpretations tend necessarily to be subjective, but are based upon the observer's knowledge of the people and situations involved.

We thought that by securing employment in Radby, two useful ends would be served:

a   It would be possible to establish friendly contact with some members of the Radby community, and to assume a position in that community and be accepted by it.

b   It would be possible, by listening to and participating in the conversation in the factory, to gather information which would be useful in the attempt to assess the modes of life and the moral standards of the people of Radby.

In addition, an aspect which was not anticipated before the observer commenced employment at the factory is important. For a period of four months he had to comply with the order of life with which the majority of working class men have to comply throughout the year. It is thought that the fact of living for a while the sort of life (at work) which the "ordinary working men" lives is of values in helping to put the situation into perspective. It helps to prevent misinterpretation of attitudes through faulty judgement resultant upon a lack of familiarity with the conditions being investigated.

Some indications should be given about the manner in which I approached the problem of gaining acceptance by the man in the factory. Other aspects of this were stated in Section II of the text, concerned with information gained.

It was necessary to give the impression to the men that I was in sympathy with their "way of life" and with the views which they expressed. It was not sufficient merely to make acquaintances – it was necessary to establish intimate social relations and not give the impression of disapproval. Thus I joined in conversations about sex, football, cinema, etc., and endeavoured to create the impression that even if I was a "student" there was no barrier between me and them arising out of that fact. "Gaining acceptance" resolved into such actions as laughing with the men at crude jokes, employing the swear words which they employed, "complaining" with them about such matters as wages and working conditions. Some of the men were not aware of the significance of such terms as "University" and "student", and seemed to

36   *The Selected Town – Radby*

assume that anyone who attended a University considered himself to be "better", or "higher in the social scale" than the ordinary workman. Not that I met with any opposition or ill-feeling from the employees: but a few of them appeared at first to assume that crude words and phrases were not to be used in direct conversation with me. In order to establish a relationship in which the men would talk just as naturally to me as to any other employee, it was essential to dispel any notions of this kind. The willingness to prefix statements with such words as "bloody" appeared to be of great use in establishing the "rapport" desired. In most factories there are probably to be found various groups of men who "cling together", also some individuals who are not liked by the remainder, and others who are disliked intensely. To an extent, I probably fell in with this situation as it applied in the Radby factory. But since I wished to converse with as many men as possible, I had the task of gaining the friendship or acceptance of all of the men. There were thus two main conditions to create

1 Acceptance by the men as an equal.
2 Friendly relations with and respect of as many of the men as possible. This in order that in conversation the men would say what they thought, with no modifications for the sake of impressing the observer or to avoid "offending" him.

The constant noise of machines in the factory restricted. to an extent conversation during working time on some of the jobs. However I was able to have many conversations. But more important was the general conversation during the 10 minutes tea breaks (which often resolved themselves into 15–20 minutes), and also during the lunch-break at mid-day. At lunch-time I went usually either to the "Co-op Cafe" or to the "Cosy Cafe", and often I went in the company of other employees. Dressed in working clothes I was thus seen in "black" area No. 1 and in the cafes in the company of other working men, and there is no reason to suppose that I was regarded as anything other than a working man by the people with whom I conversed. After lunch, I sometimes strolled round Radby with other employees. But more often the practice was to return to the factory and sit on the pavement in Wordsworth Street, outside the factory premises. At about 12.50, Dick would return, then Tim, Johnny and Dennis and Peter, until at about 1.05 p.m. there would be a large number of men sitting and lounging in the street conversing, joking and surveying the women who were returning to work at the clothing factory on the opposite side of the street.

The Selected Town – Radby   37

Such are the conditions under which the information relating to the Research was gathered.

The majority of the employees know that the observer was a student. It would have been desirable not to have revealed this information, which was however divulged for the following reasons: -

1 When securing employment it was necessary to inform the management that work for a short period only was required.
2 It was necessary to submit a National, Insurance card, and the lack of stamps on the card required explanation.
3 When I commenced work, I was faced with enquiries from the men with regard to my background – where I came from, what work I had done previously, etc. To appear friendly, some answers to such questions were necessary. A convincing story could doubtless have been formulated, but since the management knew that I was a student, it was possible that this information would become known to other employees. This as well as the possibility of an unguarded phrase, was liable not only to arouse "suspicion" but also to destroy any "rapport" which might have been established.

The following explanation of my appearance at the factory was therefore given to the management and to those employees to whom it was found necessary to give an explanation.

1 The observer was a student of economics, and required temporary employment during the summer vacation.
2 He desired employment in an engineering factory because he had not previously worked in one and would welcome the experience.
3 He sought work in Radby because it was not possible to get similar employment in the City, or, because the observer was interested in Radby with regard to its "economic organisation and social life". The latter explanation was given to three men with whom I became particularly friendly, and whom I hoped would help me particularly in gaining acceptance in some of the working men's organisations. It was impressed upon those there that it was essential for the purpose of this work that I should be regarded in Radby as an ordinary workman.

Method of obtaining information

The governing factor was the need to minimise the differences brought about within the groups of men in the factory by the presence of the

38   *The Selected Town – Radby*

observer in them. This was done by the means outlined above. Also it was decided not to appear unduly inquisitive about Radby. During the first few weeks I mostly listened to conversations at tea breaks and spoke little. No attempts were made at first to direct the course of the conversation, but later it was possible to raise topics and follow up points without occasioning surprise at the questions asked. I never said, for example, "I am interested in Carnation Street, it has a bad reputation, hasn't it? Why is that so?" But it was found possible to gain the information which such a question would hope to attract by expressing a vague interest in Carnation Street, or in bad reputations anywhere.

I committed to memory the points of interest to the research which had arisen during the day, and recorded them during the evening of the same day. Whenever possible parts of conversation were recorded word-for-word. The piece-work system in operation at the factory necessitated recording the nature of each job done, and the time taken over it. It was not unusual therefore, to see employees making penciled notes on scraps of paper: this facilitated my need to record in detail some points of conversations without occasioning interest, surprise or suspicion.

The characters in the following account of the factory are fictious.

The factory, in which engineering implements and light machinery is produced, is situated between Wordsworth Street and Spinney Street, and is thus in the centre of one of the areas in which a comparatively large number of cases of delinquency are located (Area No. 1, See Section III B). That is to say, in the streets surrounding the factory are to be found a higher number of delinquents than in other areas of Radby. The streets in this area are some of the worst in Radby with regard to general. standards of cleanliness and tidyness. The houses face onto narrow pavements and streets. Most houses have communal yards, in bad condition, behind them. These yards are shared by about ton households, and in them are the rows of lavatories, clothes lines, dustbins, etc. It is in these yards, and in the streets, that the children play and the adults gossip. The appearance of the people with regard to clothing and cleanliness is poor, and much time seems to be spent by the adults in lounging about and talking. Spinney Street provides a curious spectacle in that the backs of the houses on one side of the street face the street.

It was not to be expected that conversation in the factory would be constantly on the subject of delinquency, if ever; but it is considered that the general tone of the conversation, of the attitudes expressed and the manner of their expression, and of the topics considered, are indicative of the moral standards to which the men subscribe, of the

The Selected Town – Radby 39

cultures of which they are part, and more particularly of their value judgment as associated with delinquency.

Conversation ranged over many topics, including money, sport, religion end work. Crime was also discussed, particularly when a local or national crime was treated sensationally in the Press. But there appeared to be one topic which was referred to more than others, namely that of sex. In view of the relative frequency of discussion or talk about sex it will hero be considered first.

It is necessary to draw attention to two aspect of this topic. Firstly, the actual discussions about sex – often dealing with the exploits of various of the employees in this direction. Secondly, the preponderance of words connected with sex, such as "fucking" and "cunt", in ordinary conversation dealing with other subjects. The majority of the men used such adjectives. This, of course, is a phenomenon which is not peculiar to Radby, and which is to be encountered in factories, offices and Common Rooms throughout the country. But the use of such descriptive words by some of the men under consideration is not restricted to the times when they are in the company of other men. Such terms have been overheard in mixed company in public houses, and also in the presence of children (and, in fact, employed by children) in the streets of the town. It is thought, therefore, that the fact of the use of such language helps to illustrate the moral tone of the men and their community. If the supposition that such language is not confined to male company is found correct, it is indicative of those differences of morality which the Research postulates.

Sex

During one afternoon tea–break there was some discussion on the subject of prostitutes, and their whereabouts in the City. I followed this up with enquiries about the City, in order not to suggest too great an interest in Radby, but I then went on to enquire whether there are any public houses in Radby which act as centres for prostitutes. Peter, who lives in Dyke street, and who I consider to be a reliable informant stated that there is no open prostitution in Radby – that is, there is not an appreciable number of women, if any, who practise prostitution as a permanent source of income. Two reasons were given for this. In the first place the miners would not tolerate it and would tell the women in no uncertain terms to clear off. That is to say, there is a strong feeling against it. I consider that this is not indicative of any strong moral feeling against prostitution as such, but indicates rather a feeling of indignation which would arise were the miner to be pestered by a prostitute

40   *The Selected Town – Radby*

when he was out for a drink with his friends, or for a game of darts. Further I think that were any miner (or other workman in Radby) to desire sexual intercourse, he would probably secure it when he desired it, and probably without payment.

Secondly, the Inspector of Police is very strict about "that sort of thing". Thus, instead of women more or less openly inviting men to have sexual intercourse, they would be more likely to make the suggestion whilst walking home after an evening out. For this, payment may or may not be required.

There is an important difference in attitude revealed here, which is of significance for the Research. Although there may be an attitude of condemnation towards the prostitute, there is also an attitude of acceptance towards the woman who is prepared to have sexual intercourse without payment of fees, and without thrusting her presence upon a man when he is more concerned with drinking. Thus, Peter condemned prostitution, and Dick (Spinney Street) – who has probably availed himself of these facilities, according to his own statements and to those of other men – remarked to the effect that once a woman had started on the course of prostitution it was difficult for her, and unlikely that she would be able, to break away from it. Yet both of those men have had extra-marital intercourse with women other than prostitutes.

One morning, soon after the observer started at the factory, Peter brought to work a booklet of pornographic cartoons. Its contents showed groups of partially clad men and women performing various sexual activities upon themselves and each other. The booklet had been borrowed from a sailor at the Dyke Street Working Men's Club. It occasioned much amusement at tea-break, and was well received by all. At first the booklet was not shown to me – Peter did not think that I would be interested – but on request the cartoons were shown and this served the double purpose of revealing the contents of the booklet to me and ensuring that in future Peter would not amend his actions or conversation in order to respect any "feelings" which I might have been supposed to possess.

In May a little girl was indecently assaulted in Radby. There was some discussion about this incident, and Dick considered that in many cases of this nature the girls were as much to blame for the events as the men (although in this case the girl was only 8 years of age). Anyhow Dick "liked them himself at 15" – that is to say, he considered that much satisfaction could be got through having intercourse or sex play with a girl of fifteen. Fred, who had previously worked as a dustman, was a friend of the nan, also a dustman, who was convicted of the

The Selected Town – Radby 41

assault; his opinion was that the man presumably "felt like a bit". My impression was that although some of the men regarded the offence as morally reprehensible, others considered it foolish of a man to create such an awkward situation for himself, and they would condemn the offence chiefly for that reason.

Several. weeks after this event I was joined on the bus to the city by a youth who worked in the Assembly Shop. I established that the youth lived in Carnation Street, and then raised the above case of the dustman who had been lodging in the same street. The youth informed me that the man had been turned out of the lodgings following the event, though it was not made clear whether or not this was because of the nature of the offence. Apparently the youth's mother died in 1952 and he now lived with his grandmother in Carnation Street two houses away from his father, who was now living with another woman. The dustman had been lodging with his father and this woman.

Patrick, a single man lodging in Radby, told me after work one Saturday (he had arrived at work at 9 a.m., an hour late) that he had been out until 3 a.m. on the previous night, "shagging a woman" – at least ten times, he thought. Whereas the number of times claimed may be open to doubt, I consider that the basis of the account is true. Patrick had been in the Town for about three years and he knows and mixes with Radby people and is accepted by them. There is no reason to suppose that his habits or the principles governing them are at great variance with those of other Radby men.

There were several discussions on the subject of a woman who was found murdered in a country lane about two years ago. Patrick had been in her company some time before the crime and was questioned several times by the police: and Fred who at that time was employed by the Council, went with the dust cart which was sent to remove the body. Thus there were two men with first-hand experience of the case, and the rest were interested because of the geographical proximity of the offence. The general opinion of those who knew anything about the case was that the woman "asked for it" – that is, "she got what she deserved". For the woman habitually frequented public houses and picked up men. Also it was thought that whoever did it (and this has not been established) was foolish to go to such an extent in order to have sexual intercourse (presuming this to have been the cause). This attitude was summed up by Dick –whose statements on such matters must, however, be considered with regard to the fact that he has a certain position or reputation to maintain amongst his workmates, and are thus liable to be tinged with bravado. Dick stated, "if I want a bit of cunt, I have it". That is, <u>he</u> could get his satisfaction without going to the extreme of

42   *The Selected Town – Radby*

murdering, or causing the death of a woman, and this he considered to be the less complicated manner of resolving a need.

A few words of explanation are required about this matter, pertinent to the consideration of Dick's attitude and that of other men in the factory. Thus, with regard to men's sexual lives, some men frequently state that they are sexually active, and gain a reputation or a standing amongst their associates for such matters. They then have a position to maintain. Whether they actually do the things which they state they do, or whether they do them to such an extent, is a problem which is of interest but difficult to resolve. But in any case it is considered relevant to this Research that the fact of them saying that they do these things suggests that they have a conception of what it is "manly" to do, or what others would expect them to do, or of what they would like to do. There is thus an indication of standards to uphold, even if not a true record of them.

Dick complained at one time of the weekly burden imposed upon him by the requirement to pay £3 per week in compliance with a separation order obtained against him by his wife. What grieves him most, apparently, is that part of the order is for the upkeep of a son, of whom he declares he is not the father. He has to maintain the child until he is sixteen years of age – and he has "another five years of the fucker yet". He had become friendly with a woman in Bristol whilst working there for the firm and had had sexual intercourse with her for a month. They still corresponded, but it appeared that another employee still working in the West Country was friendly with the woman. Dick complained of this, and referred especially to the fact that the other man was married and living (when at home) with his wife. How far this is indicative of an attitude that it is morally worse for a married man to have extra-marital intercourse than for a married man who is separated from his wife, and how far it represents a rationalisation by Dick of a situation which displeased him, it is difficult to assess – although I suspect that it is largely the latter explanation.

When conversation developed on the subject of contraceptives – referred to as "French letters" – Dick stated that he prefers the "real stuff round my prick". He informed the observer on another occasion of the difficulty which he experienced in having sexual intercourse while standing up; "I can't fuck them standing up". Apparently he goes weak about the knees. He complained that he had "lost about a pint of spunk" on the previous night owing to this difficulty. Here again it is not clear whether Dick had indeed been engaged in sexual activity on the previous night, or whether he thought it time he informed his fellow workmen of a supposed recent exploit. His chief

The Selected Town – Radby 43

satisfaction might be in noticing that the people to whom he described the exploit were suitably impressed. A young man of about twenty-five, somewhat mentally sub-normal, recalled for the benefit of the group the occasion, which he had previously described to them, when he paid a girl in the City ten shillings as a fee for sexual intercourse. After the act, the girl "sat down by a hedge and pissed". This was considered as very funny by the men, and by the young men concerned in retrospect, although at the time he had been rather dismayed and apparently considered the incident as some form of adverse reflection upon himself. During the discussion on contraceptives Peter told a story (which I believe to be substantially accurate), which caused much amusement, and occasioned no surprise or condemnation. Peter and a friend went to an Inn in the City one evening, and got into conversation with two women. They did not know the women previously, but another man in the bar evidently did, for he took Peter aside and told him that if Peter required a contraceptive, he knew where there was one. He proceeded to give the directions – proceed along the river bank until a bench was arrived at. Under a boulder by this bench was to be found a sheath contraceptive. Then came the part of the story which was received so well. For Peter was told to be sure to wash the sheath out after use, as it belonged to a fishing club.

On another occasion some friendly altercation took place between Robert and Peter, which ended with the following exchange : Robert : "You have not proved yourself a man yet". Peter (who was childless), referring to Robert's physical stature : "You know what they say, the bigger the feet, the bigger the prick (i.e. penis). I've not worn mine out like you've worn yours". Robert (father of two children) : "I've not worn it, I've made it useful".

It is hoped that the above account illustrates the sort of views which some of the men have with regard to sex, and the standards which they apply to it. No conclusions with regard to the special areas with which the Research is concerned may be drawn from the account, which does indicate, however, some of the attitudes which are liable to be encountered, and which helps to set the scene for the Research.

Information relating to children

The attitude of the men towards children and their upbringing will, of course, be governed to a certain extent by their attitudes towards sex, as described above, as well as by their views on other aspects of life. The problem of tracing the precise implications which these other attitudes have for children remains to be analysed. Meanwhile it is

44   *The Selected Town – Radby*

hoped to give an indication of attitudes towards children as revealed in conversation in the factory.

In the streets surrounding the factory, I often heard children described to their faces, usually by their mothers, as "bloody nuisances" and in similar terms. Frequently these adjectives "bloody", and others such as "fucking", and terms such as "bastard" and "cunt", appear to be used not in wrath, but in the course of ordinary conversation either directed towards or within the hearing of children. On one occasion a woman shouted across Spinney Street, addressing herself to a boy of about nine years of age : "goin' ter football?" The answer was "No", and the woman went on, "Won't they let yer, the miserable bastards?" The observer considers that this incident illustrates two things – a genuine consideration for the well-being of the child, that his desire to attend a football match should be fulfilled, and further that there is no consideration by the woman as to the possible effects of employing such language with a child. Rather it seems that such language is the natural and accepted form of expression. In exactly what way, if at all, this form of expression is indicative of a subculture at variance with the normally accepted modes of behaviour in society it is hoped to establish later. But this example provides the sort of indication which is of value to the Research.

Peter described the condition of a child in Dyke Street. The mother is dead and the child is being brought up by the eldest daughter and son. The child has not yet learnt to talk: it is always to be found playing in one of the yards behind Dyke Street, with bare feet, and kicking bricks about. Peter referred to the toughness of the child, but complained that such a situation should persist. The significant point is that this condition does persist in Dyke Street, and is tolerated or accepted by the residents of that street, even if some do comment about it. Dick then referred to a boy who lives in Carnation Street. This boy is 9–10 years old, and cannot yet talk coherently. In Dick's language the lad would "shit in the street, wipe himself with his hand, and then bung the shit all over the fucking street". This description occasioned some mirth at tea-break. It is not suggested that such behaviour is actively supported in Carnation Street: the contention is that such behaviour is allowed to occur with no apparent action to ensure its non-repetition.

An incidental point ensuing from Dick's comment is that there is no embargo amongst some people in the areas with which the Research is specifically concerned on such words as "shit" and "piss" such as that which exists among other groups of people.

Herbert was interspersing some comments with the adjective "fucking". Peter told him not to talk like this, because there were children

The Selected Town – Radby   45

in the garden nearby. Herbert didn't care a "cat's bollocks"; and suggested that the children would rather hear him talk like that than be deaf and hear nothing. Peter replied "You would not like your daughter to hear that word". Herbert's retort was "Aw, fuckit". I believe that Herbert would not object particularly to his daughter hearing the word – his disposition is such that he probably employs it at home –but in any case he would not admit that he would object. His attitude was that of grievance. Things were in a pretty poor state when someone started to complain because you had said "fuckit".

It appears that the advisability of employing such language within the hearing of children is just not a subject which occurs to some of the men. Peter had the final word: he swears himself, but he stated that "swearing don't make you sound any bigger".

In the assembly shop Tom (Knoll Estate) complained about the language used on parts of the Estate by women and children. He was surprised by the extent of the bad language used, and his summary of it is that it is "fucking terrible". Jim followed up the point. Whilst he was walking home he saw two young children scrapping. He told them to stop, and received the reply "fuck off".

Both Tom and Jim regarded Carnation Street as a bad area, but as has so often been the case, when it was attempted to gather more precisely what was meant by the term "bad area", no direct information was forthcoming. (Many people have informed me that the areas under consideration are "bad areas", without being prompted to say so. But they rarely define what they mean by the term. Thus a follow-up question usually will elicit only such comments as "a lot of fuckers live down that way", etc.).

Adolescents who leave school and start work in the factory, even if they are not already accustomed to using the sort of language indicated above, appear quickly to adopt it. No attempt is made by the men to amend their manner of expression when younger people are about. It seems doubtful whether it occurs to them that there is a possibility that they ought to amend it. The position might be summed up in a phrase of ten used, in relation to a variety of matters, namely "I don't care a fuck". (I couldn't care less).

There were often comments by some of the men about the filthy condition of many of the women and children in Wordsworth Street. The manager informed me that bad language was common in the street, and remarked also about the generally filthy appearance of the street. His woman secretary who had worked for many years amongst men in factories, and was therefore accustomed to hearing "bad" language, was nevertheless struck by the nature and extent of the language of women and children in the street.

46　*The Selected Town – Radby*

Comments on expenditure and leisure time activities

Several of the employees possess television sets, probably obtained under hire-purchase agreements. It seems that this keeps them indoors some evenings when they might otherwise go out. Otherwise, many of the men spend their money and leisuretime in public houses and clubs, with occasional visits to the cinema. Friday, Saturday and Sunday (when sufficient money remains) evenings are usually spent by these men in drinking, together with games of billiards, darts and skittles. Singing round a piano is also popular. The men who spend their leisuretime and money thus consume up to ten pints of ale in an evening. Some of the single men will pick up women and buy them drinks throughout the evening. The result is that most of them will have no money left by monday at the latest, and will have to borrow small sums of money or cigarettes throughout the week. Some place small bets on horses. The local. "bookie's runner" walks down Wordsworth Street most lunchtimes, and bets are then "slipped" to him. In spite of the illegality of placing bets with cash stakes it is a widespread phenomenon. In public houses, the bets will usually be passed to the bookie in the gentlemen's lavatory: but in an hotel near the Market Place the landlord was seen by the observer with a large ledger resting on the bar. Customers went to the bar and placed a bet; the landlord then made a note of it in his ledger. The observer mentioned this to Dick, who said that this had been going on for years, and the landlord was "in with the cops". By providing a drink or a small sum to the local policemen, the landlord can avoid being reported – and also secure prior information if any Special "check up" is to be made.

During the winter months most of the men in the machine shop subscribe to a weekly football competition. For a subscription of approximately 2s., a football team is allotted to each participant. The man with the team scoring the most goals receives a prize amounting to half of the sum subscribed. The other half is kept to help pay for the shop outing in the following summer.

Such an outing was planned for a Saturday in May of this year. A coach was hired to go to Blackpool for the day. Twenty men promised to go, but only fourteen turned up – there was much comment about men not sticking to their word. Those who had let the rest down were described as "miserable fuckers".

In so far as it is possible to generalise then, those men who are in the habit of going to clubs and public houses spend an appreciable portion of their money on beer and cigarettes and much of their leisure time in the public houses and clubs.

Delinquency

There is little opportunity in the factory for pilfering, and I am not aware that any took place whilst I was there. There was not a lot of discussion about delinquency, but my impression is that the men who committed crimes such as murder were considered foolish because of the likelihood of their being found out. Also, a certain malignant feeling was expressed against a man who was recently sentenced to death after being found guilty of the bloody murder of his wife in London. But some agreed with Peter that the man must have had "something wrong with him" mentally.

As regards the views of some of the men with regard to theft, my impression is that the general view is "if a man can get away with it", then "good luck to him". Theft from, e.g., an old, poor widow is liable to be condemned, whereas theft from an employer or "the rich" may be condoned. The attitude with regard to theft from employers may be summed up in the words of a London lorry driver (not working in Radby) who, when discussing theft from work, declared that the only difference between the "workers" and the "bosses" in this respect was that "we steal in farthings, and they steal in fucking pounds"; i.e., it is accepted that theft from work takes place and this is not considered bad.

I was discussing another worker with a man from the Knoll Estate. The man under discussion had recently joined the firm, having previously been manager of a small stores. The apparent unsuitability of the man for factory work gave rise to a discussion about why he left this shop-manager job, and it was suggested that it was in order to earn more money. The man from the Knoll Estate then stated that it would be easy to charge a few coppers more on goods in the shop and thereby secure a larger income than the wage provided. The only way in which a similar view applied in practice in the factory is in the "fiddling" of time sheets, practised by some men. In this way a higher rate of pay is contrived than that permitted by the piece-work schedule. Such devices appear to be accepted forms of securing a larger income. Theft from employers seems to be regarded by many as a justified augmentation of an employee's wages.

Patrick, whilst in the Army, worked in the stores. He acquired considerable sums of money by "flogging" sheets, blankets, shirts, etc., to people in Radby. A job in the stores is generally recognised as one of the best jobs in the Forces, because of the opportunity of "making a little extra on the side".

It is hoped that some impression has been given of the activities and thoughts of the men with whom I came into contact, and of the moral

48   *The Selected Town – Radby*

code or codes. The material has been selected by me to illustrate some aspects which I consider important. In Section III the various themes suggested above are elaborated, and related, in so far as they are to be related, to the specific areas with which the Research is concerned. Here it may be said that the men concerned are not rejected socially in Radby and their views may prove to be typical of the areas in which they reside.

The following two descriptions are sketches of the sort of men I encountered during my period of participant observation:

Dick

Lives in Spinney Street. Aged about thirty-five. Tall and well built; believes himself to be "good-looking", and boasts about this, and also about his physical strength. He stutters at times, and is apparently subject to fits. Boasts of his sexual activity and of his ability to attract women. He was for some years a prisoner of war in Germany, having served in the Army. His wife has obtained a separation order against him, and she and a son now live in the City. Dick lives with his mother. In his leisure-time he dresses in a smart suit, and goes to a public house when he has sufficient money, otherwise he goes for walks in summer, or merely lays in the park. He smokes cigarettes, and frequently cadges them from those men at work who have not resolved to decline his requests because of their frequency. Apparently his reputation for obtaining drinks in public houses is comparable to that for cadging cigarettes. His intelligence appears to be low, and he is child-like at times in his statements and behaviour. Thus he is frequently "played upon" by other men at work, without his realising the position. He will on these occasions be sufficiently roused as to become bad tempered, and then the flow of swear words becomes more and more fluent.

He often goes to Radby public houses but does not belong to any organisation or Men's Club. Sometimes he goes to pubs in the City. At these public houses Dick will join in the singing and pick up women. He related to the observer the following account of one such evening. It is typical of descriptions often given by Dick. He was at the bar, and the public house was packed with people, singing to the accompaniment of a piano. A woman of about thirty approached him and talked to him. Subsequently she sat on his knee, and Dick "felt her tits and arse", etc. She told Dick she had four children but was not married. But Dick did not know whether to believe that or not. At closing time she said to Dick, "Now Dick you know it's no use coming home with me, 'cos I've got the rag on", i.e., she was wearing a sanitary towel.

The Selected Town – Radby 49

Such was the information forthcoming to my question "Did you have a good time last night, Dick?"

He likes singing in public houses. One afternoon Dick and Peter argued about the value of the monarchy. Dick was "against" it, and considered more particularly, that he was helping to pay for the Coronation celebrations with his Income Tax payments. Coronation Day was a Tuesday, by which time Dick had spent his wages received on the previous Friday. Peter referred to this fact, and said that, were Dick to have sufficient money, he would be leaning against the bar on Coronation night, and singing "In a Golden Coach there's a heart of gold". His disposition is governed at any time by the availability, or lack, of money for beer and cigarettes. Work is an unfortunate necessity to be endured throughout the week until pay day arrives.

When he loses his temper, and when he is partially inebriated, he is liable to become physically rough. Thus one evening in a pub in town, he was involved in an incident – which concluded with Dick banging the door and thereby intentionally striking another man.

He is not to be relied upon for any arrangements which he makes – nor is he a dependable workman, in that, although he works hard whilst at work, he is liable to have time off whenever he feels inclined.

Dick is an accepted member of the Spinney Street community – there is nothing to suggest that his mode of life or standards of values are at great variance with those of other residents in the street. Certainly he is not ostracised by other dwellers in the street.

Peter

Lives in Dyke Street. Aged about twenty-seven years. Married with no children. Lives with wife, mother and father. Well built and strong. Previously worked in the pit, at the coal face. But an accident caused him to have a year off work, and he no longer could, or wishes to, work in the mines. In the factory he operates a machine, but also helps the foreman in organising work. He works conscientiously, talks a lot, but sensibly and sincerely; he is quite intelligent, and keen to discuss a wide variety of topics.

In his leisure-time he cultivates an allotment holding, and also fishes. A keen member of Dyke Street Club, and the "Central Club", and plays snooker, skittles and cards. Sometimes he goes to a public house in the City, but more often to the clubs, at least three times a week. He dresses smartly when out, and informed me that he possesses five suits, two sports clothes outfits (jacket and trousers) and ten pairs of shoes. His wife works and they save regularly. However, Peter,

50   *The Selected Town – Radby*

although a non- smoker, spends probably over £3 per week in the clubs and pubs.

He is sensible in his arguments and conclusions, and always ready to see two sides of a question. He criticised those who condemn other people because they have good jobs – he realises his own limitations, and recognises that other people are worth better jobs and more money. Condemns people like Dick who will not see this point. He believes that "everyone shines at something" – whether it be only at sport or cards. Also he considers that "we are not here to judge" – it is not man's job to condemn another, for there is usually more to a question than meets the eye. But this must not be taken to mean that Peter is of a religious nature.

He enjoys singing at the club, or in pubs, and often drinks well over six pints of beer when out for the evening.

He is kindly – fond of animals, but also of men, and pleased to help a man when in difficulty. Thus he will lend money, unless he thinks that the loan will be abused. He would not like to see a man unable to buy himself a pint of beer, but would expect some effort at repayment to be made. He has a conception of fairness which he upholds. When Dick was given a ten shillings tip by a scrap merchant who called at the factory, Peter was upset when Dick did not share the tip with Fred, who had collected the scrap together. When a miner (a neighbour in Dyke Street) asked Peter for a loan, Peter asked him what he had done with the £44 holiday pay which he had drawn ten days previously. The man had spent it on beer and on a woman and her family. Peter offered him fifteen shillings, all he could afford, but the miner "turned his nose up". Peter told him not to ask again.

One of the tea-break groups always centres about Peter, and he is responsible for organising the "shop outing", football competition, and so on.

He invited me to a club one night, and told his father that the guests were expected. He asked his father to put on a collar and tie, but his father had said that Peter's friends could "take him as he was, or not at all". Peter considered this to be fair enough.

Peter is not typical of Dyke Street, but he is a useful introduction to it.

Radby, then, is a mining town, It is definitely working class in character and has fewer areas which could be designated as residential, or middle class, than have other towns of its size. The initial description of the town that was given to the research workers was not an impressive one. They were told that juvenile delinquency was relatively high and concentrated in certain areas; that the standard of educational

The Selected Town – Radby   51

attainment was low: and that Radby, to quote the local gazeteers, was a "dreary mining town of depressing ugliness". The research workers found the place less mournful than the above description suggests. Radby people appear to set about their work and play much as do English working class people in general. They seem to go visiting, drinking, dancing, worshipping and gardening on much the same lines as those who live in other urban areas of the Midlands. It was the normality of Radby which most impressed the research workers: and the point should be born in mind when considering the following section of the Report.

III A. Method

The Research was based in the town of Radby, which was chosen because :

  i It is a comparatively compact entity, and is easily accessible.

 ii Delinquency is much more prevalent in some areas of the town than in others. Certain streets have a steady load of delinquency, whereas other streets, materially comparable and in close proximity hardly ever have a youngster or adult before the court.

iii Delinquency in Radby may be studied both in the old areas of the town, and in the more recently built estates.

Information obtained from the County Probation Department's Records, and from the County Constabulary showed that there were five areas in Radby in which "official" delinquents were concentrated, and that within these areas there were "white" streets and "bad" streets. To test the hypothesis, certain of these bad streets were investigated and compared with materially similar ones which presented no cases of delinquency, or delinquency in much smaller numbers.

Information was sought under the following headings : -

1 Occupation and length of residence.

2 Standards of conduct to which children and juveniles are expected to conform by parents and local custom.

3 "Cultural patterns" of the street as a whole.

The methods adopted for the Research may be classified as follows :-

(a) Interviews with External Officials and Individuals

This approach is self-explanatory. Interviews were obtained with people who had a special knowledge of Radby and of the specific areas

Method 53

by virtue of their occupation and/or long association with the town. Much factual material was gained from these people, and from the agencies which they represent, e.g., the Youth Employment, the Probation Service, etc. There was a general agreement amongst such people with regard to the contrast between the streets in the areas which were to be studied.

On the whole, the officials with whom interviews were sought proved co-operative and helpful. The interviewers were given a letter of introduction from the County Education Officer, and this proved useful. Indeed, in one case (a Headmaster), it proved the only tool which would secure the minimum of information requested – namely a list of the boys attending his school who happened to live in the five Areas in which the Research was interested. It is perhaps not inappropriate to mention here, therefore, the vast difference noticed between the schools, The Research workers would not presume to assess the quality of the school staff; and the following impressions are only given in the belief that they have some bearing on the subject of the Survey.

Of the Headteachers with whom contact was made, some appeared to adopt modern teaching methods, and to approve of the general broadening of school curricula. On the other hand one or two, who had been teaching in the same school for perhaps thirty years, had little interest in modern methods and seemed indeed to be ignorant of them, They regarded their school (and Radby) rather as if they were their own property. Criticism of Radby was liable to be considered as a personal attack upon individual members of the community. To mention "delinquent" and "Radby" in the same sentence was in their opinion unjustified. Nor in some cases do their intellectual abilities and range of interests appear to be wide. One Headteacher, suspicious of a stranger to the town and a University worker, was most reluctant to give any of the valuable ideas which he, as a Headmaster, might have been expected to have with regard to the youth of the town. He was adamant although it was of course explained that no criticism was implied of his own school, or his management of it, and though it was stressed that the Research workers did not regard Radby as a den of vice. He did thaw a little finally, and his reasoning on the subject of juvenile delinquency was that "it's all due to the parents". Asked in what ways the parents cause juvenile delinquency his reply was "Well, they don't look after their children". Pressed further he pointed out that the parents had never been taught themselves, the blame was due to their parents – and so on.

In considering the low educational attainment in this country of large numbers of children we might perhaps more often take into account the limited horizons of some of the children's teachers, and of

54 *Method*

the special dangers attached to teaching the "twice times" table to the children of a small township for half a life-time. Men promoted to positions by virtue of their long service to the profession may yet not be competent to do the work efficiently. The Research Workers met one or two teachers who appeared to be in such a position, and who were constantly anxious because they realised the position themselves, yet did not wish others to realise it. Furthermore, the shortage of teaching staffs, adding burdens to the shoulders of most Headteachers, also accentuates the fact that the less attractive townships and schools often have to make do with the least competent teachers.

(b) Interviews with Residents in Delinquent Areas

Miss Jephcott interviewed residents in Areas A and C, and Mr. Carter those in Area D (See Section III). The object was to gain interviews with as many of the residents living in the areas as possible.

For the interviews the "oblique approach" was adopted, that is to say, the problem of delinquency was not indicated as the reason for the interview. The Research Workers stated that they were interested in a Social Survey in Radby on children's leisure-time activities, and the attitude of parents to them. When possible the conversation was led round to the topic of delinquency so that the interviewees would volunteer information and opinions.

Frequently the interviewers were invited into a house, and then the interviews generally proved to be more rewarding than those conducted on the doorstep. From some households a good deal of information was forthcoming, from others very little. After the interview in order to facilitate tabulation and analysis the information ascertained was recorded on a schedule (cf. Appendix A).

This schedule consists of two main sections. The first was concerned with factual information of a "quantitative" nature, relating to such things as age, sex, size of family and occupation. It is this section which provides the basis for the "comparisons of history of the populations with respect to occupation and length of residence". The second section related to standards of conduct upheld, and indicates aspects of the cultural pattern of the area. It is therefore concerned with factual information of a different order, indicative of such things as the interrelationships within a family, and the status of various members in it and in the local community.

This section is also concerned with such matters as the social outlook of the informant and other members of the family, his values and habits. The assessment of this type of information must of course allow

Method 55

for such complications as the possibility of interviewees stating what they think they ought to state or what they think the interviewer wants them to state, rather than what they actually think about a topic. This information recorded on the schedule is the result, then, of

i The statements of the interviewee.
ii The interpretation of these statements by the interviewer in the light of such considerations as those stated above.
iii The observations of the interviewer with regard to the physical and material appearance of the family.

The element of "subjectivity" in the second section of the schedule is checked to some extent by external information from public agencies and officials, and by fairly frequent discussions between the Research Workers themselves to establish common bases for their assessment of social situations and factors. In this connection it is of value to refer to the remarks of Plant:[1]

"To the reader who has become enamoured of a statistical approach to these problems there will be little but disappointment ... our use of the word 'findings' will be blasphemy. We use the word because of a naive notion that what someone tells us about what things mean to him – is more realistic and were a 'finding' than is, for instance, the crassly artificial matter of extracting from him his foreign-born parentage in order that he may be put into a statistical table".

The problems and techniques of qualitative interviewing are discussed in a Columbia University Guide.[2] Here it is sufficient to state that in order not to destroy or prejudice any rapport which was established between interviewer and interviewee, the research workers rarely made detailed notes but committed to memory the points arising in the course of the directed conversation, and put them into note form as soon afterwards as possible.

Three main procedures could have been adopted for the purpose of obtaining the interviews. It was at one time hoped to obtain interviews with all of the households in each of the streets compared, but this was

---

1 J.B.S. Plant : <u>Personality and the Culture Pattern</u>
2 Bureau of Applied Social Research, <u>Training Guide in the Techniques of Qualitative Interviews</u>, Columbia University, 1948.

56 *Method*

not found possible. It was therefore necessary either to take a sample number of households or to obtain interviews with as many households as possible by means of introductions, or simply by house-to-house calls. In fact, all three of these procedures were adopted. It can not be claimed that the number of interviews successfully held is in accordance with any elaborate statistical sample designed to ensure scientific veracity. The only approximation to such a "sample" was that it was decided to interview each tenth household in the streets (thus, e.g., 1, 21, 41, etc.). The digit number was chosen from the point of view of convenience. For example, if House No. 5 happened to be on a convenient corner from which to start, then the "sample" numbers might be 5, 25, 45, etc. The "sample" was employed for two main reasons. The first was in order to gain a general impression of the streets throughout their length. That is to say, it avoided being bogged down in one little group of houses in one part of the street. The second reason was to obtain the interviews themselves fairly spaced throughout the street.

The method of gaining introductions, either from people external to the streets or from people living in them who had already agreed to being interviewed, proved very fruitful, particularly in the streets in the older areas of the town. The danger of working via introductions is, of course, that one "good" family tends to give its introductions to another "good" family, and so on. In this way it might conceivably be possible to traverse the street meeting only the "good" or "bad" homes. This danger was recognised, and it was countered not only by the use of the "sample", but also by the fact that in practice introductions were obtained to households in each of the five ranges (see Section III F). The interviews on the Knoll Estate were less dependent upon personal introduction. Although in fact the Warden of the Community Centre gave one or two introductions, it was decided that the interviewer should not associate himself with the Community Association in any way. This was in order not to prejudice the chances of gaining an interview, and in order to discover what people really thought about the Association, its organisation and value to the community. But, most important, it enabled the interviewer to appear as a stranger to these parts, ignorant of the community, and anxious to hear all about it. Furthermore, the physical layout of the Estate facilitated the method of house- to-house interviews. Unlike the old parts of the town, the houses on the Knoll Estate all have large back gardens and private, though small, front gardens. Many have side entrances, and at the most, a house only shares its front gate and its garden path with a neighbour. This gives far more privacy than the contested yards of the older parts of the town. Privet hedges in the front gardens emphasised

Method 57

the relative privacy of many of the houses on the Estate, as does the fact that the houses are spaced further apart (blocks of six houses being separated by side gardens) and that the roads and layout in general are more spacious. To all this physical detail which facilitated house-to-house interviewing may be added a less tangible matter. A large percentage of the families at Knoll Estate are of a rather higher social grade than those in the older parts of Radby. They are therefore accustomed, so to speak, to some of the more usual social manners. Thus, a stranger knocking on the door of a Dyke Street house is regarded with suspicion and liable to be told to go away, or the door is just not answered. But on the Knoll Estate, whereas in some cases the same sort of experience was met with as might happen in Dyke Street, the householders on the whole were more socially at ease, more competent with the minor social graces, and more used to having a person other than a money-collector knock on the door. They were used, also, to nighbours knocking on the door, rather than walking straight in. Furthermore, it was possible to approach the Estate from two different directions, and one could visit it quite frequently without being regarded as an intruder – at any rate, not to such an extent as in Dyke Street.

Such then, were the procedures adopted for obtaining the interviews. They are thought to have been relatively successful. It was noticed that the means adopted to gain an interview had a great bearing on the quality of the interview. Sometimes the people agreed to being interviewed: but many declined at first and then, of course, it became a question of starting a discussion on the beauty of the baby or the iniquities of the local cats. Any interviewer has to be ready to assume varied roles and a variety of moods and expressions.

(c) **Participant Observation**

In this Research an attempt was made to assess "the main social facts, types of group relationships, modes of group activity, and social and moral climates of different neighbourhoods".[1] As Mack says, "to observe the special kinds of relationship and the standards of private and public behaviour prevailing in such neighbourhoods would involve a method of direct and participant group study". The method adopted in Radby, apart from that of the structured interviews, was "participant observation", described by Kluckhohn as "conscious and systematic sharing, in so far as circumstances permit, in the life activities and, on

---

1 J.A. Mack B.J. Delinquency, Vol. III, No. 4, April 1953·

58   Method

occasion, in the interests and effects of a group of persons. Its purpose is to obtain data about behaviour through direct contact and in terms of specific situations in which the distortion that results from the investigator's being an outside agent is reduced to a minimum".[1]

The "division of labour" decided upon for the field work was that Miss Jephcott would carry out the house-to-house interviewing in Areas A and C and "participant observation" in Area D, whilst Mr. Carter would do the reverse. Area D is about two miles distant from Areas A and C and is isolated from the rest of the town. This facilitated the necessity for the research workers to play dual roles in Radby – that of straightforward investigators into social conditions, and that of participant observers, endeavoring to analyse the social code whilst giving the appearance of being simply members of a local group or club.

The first objective was to get acquainted with the town and the people generally, in order to assess the social life, moral standards upheld, etc. It was desirable to get on terms with as many of the townspeople as possible – not only those from the three areas being specially studied. Mr. Carter, as has been explained already, obtained employment in a Radby factory for a period of four months. Many of the sixty or so men with whom he became friendly knew that he was a University student, but thought that his only object was to obtain vacation employment and experience of engineering. People with whom he mixed in cafés and public houses during this period regarded him as an ordinary workmen. By means of conversation, general observation and social meetings with these men (some of whom lived in the three delinquent areas), information was gathered which has proved of use in assessing the ideas, beliefs and actions of the people of Radby, and of the special areas in particular. Further, the relationships established in this way have proved of use in gaining introductions to other people in the town. The essential point of this method of research is to get access to groups and situations with a minimum of alteration to these groups end situations resulting from the presence of the observer therein.

The observers also participated in Radby life by going into Public Houses, cinemas, Clubs and Dance Halls, and by sitting around in Parks, shopping, etc.

An introduction to the Dyke Street Working Men's Club and to the Central Club was gained from some of the men with whom the observer worked in the factory. The Dyke Street Club is not extensive, but consists of one large room in which are a bar, a small platform

---

1 The Participant Observer Technique in Small Communities A.J.S., 1940.

Method 59

with a piano, a darts board, one or two pin-tables, and a large number of chairs and tables to accommodate the members. It attracts its members more particularly (but not exclusively) from its immediate environs. The following account is taken from notes made after an evening spent at this Club.

"Wednesday, 13/1/54. Pleasant evening, playing darts and dominoes. Club by no means packed but about seventy people there at one time. Importance of money – e.g., in dominoes, and. housey-housey (between 8 p.m. and 10 p.m. there were three rounds of this game). Our party of four spent seven and six- pence on this alone during the evening. Twenty-four shillings had to be won each round. Also the pin-tables were constantly in use, the object being to win a substantial sum for the outlay of one penny necessary to operate the machine. A young lad of about fifteen years of age tried to sing "Answer Me" in the Johnny Ray mode. If a member of the Club proposes someone for an audition he or she may try, and if the effort is adjudged to be worthwhile the entertainer is given a prize of £2. Other men sang, and the piano was played constantly. The evening ended with the pianist and another man singing a duet – the other man sang in a high-pitched voice to imitate a woman's voice, The song dealt with a discussion between a farmer and a young lady about their forthcoming offspring and the arrangements for the wedding. The girl wanted a limousine and a honeymoon in Monte Carlo. The farmer would not have any of this, and emphasised the essentials of a honeymoon – up the stairs and into bed. The attendant ceremonies were evaluated in detail via the medium of the song. The song was well- received and might well closely record the prevalent feelings of the clientele of the club – the "essentials" are emphasised in their lives as in the song. Peter seemed pleased to see me, and said that I must call round at his house when I wanted to see him – though he was apologetic in saying that it (his home) was rough and ready. His parents are getting old, he explained, presumably thinking that some form of excuse was necessary. He wanted to know when I was going to take my wife over to see him, as he considered it necessary to make himself specially neat and tidy. He would "put on his best manners, seeing as she is a schoolmistress"."

The Central Club is a larger organisation, and occupies extensive premises near the Market Place. It has many affiliated clubs – both sports and "interest", such as the Rabbit Club. It thrives on indoor games, drinking, dancing and music. One evening Peter and his wife, Flo, together with the observer, his wife, and his ex-foremen spent an evening at the Central Club. The observer made the following notes on the evening.

60   *Method*

"Tuesday, 19/1/54. Peter and Flo met us in the Market Place at 7.15 (7 o'clock had been arranged, but Flo said that she had kept Peter waiting). Flo explained that she does not finish work (in a town 6 miles distant) until 5.30, she operates a machine and gets as dirty at her work as Peter does, i.e., very oily and greasy.

We went into the Club, and Peter bought the first round. Flo had a port and lemon, and during the evening had the equivalent of eight or nine ports. (This was a special evening, and often she drinks only one or two halves of beer). Peter and Len (who arrived at 7.30) drank seven pints each during the evening. The bar closed at about 10.15 p.m.

Proceedings started at 8.0 p.m. It was an "Olde Tyme Music Hall", as the poster elaborately explained, and the performers were good. There was a large attendance, probably well over 200. On each table was an empty beer bottle, with a lighted candle stuck in the top. The barman and waiters wore large false moustaches. There was a convivial atmosphere, especially when the show started with some old-time choruses which everyone joined in. No bad drunkenness at all, nor bad behaviour. One man gave a clever comic turn, well delivered and holding the audience. His first act was bemoaning the lack of achievement of a local professional football club, from the standpoint of a supporter. It was based upon innuendo and double-meaning. His second appearance, towards the end of the evening was also amusing. Some stories, this kind of thing, got much laughter – he went into a butcher's shop and asked the less behind the counter, "Do you keep dripping". Also, he carried a banana, which he used suggestively with such phrases as "you know where to put this".

The barman mistakenly gave a member of our party change for a £1 instead of a ten shilling note, so that there was ten shillings excess change. Peter took commend, and said at once that the money should be used for a drink on the house – which it was.

It is unusual for so many people to attend the Club during the week. The majority were men, but quite a lot of women aged anything from 25 to 70 were present with their husbands. Peter commented that "if the Central Club does anything, it does it well". The evening's cost to each of three men (two rounds each; raffle tickets and cigarettes) was approximately £1."

A few weeks later a party was held at the observer's home. There was much solid drinking, once the men and (more particularly) the women had lost their initial shyness, and there was also some conversation useful to the Survey.

In addition to the period of employment in the factory, Mr. Carter took a temporary job with the Radby Post Office for the two Christmas

Method 61

rush periods which occurred during the course of the Research. He spent much of these periods (of ten days each) riding in a van with the driver, one of whom was from Knoll Road and another from Charlotte Street, that is, two of the streets which are considered in detail in another section. During this time he was invited into a Charlotte Street home, and had a mid-day meal there which consisted of tinned soup, custard and banana. Whilst this was being eaten, a home-perm was being given to the hostess by another young woman from down the street. Their talk was decidedly coarse. A kitten played in the general mess and untidiness on the floor. The room in which we sat was the downstairs front room, and Jim, the man with whom I was working, and his wife, rent this room and a bedroom from his wife's father and mother. The sitting room is very small and overcrowded with odds and ends, not to speak of a radiogram and a pretentious-looking modern style, light-oak piano, both of which were being bought under a hire-purchase agreement. Jim told me of the occasion when he had forcibly to restrain his father-in-law from striking his, Jim's, wife. He said to his father-in-law "She's mine now, and if anyone's going to hit her, it's me". Before his marriage, Jim lived in the City, and he told me of his exploits there during the days of the war when he was a youth. He was a member of a gang whose illegal and troublesome exploits were facilitated by the black cut and by various air-raid precautionary measures such as sand-bag barricades.

Jim took great delight in explaining to me how once his lack of height had enabled him to overcome someone of a larger physique. The rival was about to have sexual intercourse with a girl when he decided that the girl was not tall enough. He accordingly went to fetch a sandbag on which the girl would stand. Whilst he was thus absent Jim "slipped up her". This was the beginning of his adult sex history, apparently, a history which was enriched by his service in the Army, but which he now regarded as concluded. Now he has married and settled down.

Nearly every day I went with the other man whom I met to have a cup of tea in his home, and there I usually met his wife his daughter-in-law and her baby, and at least one of his sons. This family is very active at the Community Association, and I gained a lot of useful knowledge about it and about other people on the Estate.

The task of becoming accepted members of the Radby community was thus approached from various angles. The following account of Miss Jephoott's experiences describes three types of approach which she used. She went to camp for four nights with a party of girls from one of the Secondary Modern Schools. She was a regular attender (for 4 months) at the Ladies Guild and Dancing Class of the Knoll

62 Method

Community Centre: and she had fairly frequent contacts with the Youth Club at the Centre for a period of a year and a quarter. In order to facilitate contact with Dyke Street, she was able to rent a front room there. The local children came in and out of this room to paint, play with games and dolls, etc. This play room was open twice a week for about 40 sessions (July to January).

The Dyke Street Play Room

Dyke Street's reputation, both from official records and from town gossip, is bad. A few preliminary visits to the street confirmed this view. Many of the houses had ragged, filthy curtains, and broken windows. The schoolchildren playing about were untidy and raucous. Neglected-looking toddlers and blowsy-looking mothers standing on their step, contrasted strongly with the smartly-dressed younger women who made an appearance at 5.30 p.m. as they came home from work. A few lorries passed up and down the street, but apart from people who actually lived there, not many pedestrians ever seemed to enter it. Any stranger who appeared in the street for a second time was subjected to close scrutiny – "What does she want here?" It was plain that in Dyke Street interviews based on door-knocking were going to be a difficult business. And not only difficult but probably fruitless, especially in those households which had anything abnormal about their structure or history, and in the ignorant and more suspicious families – just the ones, of course, that it was most neccessary to contact. It was thought that three things might facilitate the business of making contact. The first was to provide a reason that the street could understand as to why the interviewer was constantly in it. The second was to got on terms with one or two families who would, so to speak, guarantee the interviewer to the more chary homes. And the third need was to get hold of some base from which to observe the surface aspects of the street's life.

It was decided to try to meet the above needs through the local children, and for this purpose a small, informal play room was set up in the front room of house No. – The householder, Mr. "Bates", had been secretary of the Coronation street party (which was just over) and was approached by the interviewer in this capacity. He would know, from his party lists, which houses had children, and this was a point in which the interviewer was interested as she was doing a Survey from the University on how children spend their out-of-school hours. Mr. Bates and his wife had 2 children, a girl of seven and a boy of four, as well as three young nieces living opposite. The Bates's decided that a play room might be handy for their own clan, anyhow, and they agreed

Method 63

to rent their front room (about 12 foot square) from 4 to 6 o'clock on Tuesdays and Thursdays at 5s. a night. Mrs. Bates was warned to put away any breakable objects. The Bates girl, Cissie, and three friends agreed to help the interviewer spend 10s. on paints and comics for the proposed play room, and went off to Woolworths forthwith. It was a revealing expedition, since one of the eight-year old children (while the shop assistatnt's back was turned) suggested to her sister of thirteen that they should "take" a box of crayons. The suggestion was vetoed by the older girl who probably realised that a relatively unknown grown-up was at her elbow.

That was the genesis of the play room. It moved from the Bates' front room (for reasons that are not relevant to the Survey) to a similar kind of house at the opposite and of the street. This was occupied by an elderly couple. The man, an ex-miner, was now a rag and bone merchant in a small way. His wife was a confirmed "neighbourer". Altogether about forty play room sessions were held (from July to January); the number of individual children who ever used it was fifty odd; and the normal attendance was about twenty, which was more than a roomfull. Ages ranged from two up to fifteen. Most of the teen-agers dropped out (it was too juvenile for them) and finally the eight to tens dominated the room The children came in and out more or less as they liked; they paid nothing, and no register was kept. It was deliberately <u>not</u> run as a club, the point being that any Dyke Street person who was willing to make himself known to the room would be so much grist to the Survey. With this same end in view no child was ever asked to come, or reprimanded for not coming, nor was any grown-up ever asked if she would like her children to come. A refusal, or a complaint that a child had stopped away, might have put a little tension between the home and the interviewer, and it was aimed to avoid this.

What did the children do? Mostly they painted and drew and modelled things with plasticine. Two sisters of three and four played with dolls, but dolls did not interest any of the other children. Some of them liked writing stories about a given picture, and any new comic always had a queue of readers. Games like draughts or lode were useless· No one agreed on the rules and the games always ended in a quarrel. They introduced one acting game of their own – "We're five men out of work". But apart from this one game, however, they were too undisciplined (and too varied in age) to play any game that involved a group or teams.

The play room revealed many things about the Dyke Street children's habits. One adult visitor after an evening spent at the Play Room made this comment "Poor little things – they are nice children

64   *Method*

though". Many, the majority, were poorly dressed. Some were always dirty and ragged. Their hair, especially, was unkempt. Toddlers in particular were often thoroughly grubby. Two of them used regularly to come in with black hands and faces, and clutching a cream cake. No older person ever approached with some of these toddlers, or seemed to bother where they had got to. All ages were very undisciplined and very disobedient. Two six–year olds, e.g., Edna and her friend Gloria, would take no notice whatever if told not to come down to the (dangerous) main road with the interviewer. It was useless to give a quiet instruction or a request. Unless one bawled at the child, he did not think it important. They were very aggressive too, and there were often tears. It was a mistake to leave the room even for half a minute. A fight would develop and two or three of the older ones would be struggling on the floor. Some of the older boys were always hurting the girls. A good deal of this hitting was spiteful, and not just done by accident or in play· The children disapproved of actual swearing among each other, but "devil", "bloody", etc. came out at times. The house-owner himself when too infuriated with the noise, would himself come in and swear at two or three of the bigger ones. Some of the little children were biters, and known as such by the other children. One or two others were classed as pinchers. They constantly told of each other in an "Arn't I a good girl" sort of way - "Donald has got that book out in the street", "Sallie took them crayons home", and so on. Even in the room itself a thirteen year old girl warned the interviewer not to put the latter's sweet on a high shelf for a few minutes as "Someone'll take it"· The extent to which the paint brushes, comics, small toys, etc. diminished each week suggests that many of the children regularly took things off with them. They seemed to have toys at home, but not tools like paints or plasticine or sewing things.

Money was always a topic of importance and to possess it gave great status. The stories they made up contained many references to money, lost or stolen, They constantly fingered any money they had on them. A thirteen year old boy would come into the play room on his way to the pictures just to boast of the 2s. which he had got out of his mother to go; or an eight year old would show off the £1 note he had been given with which to do Mrs. X's shopping. A three penny bit was always a more popular prize than a 6d. bag of sweets.

Their drawings and paintings[1] were very messy. Only about three of the children had any idea of tidy, clean work. They would, e.g., throw

---

1 See Appendix A

Method 65

paint on the floor and be genuinely surprised if a grown-up objected. On the other hand, they had to do their painting in a very cramped space, which made it difficult to be even relatively clean workers. One additional thing noticed was that they seemed quite unable to draw anything they could actually see. Some liked to take their efforts home, but certain children said that no one there would bother about them.

Then there were the writers,[1] children who made up stories about a given picture. Their stories revealed what things these children noticed, and what they regarded as common-place. The girls of eleven to thirteen wrote of love, kissing, and husbands, of rows between husband and wife and of remarriage. crime, hangings, jail, murder, theft, accidents at the pit, the police - came into many of the tales of both boys and girls. Considering the age of the writers (none over thirteen) they seemed to interpret the pictures they were asked to write about in a very unchildlike way. Their world of imagination was nearer that of the "News of the World" than of fairy tales and adventure stories. Indeed, with a few notable exceptions, the children themselves were very unchildlike in many ways. Little girls of six and seven had thin anxious faces and at times put on the sort of nervy giggling behaviour that would be more normal in a school girl of thirteen. The talk of some of the boys of eight and nine was sometimes more like that of sharp men, than of young children. Certain ones never got absorbed in anything, which is unusual for children.

The play room method of approach to a rough type of street had two disadvantages. It was very time consuming, and, as a means of approach, it needed more careful timing than was given in the Radby experiment. It was started primarily as a method of introduction to the families in the street; and when it had done this job, i.e., after seven months, it was stopped. The children were extremely disappointed at this, and since it was not diplomatic to tell the parents precisely why it had been held, they too probably felt, though they did not say so, that they had been let down. Apart from this, however, it certainly fulfilled its function. The play room children proved admirable ambassadors to all and sundry, including the "black" households; the room and its troubles was an excuse for talking to any of the adults about their own children; and the contacts made there enabled the interviewer to identify youngsters seen on the yards and about the town. She was able to relate them and what they were doing to specific homes (e.g., a five and an eight year old pair coming out of the pictures at 10.15 p.m.; or

1 See Appendix A

66   *Method*

a thirteen year old girl shrieking with a crowd of boys on the Market Place). Moreover, in the case of the low-level families who were very unvocal, what the adults <u>did</u> in relation to their children, was often more illuminating than anything they were able to say – and the play room gave many opportunities to observe this point.

The Knoll Estate Community Centre

The Community Centre on the Knoll Estate had been in existence for eight years. It is housed in two converted Nissen huts, and is the only non-domestic building on this Estate of well over a thousand people. Any local meetings that involved more than half a dozen people had to be held at these premises. One hut had a good dance hall and stage. The other was used only by a youth club, and is very roughly furnished. It is extremely cold at times. The Centre had a full-time secretary, responsible to various local. committees, and the youth club had a voluntary leader, a miner.

The interviewer was introduced to the Community Centre Executive Committee as someone who was conducting a survey on young people's leisure, The committee agreed that she should become a temporary member of the Centre. With this introduction she spent two to three sessions a week at one or other of the Centre's activities for a period of four months. She acted as a street-collector for the Coronation, joined the dozen solemn members of a 6d. Old Time Dancing class, became a member of the Ladies Guild, and a constant visitor (and later a committee member) of the youth club. All told she was in contact with the Centre for about a year and a quarter.

The Ladies Guild met weekly, and had from 12 – 20 attenders, of all ages. The nightly subscription was 6d. which included a cup of tea and a raffle ticket. It ran various money-making activities (sales, fish suppers); talks ("How to Ice a Cake", "Radby 50 years ago", "Home treatment of Rheumatism"); and mystery trips (bus outings to distant pubs). When hard put to fill an evening it resorted to Housey-Housey, or just chat. It had a very slow, unskilled, and anxious committee, the members of which were in terror of being accused of getting above themselves. It was obviously a major effort for these women to take on any authority outside their own home. Various ones gave up the effort.

The youth club, next door, was cold (it always had broken windows and often no fire), dirty and bare. There was practically no equipment except two table tennis sets and, sometimes, a gym horse. The youngsters themselves, by their clothes and talk, appeared to come from a lower social level than the adults of the Centre, who mostly seemed to

Method 67

represent the top level Knoll families, It was difficult to find out how many members the club had because there was no effective definition of "membership", The numbers visible, on a typical evening, ranged from half a dozen to thirty or so. Ages were from about eleven to eighteen, with a preponderance of school children. The weekly subscription was 3d. for Schoolchildren, 6d, for those at work. Payment seemed to be a hit and miss affair. The official activities included football, boys' P.T., square dancing, table tennis, first aid, and embroidery, Apart from football and P.T. there was really no regular activity. The interviewer's notes, on three typical occasions, read : (1) "8.30 – 9.30 p.m., about half to a third, mostly boys aged 13 to 18, just lolling about"; and (2) "8 – 9.15 p.m., none of the six girls in tonight doing anything except a bit of table tennis"; and (3) "turbulent rough and tumble uncivilized atmosphere - loud speaker playing - boys dirty. Two or three with their hats on all. evening. A lot of desultory back chat between boys and girls". In other words, the club was used mainly as a cheap place at which to meet other youngsters and to get away from home. So far as providing wider interests, or new skills, or any training in social relations, it was a pathetic attempt. The general talk and behaviour at the club, night after night, as well as the fact that the windows and doors were constantly being broken (on several occasions the locks were forced) suggested that the youngsters who used it might well be among those who produced the kind of delinquent behaviour which the Survey was studying.

It was found relatively easy to become an accepted member of the Community Association, and, as a practical method of observing the social life on a new estate, it was a useful approach. The difficulties encountered in Dyke Street did not arise here. Whether these months of participant observation at the Community Centre had any particular value to the Research was another matter; especially since the observer did not, later on, have to undertake her house-to-house interviewing in Knoll itself. Bits and pieces of information obtained, however, were useful, For example, the Centre showed the members' unquestioned acceptance of gambling, in some form, as a necessary part of practically every social event.

A more significant asset was that contact with the Centre put the social life of the six Radby streets to be studied into perspective. The cultural level of the recognised pleasures of Dyke Street and Carnation Street (centred on the pub and its talent nights, darts matches and so on) was definitely narrower than that of the drama groups, inter club visits, talks and committee meetings of the Community Centre, unpretentious as these were. It also showed up the difference between

68   *Method*

the entirely secular social life of the new estate, and the Church and Chapel centred social life of so many of the Gladstone Road families. At the same time it must be remembered that the Community Centre only reflected a portion of the Knoll Estate. The majority of the Knoll families had no regular connection with it. The same point, however, would probably hold good for the social life of most of Radby, or indeed for that of any artisan area, viz·, that a high proportion of the adults[1] do not attach themselves to any external social group.

The Girls' Secondary Modern School Camp

An opportunity arose for the interviewer to go camping for four nights with one of the Radby Girls' Secondary Modern School camps. It was a tent camp, pitched on a hill overlooking a river, and outside a small village about thirty miles from Radby. The weather was warm (July) and very wet. The advance party had to pitch the first tents and try to get a fire going in pouring rain. Twenty-eight girls, mostly aged fourteen and thirteen, were present, with three staff. Practically none of the girls had camped before. At the end of the week most of them voted it great sport.

The reason for going to this camp was that the school was known to be a go-ahead one, and the interviewer was anxious to get on good terms with the staff. She also hoped that some of the girls who came to camp might come from the chosen streets, in which case the camp should provide a sound introduction to those particular homes. When the final camp list was drawn up, only four of the girls did, in fact, live in the relevant streets. Two of these came from homes which had some record of delinquency. One of the four girls got on particularly well with the interviewer, and gave her a pressing invitation to go and see her home in Carnation Street. The family (Salvation Army by tradition - mother divorced and remarried, husband a miner, seven in the household) proved an admirable base from which to contact other households in the street. Another minor outcome of the camp was that the school staff began to take an interest in the Survey. The following term, for example, the Headmistress was willing to add to a series of discussion groups with her older girls, certain points connected with stealing, and sex relations, on which the Survey wanted to know adolescent opinion, When these discussions were over she was able to state the general opinion of the group, to give minority views, and to say, roughly, what social classes these represented.

A less tangible result which came out of the camp visit was connected with the relationship of the girls to the School staff. That they

---

1 *Clubs, Societies and Democracy* PEP Broadsheet No. 263, 1947.

Method 69

were on good terms with each other was established in many ways. But the authoritarian nature of the relationship was always in the background. A request, "Would you fetch the blankets please" was, in fact, an order. The point was especially noticeable to the interviewer who was much more familiar with youth organisations than schools. A certain restraint, even under the informal conditions of camp, was always present. This came out more plainly when the interviewer was able to get invited into one or two of the girls' tents, and to sit about there. Even with an adult visitor present, the girls' speech had altered. They talked with a broader accent, they were more brusque with each other, and they gave an impression of being young women (with their half serious talk of their boys and so on), rather than of being just schoolgirls. This following type of conversation, too, would almost certainly have been censored had any of the staff been present : "I've only got 8/6 left. How much have you got, Betty?" "Ten shillings; but I shall write and tell my mum I've spent all I had". Another girl joining in, "yes, so shall I". Later on one of the staff confirmed what the interviewer had seen signs of, viz. that these girls could live by two quite different standards. "Certain ones are as nice as can be in school. Out of it their speech and manners (and doubtless their codes) are entirely different", She went on to refer to a girl of thirteen who was thought to be soliciting men in the Market Place, Another Headteacher, discussing the same topic, pointed out that a child is at school for only 51/2 hours each day, for 5 days in the week, and for 40 weeks of the year. Small wonder, he said, that any good done at school is quickly countered if the out of school hours are spent amongst people with quite different standards from those taught at school. All told, the camp visit, brief as it was, suggested that the teachers 'picture of Radby children might well not be a comprehensive one.

There are several advantages of using the method of participant observation[1] in this Research.

1 It is possible by this method to obtain information which would otherwise not be forthcoming, Men discuss and elaborate their private affairs and views on society with chance acquaintances in pubs or with friends whereas they often will not do so with a person who they know to be making a social investigation.

2 Some men - particularly from areas such as those being studied in this Research - feel more at ease a public house than at home, and

---

1 and cf. W.F. Whyte, etc., for examples of use of this technique

70   *Method*

are therefore more willing to converse. For an interview at home demands that they perform the function, in a sense, of "host", and some are more prepared to divulge their thoughts and actions then to exhibit the physical and material standards of their home.

3 Allied to this is the fact that information gained in this way is likely to be more accurate and more complete than information gained in official interviews; that is to say, with interviews which are sought by the research worker as such, the situation is one in which interviewees are requested to provide information to someone who is stated to be carrying out a social survey, and the position of the interviewer is that of an "external" official. But with participant observation information is gathered whilst the informant remains unaware of that fact. The relationship is then that of "man to man" rather than that of "man to interviewer".

4 Participant observation permits of actual penetration into the social situations with which the research is concerned. Such information may be gained (by means of structured interviews) as that the male occupant of a house "goes to the pub for a game of darts and a chat with the boys", Participant observation supplements that information and enriches it, since the observer is present whilst the game of darts is being played, and, whenever possible, is actually participating in the "chat with the boys".

But there are also limitations. Chief amongst them is the fact that it is not possible to standardise the activities of the observers, and quantitative data is thus difficult to record. Also, the assessment of the situations is essentially subjective, and there is the danger of the observer becoming emotionally attached. He may thus display uncritical sympathy with the observed people's aims and ideals rather than study them in a detached way, However, the information sought in order to test the hypothesis is concerned with social standards and relations, and it is doubtful if much of the evidence which substantiates the hypothesis lends itself to quantitative statement. A problem which is of special significance in this Research is that of gaining entry into "equivalent situations" in the sets of streets being compared. Thus (to anticipate Section III D) it is comparatively easy to gain access to situations involving people coming from the black area of Dyke Street; but it is more difficult to gain entry into situations involving people coming from the good area, Gladstone Road. This difficulty arises out of one of the differences which distinguish the two streets, namely the fact that the people who live in Gladstone Road lead more private lives, and have a greater variety of interests - but more especially an

Method 71

interest in their homes. The result is that they tend not to go out to pubs and clubs as often as do the adults of Dyke Street, and when they do go out their range of interests acts against the tendency apparent in Dyke Street where they cluster together in particular pubs and clubs. The problem of effective participation in Gladstone Road is thus inherent in the social situation involved. However, the scientists' tools must be shaped for their jobs, and not vice versa, The fact that it is not possible to participate, or to participate so effectively in Gladstone Road life does not imply that participant observation is not a useful. tool for the study of Dyke Street.

As far as this Survey is concerned, the conclusion is that the method was sound, provided one recognised its limitations. The workers were well aware, e.g., that though much of the information was objective and supported by facts, a good deal rested on no more than impressions or even hunches. At the same time the hypothesis posed by this particular piece of research was such that the methods adopted appeared to be not merely the most fruitful, but possibly the only feasible ones by which to test it.

III B. Facts Relating to the Five Delinquency Areas

Having set the scene for the Research, and considered the methods employed, we must now indicate more precisely the distribution of delinquents in Radby, and examine related factual information.

During the years 1942–52 there were recorded in the County Probation Officer's Department, a total of 151 cases of juvenile delinquency in Radby, This figure relates to the number of offenders, and not to the number of offences committed.[1] The figure of 151 may be broken up as follows: -

Girl offenders	1942–52	14
Boy offenders	1942–47	75
Boy offenders	1948–52	51
Boy offenders	Unclassified[2]	11
Total		151

The decrease in the second quinquennium of the number of boy offenders is marked, but it should be remembered that the first period includes three years of war, and the two post-war years, a period notable for social maladjustment.

The following table shows the age of the offender at the time of his first offence :

Age	8	9	10	11	12	13	14	15	16	17
No. of dels.	3	5	16	9	26	22	24	19	11	16

---

1 For this Research, a delinquent is considered as a juvenile if he is under the age of eighteen years at the time of the offence.

2 The "Unclassified" boys are those who are known to have committed an offence during the years 1942–52, but the exact date of whose offence is not known. On the map they have been marked in the 1948–52 group. (of. Appendix C).

Facts Relating to the Five Delinquency Areas   73

It is seen that 91 of the offenders, or approximately 60%, were aged between twelve and fifteen at the time of the offence. With regard to the nature of the offences committed, the table below shows the types of offences and the number of offenders convicted of them. The distinction between "Theft 1" and "Theft 2" is an arbitrary one, the object of which is to distinguish between the relatively serious offence,[1] such as stealing a large sum of money or a bicycle which is later redecorated and sold, and a less serious offence, such as receiving a penknife knowing it to have been stolen, or taking a small quantity of money from a mother's purse. "Beyond control" includes those juveniles were were convicted before the Court for truancy from school, whilst "Violence" includes "demanding money with menaces".

Nature of Offence	No.
Theft (1)	64
Theft (2)	34
Housebreaking and Larceny	28
Beyond control	8
Wilful damage	7
Violence	5
Sex	5

Over the period of ten years there were an average of 15.1 offenders apprehended each year, a number which may not be considered excessive for a total population of over twenty thousand. But it is not the total number of delinquents which is of particular interest to this Research. What is of more relevance is the distribution of delinquents within the town. The incidence of delinquency was plotted on a street map of Radby, and the distribution of offenders revealed five well-defined areas of different sizes. Within these areas lived a large majority of the offenders. With regard to adult delinquency, a map showing the distribution of 83 adult offenders was provided by the County Constabulary, and this distribution was found to coincide with that of the juvenile offenders. The same position was found to obtain with regard to 68 cases proven before the Matrimonial Court. The distribution of these phenomena is indicated in the accompanying table (p.74).

The five areas together accounted for approximately seventy per cent of the total number of juvenile delinquents during the decade.

---

1 "Serious" from the point of view of material magnitude and circumstances, rather than "moral wrong".

74 Facts Relating to the Five Delinquency Areas

It was not possible for the Research Workers to assess the total number of children aged 0 – 17 resident in the areas. However, it is estimated that, at the most, the five areas might contain up to fifty per cent of the town's juvenile population in 1952. It is fair to say, therefore, that the prevalence of juvenile delinquents in the five areas does not merely reflect a concentration of children in them, but shows that an estimated fifty percent (at the most) of the total juvenile population of Radby provided approximately seventy percent of the total number of juvenile delinquents.

The total adult population (age 21 plus), as given in the Electoral Register for Radby in 1951, is approximately 16,800. There were resident in the five Areas at this time a total of approximately 5,500 adults. The figures relating to adult delinquents refer to men of eighteen years of age and over, but if we assume the distribution of adults of age 21

AREA A	Boy offenders	1942–47	11
	„ „	1948–52	11
CARNATION	Girl offenders	1942–52	1
ST. AREA	Adult offenders	1948–52	11
	Matrimonial cases	1948–52	6
AREA B	Boy offenders	1942–47	8
	„ „	1948–52	7
STATION	Girl offenders	1942–52	-
HILL AREA	Adult offenders	1948–52	9
	Matrimonial cases	1948–52	6
AREA C	Boy offenders	1942–47	9
	„ „	1948–52	11
DYKE ST.	Girl offenders	1942–52	3
AREA	Adult offenders	1948–52	7
	Matrimonial cases	1948–52	13
AREA D	Boy offenders	1942–47	15
	„ „	1948–52	9
KNOLL ESTATE	Girl offenders	1942–52	4
AREA	Adult offenders	1948–52	19
	Matrimonial cases	1948–52	9
AREA E	Boy offenders	1942–47	8
	„ „	1948–52	6
WEST ESTATE	Girl offenders	1942–52	2
AREA	Adult offenders	1948–52	6
	Matrimonial cases	1948–52	6
REMAINDER	Boy offenders	1942–47	24
	„ „	1948–52	18
OF	Girl offenders	1942–52	4
	Adult offenders	1948–52	31
RADBY	Matrimonial cases	1948–52	28

Facts Relating to the Five Delinquency Areas 75

plus to reflect reasonably accurately the distribution of adults of age 18 plus, it is seen that the five Areas, containing 5,500 adults, provided 52 adult delinquents, the remaining ll, 300 adults providing only 31 adult delinquents. In approximate figures, therefore, 33 percent of the adult population provided 63 per cent of the adult delinquents. We may conclude, as in the case of the juvenile delinquency distribution, that the prevalence of adult delinquents in the five Areas does not reflect merely a concentration of a high percentage of Radby's adult population in those five Areas.

The same holds for Matrimonial Cases, which arise out of applications for maintenance, or separation orders brought by a husband or wife before the Court. 33 percent of the adult population (living in the five Areas) provided 59 percent of the Matrimonial Cases proven before the Court.

The diagrams given on page l08 illustrate the statistical details elaborated above.

With regard to Public Health, information for the years 1942–52 relating to Illegitimate Births, Mental Deficiency, and so on was obtained from the County Medical Department. An abstract taken from the detailed statistics is given below.

	The Five Areas		*Remainder*	*Total in Radby*
Illegitimate Births	1948–52	43	43	86
Infantile Mortality	1948–52	38	38	76
Tuberculosis Notifications	1942–52	111	119	230
Mental Deficiency Incidence	1952	57	42	99
Educationally Subnormal pupils	1952	39	23	62

It is seen that the five Areas account for at least one half of the cases occurring in Radby with regard to all of the phenomena shown in the table above except that of Tuberculosis Notification, and the facts may therefore be said to correspond with the position ascertained relating to delinquency and Matrimonial Cases. But, as the County Medical Officer has pointed out, "although some of the rates for the parts of Radby appear to be well above the average, this may be partly due to dealing with such small numbers".

The information recorded above suggests strongly that there are in Radby five main Areas which may be termed "black" ones. There would seem to be sufficient a priori grounds for assuming that the five Areas have different cultural backgrounds from the rest of the town.

76 Facts Relating to the Five Delinquency Areas

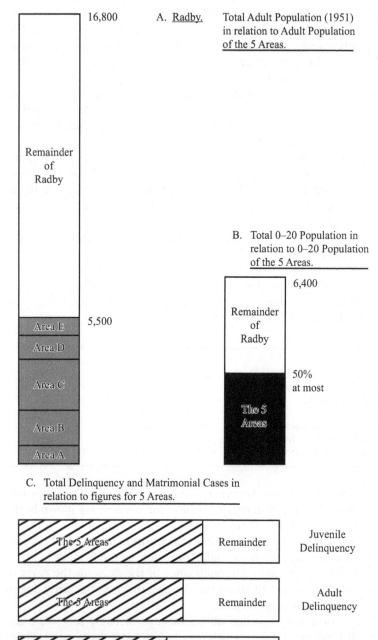

Facts Relating to the Five Delinquency Areas 77

Other preliminary enquiries supported this theory, and it was decided that the Areas would constitute a suitable field for the study of social influences in the occurrence of delinquency such as are envisaged in the hypothesis.

Of the five Areas, one was used for the Pilot Survey, details of which are given in the following Section. For the main research project three other Areas were chosen, the time factor necessitating the omission of the fifth Area. (Area E, "West Estate").

An analysis of the information about delinquency in Radby revealed that even within the five Areas there is a considerable contrast as between streets in the distribution of the various characteristics, Certain streets which were materially comparable with the streets which contained a concentration of delinquents, were found to be either free of official trouble, or to have had a very light record for years past. It looked as if certain factors were operating in one street but not in the other. Were such factors of sociological order?

To try for an answer to this question it was decided to concentrate on a single pair of streets (one "black", one "white") in each of the five delinquent-prone areas. The details of the first attempts to distinguish between the "black" and the "white" are given in the following account of the Pilot Survey.

III C. Pilot Survey

The Pilot Survey was undertaken during five weeks in the early summer of 1953. The area was in an old, outlying district of Radby known as Station Hill. The reputation of Station Hill, and of several of its streets in particular, is not good. People who live in Radby itself don't much like to admit it if they were born in Station Hill. Within this area, two streets, Chapel Street and John Street were chosen for a comparative study. Chapel Street, is one of a network of similar rows of terrace houses, several houses sharing a common yard. The street was built about 1870 and is typically bye-law in looks. John Street is more modern (c. 1900). The south side has terrace houses which, as in Chapel Street, open directly onto the pavement. But the north side has the semi-detached houses of the 1930s, with little plots in the front and small gardens at the rear.

The following are some of the more obvious facts relating to the two streets.

	John Street	*Chapel Street*
Street	A through, one-way street. No shops. Tidy.	A cul-de-sac street; one other street leading into it. Some traffic (vans delivering to shops and wood-working firm). Decayed.
Houses	26	75
Houses Interviewed	<u>12</u>	<u>32</u>
Date	1900 Terrace houses 1930 Semi-detached	1860–80
Type	Terrace houses. Two storey, yard or garden shared by two houses. Semi-	Two and three story terrace houses. Yard for 2–12 houses. A few

Pilot Survey 79

	detached. Front garden and self-contained garden at rear. Bathroom in about half the houses. Indoor lavatory in all.		unfenced earth plots. No bathroom or indoor lavatory. Some houses in bad Structural condition.
Owned/Rented	No information		No information
Rent	No information		5/6 – 8/6 (top and bottom figures quoted).
Length of Residence in immediate neighbourhood.	1 household 5 ” 2 ” 1 ” 17 ”	0 – 10 years 10 – 20 ” 20 plus ” “many” ” No inform. 54	6 households 9 ” 2 ” 4 ”

Population : Adult[1]	54 ⎫		166 ⎫	
Adol. (15–20)[2]	24 ⎬ 85		115 ⎬ 301	
Child (−15)[3]	7 ⎭		20 ⎭	

1 Electoral Register 1951.
2 Estimated
3 Coronation Street Party Lists 1953.

	John Street	*Chapel Street*	
Household Structure	1 household of 2 3 3 2 2 - 14	1 person 2 persons 3 ” 4 ” 5 ” 6 ” 7+ ” No inform.	1 household 15 ” 3 ” 4 ” 8 ” 7 ” 11 ” 3
Relation living in street	No information	At least 23 households with 1–5 related families.	
Employment	About half estimated to be colliery employees; some surface workers.	At least half estimated to be colliery employees; mainly under-ground workers.	
Education I.Q. records at Secondary School Admission Exam: 1947–51. Av. I.Q. for Radby 96.6	2 entrants only I.Q. = 99 : 113	21 entrants. Av. I.Q.= 91 (of whom 3 were −80; 5 were 100 or over).	

80 *Pilot Survey*

Facilities within 3 mins. walk of both streets.	Schools 1 Primary, 2 Secondary Modern (Boys, Girls). Churches 1 Anglican, 3 Free Churches. Youth Organisations attached to all four of the churches. Pubs 2. Constitutional Club, Recreation Grounds Park, open field.	
Facilities within 3d. 'bus fare	Central Radby	Suburbs of City
7d. 'bus fare	City	City

The interviewers aimed at contacting as many families in the two streets as was possible in the five weeks. They wished to obtain certain factual information (structure of family, employment, etc.) and to sound the family's attitude (or that of at least one adult in the home) on certain Subjects.[1] None of these subjects had any very obvious bearing on delinquency, and a direct question on it was seldom asked. The interviewer's questions were carefully framed so as to sound practical and not more idle curiosity. E.g., "Do you think youth clubs are better mixed, or for boys and girls separately ?": or "Do you find it wise to give children regular pocket money, or is it better to let them ask for money when they want to buy something?" The following is typical of the material on the above two points that was forthcoming by the method of direct question.

The women interviewed lived in John Street, was about 40, a miner's wife and had three children, Barrie 13, June 9, and Teddie 8. She thinks youth organisations keep the children up too late. She likes Barrie to go to the Bethel Club in spite of the girls there because it helps him to be less shy. The children are in their own gangs (street ones)· Thinks perhaps school teaches too much about sex. Is amazed at what June and Teddie know. Her children seldom go to the pictures, but they have TV instead. Barrie (or all three?) gets 2/6 savings stamp a week plus 6d. to spend. Mrs. X buys the children's sweets and comics. She feeds the children well and says this stops them from always wanting cakes, ices, etc. She definitely teaches them how to handle money. Thinks the Chapel Street children are given money as a solace.

In the more illiterate homes direct questions were avoided· Youth organisations, e.g., were talked about in a general way and produced this kind of material from a Chapel Street mother (age 45), a miner's wife. "Crowded kitchen into which I was invited. Two sons and friend sitting in row on a settee. Daughter (6) also present. Untidy. Broken window. Preferred children to play in yard or street. 'Nice to know where they are'. The older children should be 'kept under', i.e., kept off

1 Appendix B Notes for Guidance of Interviewer

Pilot Survey 81

street when in their teens. Not so much the boys as the girls, for a few doors away, a girl had a baby at 17 years of age, and 2 (?) more before she was 20 (22?). Girls should be watched because of delinquency in Radby 'if you know what I mean'. Another girl over the road, 'had one' (i.e., a baby) when only 15 years of age. Thought that there should be more youth clubs because of that sort of thing. Parents should be stricter with daughters. Her children did not belong to clubs - interests were cycling and cinema."

After forty-four interviews had been held (in some cases several visits were made or the first talk was supplemented by chance contacts in the street) the following points relating to the social life of the two streets were noted :

John Street adults exchange news with neighbours mostly in their back gardens. The older children, but not toddlers, play in the street. Chapel Street is a meeting ground for people of all ages, at all times of the day. Street gossiping is accepted as correct behaviour. Children of all ages play in the street and are said to prefer it to the yards, or to the Park and Recreation Ground. This street play causes a certain amount of nuisance, e.g., window breaking. It is a source of anxiety among many mothers because of traffic dangers. The bottom, bad, end of the street seems to have a more vigorous street life than the top, main-road end. This bottom of the street is assessed as bad (by residents at the top end) on such grounds as these - the people are "ignorant", i.e., the wife lives in another part of the town; a girl of 15 has had a baby; the children "give you a mouthful if you say anything to them, and so does their father"; the boy is away in Borstal; even the small children are not willing to do any work to earn some pocket money. The attitude of the two streets differs markedly in what they think and do about youth organisations. In John Street a considerable proportion of the children are or have been in organisations. Parents, almost without exception, favour youth organisations, though they would not force the children to belong. Chapel Street parents regard them as places just for enjoyment, on a par with any other of the children's ways of entertaining themselves. The youngsters on the whole regard them as too classy ("they are for the top end of the town"); too strict; too like school; or tied to a church, "which would put some off."

The attitude to education also differs. Chapel Street parents have less ambition than John Street about their children's education. Some would favour compulsory schooling from 4 – 14 rather than 5 – 15 on the grounds that school at the age of four would relieve parents of anxiety; it would enable mothers to go out to work; it would encourage those of fourteen to do some work (instead of idling as they are said

82 *Pilot Survey*

to do in the new extra year at school); and it would allow them to be earning which would both help the parents and be good for the children. The extra year at school was said by two people to be a cause of the increase in delinquency.

On the whole the Chapel Street people are less contented with their environment than the John Street people with theirs. But the formers dislike is more often related to damp, old, crowded houses and earth yards, than to any feeling that Chapel Street is socially inferior or produces bad companions for the children. Part of their relative content with the street is possibly related to family feeling and to questions of convenience. At least twenty-three of the seventy-six households have relations living in the street. This means, e.g., that children can be parked with an aunt while the parents go to the pub; or that a mother can go out to work because her own mother will obligingly see to the dinner, and so on.

If the Coronation celebrations were any clue to the vigour of the social life of the two streets, Chapel Street certainly held the palm. Every house but one was said to have contributed to the collection (£70 from seventy-six houses) and most households also spent money and time on individual. decorations. John Street, with only a third of the number of houses, raised about the same amount, but much less trouble was taken over private decorations, and the preparations produced nothing like the excitement and competition (or the practical results, as far as gaiety went) of the "bad" street.

Chapel Street, too, has a kind of club in the local pubs. It is considered respectable for Chapel Street women to go to a pub with their husbands at the weekends and for special occasions, though not during the week. The local pub is used by many inhabitants of the Station Hill area, and there is an accepted phrase, "Gone to Dicky's" (Dick being the landlord). In the pub a person who is familiar with the district may notice that the residents of the various streets from which customers come tend to cluster together in small groups around the tables. John Street women do not appear to go to the pubs and certainly not to the Station Hill ones. On the other hand cost of the John Street families encountered seem to be connected actively with the local churches· Chapel Street has practically no connection at adult level, though adults go to some of the Chapel's social events.[1] Despite the pub-going of Chapel Street women (and not all go to pubs) they seem to have less contact with the outside world and less opportunities for receiving new ideas generally, than do the John Street mothers.

---

1 Attenders at local churches or organisations connected with them.

Pilot Survey   83

Adults responsibilities towards children

The appearance of all the John Street children (clothes, cleanliness, etc.) suggests that they are well looked after. Chapel Street children show marked differences between families. Some of the children, especially the toddlers and the adolescent boys, look very neglected.

In Chapel Street the physical safety of the children (toddlers and traffic; girls and sex dangers) seems to be the parents main concern. They do not regard children as having specific needs in the way that John Street does. On the other hand some do a lot to give the children pleasures.

	Adults		*Juveniles*			
	Chapel Street	*John Street*	*Sunday School*		*Youth Organisations and Choir*	
			Ch.St.	*J.St.*	*Ch.St.*	*J.St.*
Free Church No. 1	–	5	8	4	1	1
” No. 2	–	–	–	–	No	inf.
” No. 3	1	2+	2	4	–	2
Anglican Church	"Practically none"	No inf.	8	3	4	3

John Street has strong views on the need to train children in such things as spending habits, and Sunday School attendance. In general Chapel Street does not seem to distinguish between training and forcing. It is strongly opposed to employing compulsion· This attitude seems to be related to the hard, authoritarian upbringing and the physical deprivations of their own childhood. They are determined that their own children shall not suffer as they did. One mother pointed out that the big families so common in her childhood made some discipline essential even in "bad" homes.

Views on specific subjects

Money

Money cropped up in many conversations, There was a good deal of disparagement among Chapel Street housewives of the families who do no planning or saving even for a few weeks, e, g., for a TV set. External evidence suggested that a good deal of buying of clothes, etc. is done through clubs, Both streets had plenty to say on children's pocket

84   *Pilot Survey*

money. John Street regarded it as an important part of children's training, and favoured regular pocket money. Examples given were : Age 8 (6d, and "what she asks for"); 13 (2s. Savings Stamp plus 6d. to spend); 15 (4s.6d. and saves about 2s,); 8 (9d. and "no more for the asking"); 13 (1s,). In Chapel Street most children probably have no regular pocket money until they are about 13 at least. John Street disparaged Chapel Street as a place where a mother would give a kid 2s.6d. to get him out of the way, Chapel Street often spoke of the modern child's constant demands for money and contrasted their own spending, as children, with that of the child of today. They did not suggest that it might be bad for the child himself to have too much money.

Sex

Chapel Street girls often marry in their late teens. Seven instances of recent marriages at this age were given. A local small shopkeeper, who seemed reliable, talked at length on the bad behaviour of the children of the area. She said, that there was sex misbehaviour "in the gardens", i.e., a rather cut-off place beyond the railway. She gave a specific instance that related to a boy of 15 and a girl of 12. The "fee", said the shopkeeper, is a shilling. "Doesn't the girl's mother stop it?" "She'd do the same herself". The John Street parents did not normally raise the subject of sex themselves. In Chapel Street they did so on several occasions, e.g., two mothers volunteered the information that they had had to get married. One regarded this as a nuisance with no suggestion of any moral issue; the other justified it with "lots do". Several brought up a recent assault case on a local girl of about twelve in the Park. Some parents had stopped their children going there; one said that it had happened before, so why worry. On sex relations with older girls this comment was made :

"If a man gets browned off about the girl he wants, he'll take it out of the next one he meets - rape her perhaps".

Delinquency

The interviewer raised the subject of "official" trouble, i.e., cases in which the police had been brought in, at most of the John Street conversations. The general opinion was that delinquency was more due to lack of training at home than to anything else. An instance was quoted of one home where the child was the master. Several parents who were pleased that children were less frightened of grown-ups than they used to be, nevertheless thought it a pity that children had lost their respect

Pilot Survey 85

for people like teachers and the police. Chapel Street often referred to the nuisance that children caused (broken windows; fireworks; "bow and arrowing", at the washing; late bedtimes because of the pub; rowdyism in the shop; disturbing Guide meetings; bad language). Troublesome boys were often named but only one adult referred to anyone as having been actually involved with the police.

Two Chapel Street girls (aged 11 and 12) made the following comment about bad behaviour in general, In their view the "bad" ages are 8, 9 and 12–14. The younger children are really scared of the police; the older ones are not, nor the adults of their homes. The younger ones take notice of what another child. says (e·g·, about stealing) if they like him. The younger ones mostly do bad things to show the gang they dare. Some children get really desperate for money; they steal from each other.

As regards their own pocket money, the two girls both preferred not to have regular pocket money. One gave this example : "If I ask my father for some sweets and they cost 6d. and then I tell him they were 9d. I can make 3d.".

III D. Dyke Street and Gladstone Road a Comparison

The Pilot Survey suggested that the hypothesis was correct, viz. that contiguous and similar-looking working class streets might live by different codes and have different habits. The enquirers therefore proceeded to make a study of two more streets in another the "black" areas of Radby. They used the methods already described in Section III A.

The streets in question, Dyke Street and Gladstone Road, were comparable in length. The former contained 108, and the latter 102 houses. But the number of people living in the two streets was not the same. Dyke Street had 474 (in 115 separate households), Gladstone Road 316 (in 104 households). Certain basic information was obtained for every household and is given in the following table :

Information relating to Dyke Street and Gladstone Road

	Dyke Street	Gladstone Road
No. of houses	108	102
No. of households	115	104
No. of people	474	316
No. of adults 15 plus	338	248
No, of children 0–14	136	68
Households on which sufficient information obtained to make an assessment	84	58
Structure of household		
1–3 people in home	50	62
4–6 ” ” ”	48	42
7–9 ” ” ”	17	0

Other people living in household

Married children	9	10
Grandchildren	9	8
Parents	9	6
Other relations	15	8
Non-relations	4	6

Yard shared with :

1–3 other households	35	–
4, 5, 5 plus, other households	30	–

Employment (past or present) of chief male

Miner	74	63
Labourer or unskilled factory	17	7
Skilled factory	2	3
Transport	4	5
Clerical	0	4
Self-employed	6	6
Miscellaneous	9	13
No information	3	3
Position of responsibility	6 (of which one = minor)	17 (of which 8 = minors)

"Official" Delinquency

Households with an adult known to have been brought before Court 1942–52 :	2	0
do. Juveniles	6	2
do. Matrimonial Court	2	2
do. Divorce Court	2	0
Households with some known irregularity, e.g., delinquency, matrimonial trouble, excessive drinking, sex, (in addition to above).	32	2

Although the two streets lie within two minutes walk of each other, they have few contacts. Both streets have numerous relations living in their own or neighbouring streets, but only six Gladstone Road families were found who had relations in Dyke Street. The latter is relatively unknown to Gladstone Road women, though the men meet at work of course, Mrs. D, e.g., who has lived in Gladstone Road for 21 years, has never been in a Dyke Street house. Several said that they never entered the street. One or two spoke pityingly of "those poor Dyke Street children". Others disparaged the street, "those women would

88 Dyke Street and Gladstone Road a Comparison

go out to work, I dare say". Dyke Street people don't bother to discuss Gladstone Road ones, though many of the Dyke Street children walk along it daily as their school entrance is actually in Gladstone Road.

Both streets are terraced ones. The majority of houses have two bedrooms, two downstairs rooms, and a small scullery. Some Dyke Street houses have an attic that is just habitable. Gladstone Road has indoor sanitation and bath rooms in many houses; Dyke Street has neither. Housekeeping standards vary greatly. Gladstone Road serves food more or less on middle class lines, i.e., the family sits down to meals together at fixed hours. In Dyke Street it is more a question of "He must be fed when it suits him". Mrs. X, for example, fries eggs and bacon separately for each of her three men who eat it, as it is ready, and sitting wherever they happen to be - on the sofa, or by the fire. Mrs. Y finds it impossible to get her children (aged 3 and 5) even to sit at the table. Her neighbour can, but she can't, and it don't much bother her. Meals, like other activities, overlap and fade into each other. You have your tea, rather than "now it's tea time". As far as the actual cooking goes, Gladstone Road habits seem to conform to middle class customs. They bake cakes, make jams, and pickles, etc., more than do the Dyke Street housewives. By mid-week a Dyke Street mother may have so run out of food that she can give her child nothing for a picnic but bread and margarine. That particular house evidently keeps no stock whatever of jams, pastes, etc.

The important point is that while Dyke Street has a certain number of houses which are well kept (and working class standards can be very high), Gladstone Road has none that could possibly be described as feckless or dirty. Most are spic and span, even though the housewife may feel that she is short of goods and chattels, and is saving up for them. It is indicative of the artisan character of both streets that the houses have practically no possessions that have been handed down from an earlier generation. Neither street makes much use of the front room, though less pride goes into "the front" in Dyke Street, where people use back or front door indiscriminately. Gladstone Rond, for ordinary use, comes to the back door.

The average space occupied by the house and yard or garden is much more limited in Dyke Street than in Gladstone Road. In the case of some houses that were measured up roughly, the total enclosed space per house available was nine times greater in Gladstone Road than in Dyke Street. And that was for one of the few Dyke Street houses that has a tiny enclosed yard and garden. Although only 14 Dyke Street households (as compared with 4 in Gladstone Road) share a house with one other household, 80 share a yard with four or more other houses. In Dyke Street, therefore, privacy has to be fought for outside

Dyke Street and Gladstone Road a Comparison 89

the house as well as in. Here, too, Dyke Street has less space – 474 people in 115 households (108 houses) as compared with Gladstone Road's 316 in 104 households (102 houses). The Dyke Street children almost certainly seek the relative privacy of the street to help avoid the publicity of a packed home, especially if this contains one unsympathetic person. It is physically impossible to avoid such a one indoors. The very small children, are even more subject to lack of privacy or quiet since they are relatively immobile. The only world they know is the immediate one of the congested room, the common yard, and the bit of street within earshot of their home. Part of Dyke Street's low standard of housekeeping is undoubtedly due to the fact that so many people have to occupy not only inadequate, but shared space. Next-door children with dirty habits inevitably pull down the work of the most careful housewife. It is no use to teach your children only to "wee" in the yard, if the ones next door do it against the door.

It is dangerous to attempt any comparison as regards the actual health of the two streets. Two Gladstone Road men were killed in pit accidents. In Dyke Street one man died suddenly at work, two people had serious accidents, and another committed suicide. Dyke Street talked much more about illness than did Gladstone Road, and, to a casual observer, more people seemed to be involved in physical troubles there. Such things as miscarriage, suspected polio, mastoids, stomach trouble, sore eyes, bad feet (two children aged 13), "me nerves", etc., cropped up. Certainly the children constantly said they were, or had been, "badly".

The day-to-day appearance especially that of the toddlers, probably reflects the general physical standards of the home pretty closely. Gladstone Road has no really uncared-for looking children, and few who are even untidy. The older schoolboys have begun to take a pride in their looks, have smooth hair, tidy ties, etc. Many of the Dyke Street boys of 13 and 14 are oddly loose-looking. They hold themselves badly, and go about in plimsoles in all weathers, in old and torn trousers, and with dirty shirts. Some children never seem to have clean hands. It is obvious that no grown up is bothering much about them. That is the normal picture. For special occasions, a trip, or of course a wedding, they smarten up so much that sometimes they are literally unrecognisable. The older men, too, can look very dandy, with button-holes and gay neckerchiefs. Clothes are not unimportant to Dyke Street. A smart appearance is much admired, among both men and women. But no one thinks the worse of you if you are dirty and badly dressed "just in the street", whereas Gladstone Road is tidily dressed at any time of the day. One of the children expressed the typical Dyke

90 *Dyke Street and Gladstone Road a Comparison*

Street outlook. She was describing an advertisement, a picture of a middle-class working man. He was "someone who dresses nice <u>every</u> day of the year".

Except that they suggest that Dyke Street has more children living in the home than has Gladstone Road, the figures do not show up what is a characteristic of Dyke Street, viz., the complexity of the household structure. The impression given is that a larger number of people of different generations live in one household; more in-laws are present; and more "odd" children (illegitimate, orphaned, etc.) are included. In Gladstone Road the typical household is father, mother and two children. "I feel quite odd in this road with my three", was a typical remark. Moreover, in Dyke Street relationships are so mixed that children know a particular child by a variety of surnames. Even older people are often uncertain, or they may explain "They call her Mrs. A. but really I think she is ... " The household may be as fluid and relatives so often coming in and out, that children of seven cannot readily say who does actually live in their own house. They will include "our Sammy" or "my Grandad" until pinned down as to whether the person mentioned actually sleeps in the house. The relationship between the two heads of the household is also more varied than in Gladstone Road. At least thirteen families are known by everyone to have a father or mother who is living apart from their partner or is or has been cohabitating. The children of previous alliances are brought up alongside the present set of children.

One most noticeable feature of Dyke Street life is the number of families who have relations in the street. At least 37 homes have relations living within a few doors. On the whole the relations seem to be on good terms. Gladstone Road, too, has related families (at least 26) but the kind of tribal life that exists in Dyke Street is much less obvious in Gladstone Road. The larger size of the Dyke Street families probably has a good deal to do with this, as well as the informal habits of the street. Children and adults move in and out of the related houses as if they are their own. They eat indiscriminately at each other's houses, borrow extensively, feed each other's babies, etc. They also adopt a common front on issues like the Coronation Party, or disapproving of a neighbour's behaviour. Gladstone Road's related households are much less obviously related, e.g., the family had to be asked if it had relations in the street, whereas in Dyke Street relations were likely to pop in and out while the interviewer happened to be at the house.

Gladstone Road is alleged by some of its older householders to have declined socially but its houses are still regarded as a solid investment and as many as 33 people own their home. Dyke Street people, on the

Dyke Street and Gladstone Road a Comparison 91

other hand, are nearly all weekly tenants (at a rent of 7s. to 9s.). Only a few of the old tenants have bought although the present-day selling price of a "two up and two down" typical house may be no more than £150. But they appear to find the £50 deposit an insuperable difficulty. It is, of course, true that the street is in a clearance area, but it is likely to stand for many years.

Both streets are full of "old" residents. Of 46 Dyke Street homes, 21 of the husbands or wives had been born in the street or lived in it most of their lives. Fewer Gladstone Road heads of households appeared to have been actually born in the road, but they had fairly often been connected with it. In some cases they said with some pride that their father had built the house. As many as 43 of 83 had lived there for over 20 years; and only 8 of the 85 had lived there for less than 2 years. At the same time more people appear to have moved into the road fairly recently than is the case with Dyke Street. They are people on the upgrade who are delighted to have got into such a nice street. The older residents feel that the road's not what it used to be, socially, but they are secure enough themselves not to bother about this. No one suggested that he would like to move to a better road. Nor did Dyke Street really disparage itself. They wanted a better house, often enough, but there was seldom reference to any wish to leave the street. The new families in the street had often bought the house and seemed pleased to be there.

On the whole Gladstone Road can be classed as an artisan street, Dyke Street as a labouring class one. The typical householder in both streets is a colliery employee (74 out 115 in Dyke Street, 63 out of 104 in Gladstone Road). The great majority of these are manual workers. Dyke Street, e.g., has only one miner in a position of responsibility, Gladstone Road eight. Whereas Gladstone Road has a sprinkling of black-coated workers and of self-employed artisans, Dyke Street has practically none. Neither street has professional men, except for a librarian, an ex-miner, in Gladstone Road. The adolescents of Gladstone Road tend to go in to jobs that are more skilled (and less highly paid) than the Dyke Street youngsters. This applies rather to the boys than the girls. A good many of the latter seem to be in exactly similar factory jobs to the Dyke Street girls. Both streets have a high proportion of men on shift work but few people who work outside the town. Women's employment shows more variation between the two areas. Only 8 of the Gladstone Road women interviewed went out to work, and 4 of those were only to part-time jobs. Moreover, they are content to stay at home. They emphasised that homemaking is their pleasure as much as duty, though a few did say that their husbands

92 Dyke Street and Gladstone Road a Comparison

would not hear of it, "If you go, I shan't". In Dyke Street 18 women (all married) were in Jobs (13 of them full-time): and pretty well any able bodied woman toys with the idea of going out to work. If only she could get someone to look after her man and the children. Some of those who cannot go feel bitter about it. The working class character of even Gladstone Road is reflected in the pre-marriage jobs of the women. Certain of the older ones were in service as girls. In both streets, unskilled, but clean, factory work had been the typical, pre-marriage, type of job.

A noticeable feature of the Dyke Street adolescents was the sudden change in their clothes and general appearance when they started to work. The point is mentioned because it probably reflects a similar change in their status. They are obviously adults now, and presumably are expected to conform to adult codes. Several cases were met where a boy had gone to the pits against his parents' wishes "because he was after the big money". In Gladstone Road too certain parents emphasised that they had not stood in the way of their child going to the job fancied. But there the argument was that the youngster had been allowed to have his way although the parents would suffer financially.

Household incomes are probably higher in Dyke Street than in Gladstone Road since more adults live in the one household, and if there is more than one woman in the house, the others will be likely to go out to work. The adolescents, too, are in the non-apprentice, higher wage type of work. Dyke Street is more openly pre-occupied with money than is Gladstone Road. Prices of goods that might be acquired are a constant subject of talk. The children, too, seem to translate everything into terms of money. A small instance of the Dyke Street general attitude to money was the following. It would be no use, said a young woman and her husband, getting up a small fund to put up some swings for the children because the families who had not contributed would use them just the same. The safety of money, too, is a constant source of anxiety. It tends to be kept in the house and if it should be stolen, no one likes to bring in the police. This happened. in the case of a house where the holiday hand-out (£20) had been taken from a locked box. The adolescent girl of the house in question thought it was probably friends who had taken it. She did not envisage the possibility of bringing in the law.

In Dyke Street spending, as is life in general, is geared to a weekly pay-day. It declines noticeably towards mid-weed and is the main feature of many homes on Friday. Goods are largely bought through clubs, a type of buying that, according to local shopkeepers and an insurance agent, has increased with higher wages. Gladstone Road

Dyke Street and Gladstone Road a Comparison 93

spending is planned ahead and includes an attempt to save. Mrs. X, e.g., puts her money for the rent, clothes, electricity, etc. in separate boxes "so as to have it ready in time". Not much haphazard buying is done. In some homes this often extends to such things as sweets. Certain Dyke Street homes pretty certainly have no reserves of money. The difficulty of finding the £50 deposit necessary to buy a £150 house, is an evidence of this. At the same time an insurance agent of the town believes that very many miners, even from the Dyke Street area, now save something each week through the colliery savings schemes. A certain amount of saving for holidays is now common. It is probably harder for the Dyke Street women to save than their husbands as there is some evidence that the only money they have to handle (unless they go out to work) does not increase in proportion to the general rise in wages. Moreover it is considered mean for a mother to increase the "board" money that those in their late teens pay her. So that higher earnings from this source also do not get to the housekeeper. One thing that does favour the mother is that the high wage families tend to be the ones where the children go on "board" early. Anything that deprives a child of any age of money, however, reflects poorly on the nether. In Dyke Street, too, it is rare for husband and wife to have a common policy about the family income and spending, whereas this is often done in Gladstone Road. In Dyke Street one woman talked with envy of another whose husband gave her, in addition to her regular money, so much each week for herself. It was unheard of generosity. It is difficult to guess at what the women's pleasure spending, apart from the family needs, does go on. If Knoll Estate habits are similar to Dyke Street a good deal must be spent on smoking and minor gambling. This is not so in Gladstone Road where the women often say they cannot afford to smoke. Smart clothes are not particularly evident in Dyke Street, so the money does not appear to go on that. Indeed such old-fashioned institutions as jumble sales are regarded as highly desirable and second-hand personal goods are not despised.

Dyke Street seems to attach more importance to presents than Gladstone Road. A Dyke Street mother, e.g., quoted as an example of her grown-up sons' goodness, all the presents they bring her back from the holidays. Here it is cost, rather than suitabillity, that reflects credit on the giver. This comes out Strongly in the children's Xmas presents. A Dyke Street father, e.g., gives his most destructive 4-year old boy an elaborate electric train though he admits that, of course, the kid will smash it up. A fancy goods shop just off Dyke Street runs a special club for holiday-bring-back-presents, so that one actually buys the presents from Radby, and before one goes away! Birthday presents,

94 *Dyke Street and Gladstone Road a Comparison*

on the other hand, are considered of little account. Even the children don't expect much except three or four cards, and a woman who always gave her brother a birthday-present excused herself "it sounds so daft". Gladstone Road seemed to have middle-class customs about present giving.

The children in Dyke Street are very money conscious. In both streets it is remarked that children depend more on money today (for their pleasures) than they used to do. In Dyke Street they are given money for the asking, if it is possible, even in the knowledge that it is just going to be wasted. But this is "kind", "not mean", as well as being the obvious way to get shut of a troublesome child. The children ask for money, not things. They are not expected to say what they propose to buy, nor expected to say what they have bought. They also do a lot of the shopping and are therefore accustomed to handling quite big sums, and are more familiar with the power of money than the Gladstone Road. children.

The children get hold of money in any ways they can. Not many appear to have regular pocket-money. Some of them get three penny bits to half-crowns, just for the asking. A couple of twelve-year olds, asked if they could raise the 8d. child's fare to come to the City, said "I can get 10s.", and "I can get £1 if I want it". One of the children in question had recently had a 35s. perm., but alleged that she had no footwear except gum boots. She never appeared to wear anything else, so she may have been telling the truth. She seems to get about 10s. a week spending money. Tiny children, not old enough to count up to three, are seen clutching the coppers they have wormed out of a grown-up: and certain boys of 12 and 13 often display the two-shilling piece that their mother has just given them. It is noticeable however that even boys of this age do not save up for such looked- for events as the local Wakes or town fair; "Me Dad will pay", they say. The children are prepared to work for their money. They mostly expect to be paid for jobs they do. A girl of twelve, e.g., expects her father, the Club Steward, to give her 1s. for helping him sweep out the club room. Some will do jobs, especially for their mother, just for love. Money making jobs are jealously guarded. A fourteen-year old girl would not go away to the sea for a week because she would lose her 9/6d. a week paper round. The Gladstone Road attitude to children's money is very different, both from the adult's and the child's point of view. Here the children are definitely taught how to handle money. Parents have a deliberate policy about their training in this. Some give money for special purchases, others prefer a weekly pocket-money system. But most of them are shocked at the idea of children getting money "Just for the asking", or

Dyke Street and Gladstone Road a Comparison 95

of small children having big sums in any form. Saving is encouraged, and parents often expect the child to put by so much a week of what they nominally give the child for himself. The children themselves obviously handle less money and it appears to be rather less of a social disgrace not to have money to display to your friends.

The chance statement of a Dyke Street woman that she herself had never known any youngster from the street go to a Grammar or Technical School, is indicative of the educational level of the street. It means that practically all the children, and most of their parents, know only the three or four elementary schools which are Situated within a few minutes walk of their homes. Gladstone Road, though the bulk of its children attend these same schools, has a sprinkling (small – see Table) who go to Grammar and Technical Schools. A few of its adolescents attend evening classes or are in jobs that allow day release for educational purposes. Formal learning does not stop short for everyone when they reach their fifteenth birthday, though, in the case of practically all the parents in both streets, it did so at fourteen, thirteen, or occasionally twelve. Even today, though the educational ladder is available for all, it is Gladstone Road, not Dyke Street, who does or can take advantage of it. Gladstone Road is even willing to pay for the child to get a little extra teaching – music lessons, dancing classes, and so on. A Dyke Street aunt pointed out that her niece had had a grammar school education, although as an aunt she thought it pointless. She probably expressed the views of a good many of her neighbours. Moreover the odd ones who do get to a Grammar School tend to be disgruntled with it and to leave early. They wish to start earning, or, as in the case of one boy met, who passed the scholarship but would not leave his pals to take it up.

The two roads showed a marked difference in the extent to which parents co-operated with the school. It was not only the figures for such things as bad attendance (15 references to Dyke Street in the School Attendance Records for 1949+ as compared with 1 for Gladstone Road). Cases were met where, e.g., a girl of twelve was kept from school just to help her aunt do a bit of cleaning. Gladstone Road on the other hand was definitely out to see that the children not only went to school but profited by it. One mother instanced the way in which each of her three girls came in from school at a different time and said how helpful this was because she could talk over what each had been doing. Another was willing to spend £15 (in instalments). to get an encyclopedia for the boy. They were all out for him to get the scholarship. Another home took the two children to London, and made them see places like the Houses of Parliament "because it will help them at

96 Dyke Street and Gladstone Road a Comparison

school". In one or two homes there was constant anxiety for at least six months before the ten-year old boy or girl was to sit the scholarship exam. Parents would go to see the teachers, too, and talk over problems about the children with them, The children in Gladstone Road certainly give the impression, even to an outsider, that they are profiting from their education. They talk about school, display their lesson books, "do hope I'll get through the exam. when I'm eleven", and so on. A Dyke Street child's comment on school is confined mostly to remarks (often friendly ones) about the teachers. Lessons as such are hardly mentioned.

One interesting point that came out was the common attitude that the two streets adopted on the question of the extra year (14–15) at school, The subject cropped up constantly and of 38 adults with whom this point was carefully discussed 28 definitely thought the extra year undesirable, The proportion in the two streets was about the same. They put forward such arguments as these: at 14 the child is old enough to recognise the poor teacher; children mature earlier today, yet are kept at school longer; a job is a steadying influence at the difficult age of adolescence; at that age children, especially boys, need money to hold their own with older boys; the children don't feel, themselves, that they are advancing, which is bad for them; or more often, they just waste their time that last year. As one parent put it, "It just gets them accustomed to idling"!

The difference in the leisure-time habits of the two streets can be illustrated by saying that the local weekly paper mirrors the life of Gladstone Road more closely than that of Dyke Street. It is adults from the former street who go to the Eve of Poll Rally, the Church Welcome to New Minister, and to the Parent-Teacher Association. Apart from weddings and funerals (reports of which have to be paid for) the paper mostly disregards the social events that mean a good deal to Dyke Street. These include bonfire night (a semi-adult festival); the local Wakes; the Dyke Street Club's produce show, darts matches, mystery trips, Old Age Pensioners' outing, etc., etc. The Coronation Celebrations were more important to Dyke Street than to Gladstone Road and it was, in fact, one of the top prize-winning streets for the whole of Radby. Gardening and sport for the men; gossip, window shopping, visiting relations, for the women; and the pub and the cinema for most, cover the recognised leisure-time occupation of most of the adults of Dyke Street. There is a sprinkling of hobbies and about half (52 out of 115) the homes have a pet - dogs, birds, fish, etc. Reading, except for the evening paper, the kids' comics, and the 3d. women's' magazines, is practically nil. In Gladstone Road, books, especially ones for the

Dyke Street and Gladstone Road a Comparison 97

children, are slightly more in evidence than in Dyke Street, but the level of Gladstone Road adult reading appears low. Few adults ever talk about a book of any kind. T.V. is highly popular but only about twenty homes have as yet acquired it. It has a definite snob value, on a par with going away for the holidays or the new tiled fire grate that the best people are putting in whether they own the house or not. Cinema going is often a family affair, on a "once a week" basis. Most of the women do not go to pubs. A few go, but only with their husbands. But the adults, as compared with Dyke Street, have more resources <u>inside</u> the house. The mothers, e.g., get a lot of pleasure from things like embroidery, making dresses for their little girls, and so on; while some of the men do jobs about the house such as fitting electrical gadgets. There does not seem to be much membership of voluntary organisations in either street - certainly not among the women. What there is, is connected with the Churches. A marked difference is discernable in the womens' leisure and pleasures. Dyke Street women seldom seem to get a stretch of leisure during the day: nor do they seem to do a steady household job that takes some time (like a whole morning's cooking) as Gladstone Road women do. The point came out in the course of interviewing. Most Dyke Street women would be willing to chat (and not be knitting even) at any hour of the day, except when actually frying a meal perhaps. Whereas Gladstone Road gave one to understand at once that they could not possibly just stop to talk, if a domestic job was on hand. In actual fact, some of the Dyke Street women, for all their lack of leisure-in-a-stretch, are not really busy, The houses are tiny and they are no great shakes as housekeepers. Yet things seem to get on top of some of them. They have no pleasures, they move in a terribly narrow world, and with only two or three children they have not the justification for this tied-to-the-house life that, e, g., their mothers had with eight or nine children to bring up. Perhaps this helps to account for some of their bad temper with the children and their generally less equable frame of mind than the Gladstone Road mothers. At the same time Dyke Street women feel that the mother works hard, (especially if she goes out to a job) and has a right to some recreation even at the expense of the children (e.g., the children must manage alone, till after 10 p.m., if she is at the pub). Gladstone Road, on the other hand, puts the children's welfare before any idea of the parents' pleasure (e.g., Mr. and Mrs. X say they have only been out together half a dozen times in the last six years).

Most Gladstone Road households allow their school-age children to play in the street, but not the toddlers. The latter, therefore, are not the constant drag on the older boys and girls that they are in Dyke Street.

98   *Dyke Street and Gladstone Road a Comparison*

Partly as a result of this the Gladstone Road street play appears to be better tempered, can involve bigger numbers and is perhaps more fun than in Dyke street. The point may have an indirect bearing on delinquency. Dyke Street has a great many children visible in the street at all hours; but many are sitting about on steps (if tiny) or propping up a doorway: or racing about aimlessly, i.e., not actually playing at a game. Nor do they make much use of the official recreation grounds. The boys use a derelict field bordering on a pit-heap for scratch football, but there is nothing there to attract the girls, except of course the boys. The little children, with or without their mothers, wander up there sometimes, but it is a dismal spot. The girls of twelve and thirteen do a lot of hanging around the Cinema entrance, and both boys and girls are almost certainly among the crowds aged twelve to seventeen who congregate each night on the seats under the Church wall. As far as possible Dyke street lets the child do what he himself wants about his non-school, non-errand filled hours (e.g., adults sometimes question the good influence of the cinema but "the kids enjoy it"). Gladstone Road, on the other hand, definitely directs and supervises leisure. Parents <u>take</u> the young children to the cinema - not send them off with another eight-year old. The point comes out strongly in the children's friendships. Here, too, Dyke Street is unwilling to interfere, especially in the case of the adolescents. Courting, or pre-courting, unless flagrantly unsuitable, is the girl's or the boy's own business. "I don't know (says a mother of a girl of fifteen) but I think she's got a boy". Gladstone Road vets the Children's playmates; selected friends are asked inside the home to play. It also vets the boy friend of the adolescent girl.

How do the children of the two streets react to the local youth organisations? In the first place Dyke Street adults know very little of the local organisations and do not know personally the adults who run them. These adults regard youth organisations as on a par with the cinema (mere recreation), and only for school children, Attendance is left entirely with the child, "He goes when he thinks". The same applies to Sunday School attendance, Gladstone Road puts some pressure on children about formal organisations, and thinks them of value to adolescents too, Parents are interested in what the children do at their societies. They regard them as of positive value, and more than just a means of keeping children off the street. In many cases it is a family link even if the parents do not go to Chapel themselves now. Dyke Street schoolchildren and adolescents are firm in the belief that youth organisations are "not for our sort". The clothes, speech, ethical standards and manners of the typical Radby youth organisation, more

Dyke Street and Gladstone Road a Comparison 99

than its actual activities, are rather above that of the average Dyke Street youngster. Some of the boys, too, regard youth organisations as "sissy"; also they smack of school where these children, mostly, do not shine.

All the above is probably related to the fact that practically all the youth organisations of Radby are closely connected with some religious body, or, as the Boys' Brigade, have a strongly religious flavour. One Dyke Street woman said, it is the other children in these church groups who are the snobs and keep the Dyke Street kids out, not the grown-ups there. Whatever the reason, the figures for just one set of organisations (the ones for the nearby Anglican Church) are revealing, even if small. Four Dyke Street children figure in the current registers for Sunday School, youth organisations and confirmation class; twenty youngsters from Gladstone Road. And this concerns children nearly all of whom attend the Church School, and relate to a Church which has an active and friendly rector.

One noticeable feature of the Play Room children was the extent to which they talked about love. ("She thinks he don't love her"); marital troubles ("they were rowing - he's left her"); and irregular sex relations which they hardly understand ("that lady, she has heaps of clothes men give her"). A girl as young as twelve, but from a household with a very dubious reputation, writes about a picture of two smart looking women talking, that "perhaps they are thinking of men". A certain amount of sex play probably takes place in Dyke Street. A girl of seven, e.g., is found in the entry with her knickers pulled down and the boy opposite is suspected by the girl's parents. Older women complain, too, of the filthy talk they overhear the boys using sometimes. The girls of twelve and upwards do a lot of boy hunting on the Market Place which has a bad reputation and is a place the Gladstone Road girls would not think of going to. One thirteen-year old Dyke Street girl was suspected of soliciting men there but nothing was ever proved and in the interviewer's opinion the suspicion was unjustified. General talk with women in Dyke Street did not suggest that there was much sexual irregularity among children or adolescents.

"Going with boys" on the other hand, is accepted as the proper thing at about any age. On the point of early courting the difference between the two streets is marked. Dyke Street accepts it as a proper occupation that is not to be interfered with, and demands no supervision except that certain mothers felt they had not done their duty until "I'd given her (it was always 'her') a good talking to", i.e., told her the facts of life and, so to speak, warned her. That done, the mother's responsibility ends, In Gladstone Road however early courting, though

100 Dyke Street and Gladstone Road a Comparison

not stopped, is subject to supervision and is, in some cases, definitely a cause for anxiety, "I've worried and worried" said 40-year old parent whose only girl had begun going out with a boy at fourteen, "but I've decided it's best to let it go on". Marriage itself, of course, is regarded as about inevitable in both streets. "Miss" is a practically unknown status in Dyke Street, and an oddity in Gladstone Road. Both streets expect marriage to take place in the early twenties at least, and Dyke Street is prepared to make it earlier than this. At least 16 Dyke Street households were met where some one in the house was believed to have married at twenty or under, though it is sometimes thought a pity for the girl· "She ought to have a good time while she can". The implication is that, once married, she will inevitably have a poorer life. The newly married frequently make their home in one room of a parents' house, and the girl continues to work. This persists till about the second baby, when the couple move to a home of their own. The real change, in the girl's life anyhow, takes place at this stage, not at her actual marriage. In Gladstone Road, marriage seems to be less of an inevitable stage than something which is deliberately chosen. Marriage itself is probably more often a break with former life than in Dyke Street, even if the married son or girl does continue to live with the parents.

Apart from what is said and talked about, general observation suggested that there are far more irregular sex relations among adults in Dyke Street than in Gladstone Road. At least 32 families in Dyke Street, as contrasted with only two in Gladstone Road, are known to have someone who has been involved in "trouble" which, in most cases, concerns sex. Co-habiting is known in at least ten of these households. The children's vagueness about surnames, "He's Johnny Alan", "No he's not then, his name's Hardy", was the kind of argument that arose constantly: or (from an adult, and with a smirk) "calls herself Baker now, does she?" A story of a woman leaving her husband to go off to another hap, and getting a neighbour to have the suitcase packed and ready at the neighbour's house would be unheard of in Gladstone Road, It is accepted as a commonplace (even if condemned) in Dyke Street.

As far as pre-marital intercourse goes, as has been said, people seem to think that there is not very much of this among Radby girls. "The local boys have not much glamour to offer". It is the older girls who are concerned. Dyke Street <u>area</u> had twelve illegitimate births for 1948–52, although this was a quarter of the total number for Radby. Illegitimate births, however, are not necessarily a clue to extra-marital intercourse, though they are perhaps more likely to be so in the case of adolescents than of older women. The big, extended family of Dyke

Dyke Street and Gladstone Road a Comparison   101

Street can absorb the illegitimate child more readily than can a Gladstone Road home. The following conversation may be quoted : Mrs, C said that only last week she had moved off a man (a Pole from the next street) and a woman who were standing up against her front door at 11.30 p.m. The woman lives up the street, is about thirty, is waiting for a divorce, and has a three months old baby by the Pole, whom she has taken to Court for a paternity order. In the morning Mrs. C found a "rubber goods" among her coal, fallen through the grating. She did not know what it was. Her son told her "What you use if the woman don't want her husband to find out". A neighbour Mrs. R confirmed the story, and said they were always sweeping "rubber goods" out of the entry opposite her house. They "makes you feel dirty" according to the speakers. They were all elderly women who had lived in the street for many years. The general attitude to sex also differs in the two streets. Among Dyke Street men it is considered good manners and a definite sign of friendliness for men (especially strangers) to chaff a woman about any casual dealings she happens to be having with any male. Co-habiting and irregular relations are spoken of fairy freely to a relative stranger, by people of all ages, and are often introduced by the speakers themselves. Occasionally Dyke Street talk suggests a *News of the World* atmosphere. For example, three women, in one conversation, brought up the following topics in relation to people in the street whom they know, and know well : - a girl of twenty who had a baby in the factory lavatory "on a Friday afternoon", and had tried to put it on the fire; a boy in Borstal; the man and the woman next door who "have got married at last, now there's no risk of children"; and a particular friend whose first husband had so kicked her about "in her privates" that she got abesses. In Gladstone Road the subject has to be brought up by the enquirer, who was often fobbed off, especially by older women. They were embarrassed. Even among the young women certain ones object to the idea of talks on sex being given at school; and say "I could not tell my boys of course". They don't find the subject dirty, but they suggest that they want to keep it very special, so to speak. Dyke Street is inclined to find sex a dirty subject that should be kept away from children. The older women in particular think it highly improper that children should know the physical facts of birth. Even a girl of thirteen ought not really to know that her mother is pregnant. The mother should not mention it anyhow. Another woman was equally embarrassed about menstruation. "I couldn't tell my girl. Her Aunty had to". Some have a high sense of decorum and of what is, and is not, proper. An old age pensioner, e.g., should not be expected to nurse his still older mother-in-law; it would not be decent.

102 *Dyke Street and Gladstone Road a Comparison*

In Gladstone Road the Chapel code on extra-marital relations would probably hold good in the majority of households, though it is difficult to confirm this because people are so reluctant to discuss such matters, They are certainly much less apprehensive about the girls' safety than the Dyke Street people. They are more inclined to blame the man and to excuse the girl. "There's no harm in her. She just longs to look grown-up". In Dyke Street the boy is almost expected to try his hand. "A girl should have more self control if she goes with boys", says a thirteen-year old girl. The girls of fourteen and fifteen who make themselves look older than they really are get heavily censured. "The girl, not the man, is to blame if there's trouble". All told Dyke Street seems much more aware of sex than Gladstone Road. It is more imminent both as a source of pleasure and as something to be feared, but feared on grounds of inconvenience, trouble or disaster rather than moral ones.

Examples of behaviour that borders on delinquency were met with occasionally in Dyke Street, not at all in Gladstone Road. Some of the play room children took the pencils, plasticine, etc., away with them. Certain ones were so tiny that this was to be expected; but the older ones knew that they ought not to do this, because they accused each other of doing so, or were indignant if accused themselves by a grown-up. A six-year old (illegitimate) child brought in an obviously new wrist-watch one evening. He said he had been given it for Christmas. He had, in fact, gone into a neighbour's house, got up on the bed, and taken the watch from a shelf. It was found, later on, lying on a doorstep in the middle of the town. The child is known to have already got a reputation, among the children them selves, as a "pincher". Some of the stories the children wrote suggested that they were quite familiar with the idea of ordinary people stealing. Their own habits too, were spoken of openly, such as taking wood off the pit heap (known to be wrong); telling each other how to undo a gate so as to get into a garden to scrump, and so on. Adults said less about wrong-doing (people in prison were not referred to as was the case of, e.g., people co-habiting).

The children were not clear, often, as to what stealing really meant. Pinching little things was not stealing. A person who would not steal £20 lying about in the room, was described as almost odd, or anyhow one of unparalleled honesty. A good deal of what looked like stealing is put down to "just roguery" and excused altogether. In fact, therefore, the children might well be excused for a certain amount of thieving since what was, and was <u>not</u> stealing, was so vague. Nor did some of them seem to get definite teaching not to steal. While some were encouraged to do so (from woodworking, e.g.) by their parents. Or if they

Dyke Street and Gladstone Road a Comparison   103

found another child's toy they would bring it home and not be made to take it back. In Gladstone Road there was none of this vagueness. Stealing is stealing, and children have to be taught that it is wrong as early as possible. It is a test of a family's character that the child shall not even be suspected of stealing. That stealing is something not altogether removed from Gladstone Road experience is suggested by the emphasis they all put on the importance of teaching the children to be absolutely honest. Behind all this probably lies the Church training and standards with which Gladstone Road as a whole has had first-hand contact, though the adults may not be Churchgoers now. With the children, too, the parents' moral teaching is reinforced by what they hear at Sunday School and the (church) youth organisations. Moreover Gladstone Road supports the law (some parents would like the police to have more power) , while Dyke Street children laugh at the idea of being soared of a policeman. Even a child of seven will pooh-pooh the idea of taking any notice of what a bobby might do.

Physical force was more of a menace and more common apparently in Dyke Street than in Gladstone Road. Several cases of physical assault were mentioned (two women neighbours fighting; a husband who had kicked his pregnant wife). And these were not regarded as especially disgraceful. The children, too, seemed to do a lot of bad-tempered hitting and fighting among each other. Arguments were expected to be settled by force. A girl of eleven would tear a note book from another child's hands rather than talk over who should own it. For children to use physical force is obviously a less unnatural thing in Dyke Street than in Gladstone Road; and it may have some bearing on their attitude in later life to delinquent behaviour that involves violence.

The preceding section has dealt with factual information, matters which, on the whole, could be measured and checked, and which were relatively easy to talk over with the people concerned. The following section deals with such intangible matters as personal relationships and attitudes, subjects on which many errors of judgment are likely to be made - especially in the case of Dyke Street, where people are less accustomed to analysing their doings, and less able to express their thoughts than in the rather more literate Gladstone Road.

Plenty of couples in both streets "live comfortable", as Radby expresses it when husband and wife are known to be on good terms. Wives may speak lovingly of their husbands even in the most slovenly looking house. On the other hand, so many families in Dyke Street have irregular unions, and there seem to be so many cases in which a husband or wife has been abandoned, that the marital relationship does appear to be less satisfactory than in Gladstone Road. Of course

104 *Dyke Street and Gladstone Road a Comparison*

it is easier in the latter to hush things up, and people would be more concerned to do so. In the "good" street, too, the husband or wife who loses their partner (for whatever the reason) often remarries. In Dyke street a new partner is often brought in without bothering about marriage. If it is the woman, she comes in primarily to run the house; if the man, to support the woman in every sense. The sex relationship seems to be a secondary and later consideration, wife beating is definitely on the decline, A good many men even take on a share of the domestic chores. They look after the small children, for example.

Kids are a worry in Dyke Street however fond adults are of them. In Gladstone Road they are troublesome, certainly, but on the whole parents appear to enjoy their offspring, That is the general impression which the two areas present. Moreover Gladstone Road likes children as such, and not merely their own. The worrying in Dyke Street is partly connected with the inadequate physical environment. The children must be stopped from being an intolerable nuisance to the neighbours. That is a prime consideration and it is an excusable one. Gladstone Road does not have to contend with the difficulty of so many and so close neighbours. In Dyke Street children are also regarded as a grievance because they cramp such things as pub- going, a legitimate bit of recreation especially for the woman who goes to work as well as running her home. Their attitude to nursery schools brings out the different approach of the two streets, Dyke Street supports the idea of a nursery school strongly - it would relieve the mother of the bother of children, and it would allow her to go out to work. Gladstone Road has no use for nursery schools except perhaps for a widow or for an only child who needs company. "I <u>like</u> to look after my children", the mothers say; or "We want lots of things for the home, I know, but the children must come first".

Gladstone Road also sees Children as children, not just as small-sized adults. As children they need a specific kind of treatment and a training that may well include denying the child's wishes at times. Dyke Street thinks an adult who does not respond to a child's demands (unless this would annoy the nighbours) as callous and inhuman. Of course they recognise the need for the child's physical safety, but not much beyond this. They are more inclined to feel responsible for the child's present satisfaction than his future welfare. Nor do they give it much conscious direction, or take any particular interest in its doings. Some of the Dyke Street children never take their paintings home "to show me mum". She wouldn't be interested. This seems to be true of the average "happy" home, and is not confined to the occasional child who definitely dislikes his mother for some such reason as that "she's

Dyke Street and Gladstone Road a Comparison   105

always hitting him". The Dyke Street babies certainly do get rather special treatment. "Everyone loves a baby", they say; its helplessness is so apparent. But the toddlers often get scant attention, and any deliberate training decreases as the child gets older. By the time the child is adolescent, it comes under almost the same treatment as an adult - "She's sixteen, she can do what she likes, can't she?"

Dyke Street enjoys giving the children pleasure. That is certain. It believes firmly in presents, though these, of course, also demonstrate how good a parent the giver is. Much of the present giving (which is constant) is probably determined by this and is not a matter of particular affection. It is a nuisance stopper too, of course. The children are aware of both points. They often seem to regard adults (Grandmas, for instance) just as providers of things. The way to get money or presents out of such people is to be aggressive.

The streets agree on one topic, that children are less disciplined now than formerly. Dyke Street children are flagrantly disobedient by middle-class standards, and even Gladstone Road adults say that there is much less implicit obedience from children now than when they were children. Insolence, not just sauciness, is more common and the old unquestioned respect for adults, just because they are adults, has gone. "We would never have dared", is the line the adults take. The change may be partly due to the fact that today's children are better able to stand up for themselves. Also the parents are less the sole source of provision now than formerly. Dinners are got at school, the child goes to the nurse at the clinic, he gets his holidays at the club camp - and so on. Perhaps a more significant cause of the changed relationship is that the old rule-of-thumb, authoritarian regime, almost inevitable in the big family, is now discredited. School, the women's magazines, the wireless, all preach a democratic treatment of young people. The old fixed rules have gone. It is no longer "You come in at nine, my girl, or you don't go out tomorrow", which, of course, was an easier technique, especially for the less intelligent parent, than the modern one of weighing up each situation on its merits and deciding what rule to apply.

Both Dyke Street and Gladstone Road children play in street groups of course. But in Gladstone Road the youngsters, especially the little children, often have one or two particular friends who play regularly in each other's houses and back gardens. The older Gladstone Road groups are said to be "proper cliquey", i.e., the top-end children don't play with those below the middle lamp-post. The Gladstone Road street games appear to be more satisfactory than the Dyke Street ones, and on a rather bigger scale. Dyke Street children are perhaps too

106 *Dyke Street and Gladstone Road a Comparison*

undisciplined to be able to manage a game that involves more than three or four children. This does not apply to the boys' scratch football, but that often has a few older fellows in it. A lot of rough play, hitting, etc., upsets the Dyke Street children's play. There are constant tears and accusations. The girls, especially, get knocked about. It is regarded as inevitable. They also becall one another a good deal. Children of four and five accuse each other of being "biters" or "pinchers". At nine or ten "you're a liar" is regarded as an insult, and they are greatly offended if another child swears at them. Certain standards, perhaps schools', are evidently acknowledged if not kept to. They are extremely jealous of each other over any small privilege: and equally irresponsible (by middle-class standards) over jobs they have undertaken to do. On the whole however they achieve a rough justice among themselves, and don't too often have to appeal to a grown-up.

Dyke Street as a whole knows a lot about each other. Families have lived there for so long, and at such close quarters that it would be difficult to keep one's affairs private. Mostly they seem on pretty good surface terms with each other. Occasionally they come to blows, and do not hesitate to say so to a stranger. Gladstone Road would regard such a thing as disgraceful. There people seem to be on less black and white terms with each other. In Dyke Street one or two tiresome households (e.g., a "simple" but very aggressive woman, or a super-tidy one) act as a common and unifying target. Mutual services, from assisting at a birth, to borrowing the gravy salt, are a regular feature of the street. In pretty well any of the houses visited it is common for one or more neighbours or neighbours' children, to open the door and come in - no knocking, and of course Christian name terms. So many of the households are related that some of this apparent "neighbouring" is really based on actual relationship. People often say they don't neighbour as it is considered rather a low thing to admit to even in Dyke Street. But while they are saying this, often enough, the door opens and in pops Mrs. G from across the road; and then five minutes later the Brown child comes in to ask for the loan of some milk. The street telegraph (news spreads like wildfire) must be based on neighbouring. Whatever the cause, it is a significant feature of Dyke Street life and is in strong contrast to Gladstone Road, where there is little dropping in, except perhaps by one specially friendly family. Gladstone Road puts it this way "I don't neighbour, but of course when young Mrs. A next door was ill I did all I could for her". No housewives are to be seen talking on the front, and there is no question of sitting on front steps. At the same time, Gladstone Road people are pretty knowledgeable about each other's affairs, especially the residents who are old stagers, as so

Dyke Street and Gladstone Road a Comparison 107

many are. A family in the end house of the street, e.g., could give the names and approximate age of the children in pretty well every house. Another woman, with her sister's aid, could do the same as to which of the 102 houses was owned or rented.

Dyke Street, on occasion, likes to do a good turn, to give the children pleasure; to organise an outing for Old Age Pensioners at the Club; to collect (from nearly every house) for a wreath, and so on. Their public spirit seems to be confined to the street itself, whereas Gladstone Road, through its Church affiliations, probably accepts social responsibilities in a rather wider sphere. It is noticeable, however, that it feels no obligations to its neighbours in Dyke Street. They are a feckless lot, according to most Gladstone Road people, and "we prefer to keep clear of them". One Gladstone Road women was genuinely surprised that anyone respectable could be found in Dyke Street.

The social level of Dyke Street appears to be fairy stationary, or even on the rise. Fights are less common, and so is wife-beating generally in Radby. Dyke Street know that they are a rough lot, but it does not worry them. Gladstone Road opinion on the status of their road varies. Most of the newcomers feel that they have stepped up. No one expressed a wish to leave the road itself, though one woman, not a Radby native, did think poorly of the town itself. Both streets regard mining as a normal occupation but Gladstone Road is sometimes careful to distinguish between different grades. "My husband, he's not a face worker of course". This is said in self-defence, e.g., "You may think because he's a miner we are well off. It's not so". The wives of the non-miners in both streets often voiced some bitterness against the mining homes because of the high wages. Both streets, too, often refer to the hardships of their childhood, or with the older ones, of their early married life. This came out time and time again. But the reaction to these memoirs was different. Dyke Street will give the children anything they ask if possible because they had such a rough childhood themselves. Gladstone Road sees the danger in this. It wants long distance benefits rather than immediate pleasures for the children. Their children have got to rise educationally and financially. "We want them to have a little bit more than we had ourselves". Another difference is that they not only recall the bad old days, but are proud that their parents, by hard work and thrift, made a relatively successful fight against their difficulties. It is a more pugnacious, optimistic and fruitful attitude, really, than that of Dyke Street.

Both streets have raised their standards of living as far as income goes. Dyke Street spends more on clothes, shoes, better quality food, fruit, etc. But Gladstone Road, besides this, uses the extra money for

108 *Dyke Street and Gladstone Road a Comparison*

the children rather than the parents. The adolescent daughter, e. g., is allowed to take a nice nursery school job, rather than a factory one as her mother did, even if the wage is only 30s. Gladstone Road people are ambitious for their children in other directions. They will stop their little girl from playing with "that Davies child" who swears. They will go and see the teacher to see if David can be pushed on to get the scholarship; a father will even send his girl's boy-friend packing if he feels that the latter does not come up to the standard he had set for her. In other words while Dyke Street appreciates the extra money, it mostly spends it forthwith. Gladstone Road uses the extra money as a tool for long term improvements. They see their children getting more advantages from the Welfare State than just a bigger pay packet.

Another difference between the two streets can be summed up, simply, by the statement that one would know what to expect in Gladstone Road much more than in its neighbour. This lack of predictability about Dyke Street arises from the fact that it presents so many different faces. There is a vast difference in physical standards as between household and household; the Dyke Street individual house will be ship-shape one day and unwept and cluttered up the next; the mother will be smartly dressed when off to the pub, a slattern during the daytime. A similar inconsistency rules in other fields. in Dyke Street matters that are talked of openly (e. g., a theft of £20 from the house) are never mentioned again; the adolescent boy is a member of the Boys Brigade one month, and has stopped going the next; the little girl in the play room who tells on another child "Barrie takes the plasticine home", is known to be a "pincher" herself. Nor can their promises be rolled on. Of nine adolescents who said they would come to a little meeting in the street, one turned up. They had not been busy, just gone to the pictures, and so on. For people who live in Dyke Street and know its habits it may be different, but the stranger can never trust Dyke Street; Whereas Gladstone Road, though it doubtless has its inconsistencies and even skeletons in the cupboard, (who hasn't!)on the whole presents a reliable and consistent pattern of behaviour.

Allied to the above is the general atmosphere of uncertainty that hangs over Dyke Street. Anything (in the sinister sense) might happen there. They are on the edge of trouble all the time. The mothers, e. g., are always apprehensive about possible ills befalling the children (the toddler will be run over; or the adolescent boy will surely get led into trouble by those bad boys who live opposite). Gladstone Road people seem far more secure. Difficulties will come to them doubtless, but they expect to weather them. In Dyke Street the chances are that difficulties will swamp one. It is perhaps this fearful attitude that helps

Dyke Street and Gladstone Road a Comparison 109

to account for the readiness with which Dyke Street seizes on any bit of relief - two bob (for the wife) on the 3 o'clock race; the ladies' Mystery Trip next Saturday night or the slap-up wedding at the Newcastle Arms for an eighteen-year old bride.

The above description of Dyke Street and Gladstone Road does no more than outline the more obvious aspects of the life of the streets. The interviewer herself was very conscious that she saw the surface only. But even this surface did suggest certain different trends, and justified the belief that if a longer and closer contact had been possible the suspected difference in the deeper attitudes of the two of people would have only been revealed. The relevance of the above to delinquency has only been hinted at. The theoretical implications of the comparison will be discussed more fully in the section on conclusions.

III E. Carnation Street Area and the Knoll Estate Introduction to the 5-Point Scale

The findings in Section III D suggested that the two streets in Area C were conditioning those growing up in them differently. As will be shown later these two types of conditioning might be thought to affect, amongst other things, the children's expectation of delinquency. When the Enquirers came to make a closer contact with the two remaining Areas, A and D, they found less clear-cut differences between the selected "black" and "white" streets. While certain families in the so-called black streets were on a par with the average Dyke Street home (or in the case of the good streets, with a Gladstone Road household), there was less evidence of a homogeneous blackness or whiteness, so to speak. At the same time individual families were found to have closely similar "patterns" to the average Dyke Street or Gladstone Road family, and none were much above the top Gladstone Road home, nor below the bottom one in Dyke Street. The Enquirers therefore decided not to study the pairs of streets in Areas A and D as geographical units, but to substitute a comparison between the families within these streets. They decided to include also the families in the pair of streets (Dyke Street and Gladstone Road) which were described earlier (Section III D). For this purpose they ranked each family about whom they could obtain sufficient information (225 in all) on a 1 to 5 scale. The assets, and the dangers, of this "ranking" are discussed in the following section, preceeded by a short description of Areas A and D themselves.

The above table gives the essential facts about the two streets chosen for comparative purposes in Area A. Carnation Street[1] lies within two

---

1 Charlotte Street is, in fact, two streets. For the purpose of this Report they have been treated as one. This is felt to be justified since they lead off each other and have a common social life (e. g., they shared collectors for a joint Coronation party).

Introduction to the 5-Point Scale 111

Area A, The Carnation Street Area		Compaction St.	Charlotte St.
No. of houses		59	65
No. of households		59	65
No· of people		224	227
„	Age 21+ years	127	148
„	15–20 years	23	22
„	5–14 years	45	33
„	0–4 years	24	20
„	No information re. age	5	4
Total no. of households where contact made with at least 1 adult and sufficient information gained for grading		16	17
Households not contacted but information obtained from other source		43	48
Structure of household for whole street:			
	1 – 4 persons	44	48
	5 – 8 „	14	16
	9 plus „	1	1
Delinquency:			
Adults	1948–52	7	0
Juvenile	1942–52	11	0
Matrimonial cases	1948–52	3	3
Employment(of chief male in household):			
Miner		24	31
Factory skilled		2	1
„ unskilled or lab.		3	10
Transport		5	10
Clerical		0	0
Self-employed		2	1
Miscellaneous		3	5
No information		20	7

minutes' walk of Charlotte Street though a main road runs between them. They are about equal in length and much of a muchness in looks. Both are typical, terrace streets of the 1880s with rents in the 7s., 10s. range or a buying price of £200 or so. One Carnation Street buyer, e.g., had paid a deposit of £75 and is to pay 25s. a week for seven years. Incomes are probably fairly similar since the employment pattern and the total number and age structure of the residents shows little difference.

More difference is to be seen in the backs of the houses than in their faces. Charlotte Street has one block of older, stone houses which have

112 *Introduction to the 5-Point Scale*

no doors onto the street itself. They have very small gardens, as do most of the Charlotte Street houses. Though the gardens often have little, home-made palings, there is no privacy about them. The lavatories, too, in both streets, are outside the house. Carnation Street has yards, and ash yards, more often than gardens: or if there is any strip of earth, it is unfenced. There is no spic and span look even about Charlotte Street, but it has not got the scatter of squalid looking houses with broken windows and bedraggled curtains that occurs in the other street.

The streets do not have much to do with each other. The children do not play together and do not seem to know each other. The busy main road that lies between them is probably the real barrier though Charlotte Street has not much opinion of Carnation Street. "It's very quiet up here", say Charlotte Street residents, or, "they are a rough lot in Carnation Street - you should hear them round at the Plough". The speaker in this case was a Charlotte Street man whose garden wall is that of the Plough's backyard. The reputation of Carnation Street has been chequered. Sixty years ago it was a normal working class street, according to what the local people say. Then, for reasons that have not been ascertained, its character deteriorated. One of the present householders, e.g., talked of the 1926 strike and of the line of taxis he saw draw up off the street to disgorge a load of police brought in from another town. He remembered the rough reception that Carnation Street gave the visitors! In more recent years this reputation for roughness has been maintained. The local senior girls' school, e.g., has plotted the areas from which two thirds of the bad attenders come, and Carnation Street is in the centre of this (quite small) area. The Enquiry's own set of figures for the juvenile and adult delinquency of the street were also relatively high.

With the above picture in mind the interviewers were surprised to find that Carnation Street did not present the uniformly black set of households that had been expected. On enquiry, however, they found that the street had experienced much change recently. Local people kept on saying (when hearing that the interviewer was interested in young people's leisure) how quiet the street was nowadays. "No children about now"; "Not the shouting there used to be"; "Less rowing". It was found that about 100 people had moved (mostly to new Council houses), and that at least fourteen families had left since January, 1954. It was the big families that had gone and they included at least seven of the households known to have had a delinquent member between 1942–52. Families that had been publicly regarded by the street as a nuisance were often referred to.

As a situation of this kind had arisen, the Enquiry decided not to go on with any attempted comparison between Charlotte and Carnation

Introduction to the 5-Point Scale   113

Streets as such, but to substitute a comparison between the families within the two streets. Before this decision was finally taken they had, in fact, come across plenty of families which could, presumably, have fitted comfortably into either street; and they had only met a few which would have been markedly out of place in either street. One small aspect of the actual interviewing illustrated this. In Dyke Street and Gladstone Road the interviewer often made a rough guess as to the kind of households she would have met with by the end of an afternoon's work in one street. Normally this guess turned out to be more or less correct. In Carnation and Charlotte Street on the other hand, the guess was liable to be quite wrong. It was upset by the a-typical family that kept on turning up in both streets indiscriminately.

Area D The Knoll Estate Area	*Knoll Drive*	*Knoll Road*
No. of houses	74	70
No. of households	74	70
No. of people	280	261
„ Age 21+ years	160	158
„ 15–20 years	21	9
„ 5–14 years	74	80
„ 0–4 years	25	14
Total No. of households where contact made with at least one adult and sufficient information gained for grading	28	21
Structure of household:		
1 – 4 persons	50	55
5 – 8 „	23	14
9 plus „	1	1
Delinquency Court cases:		
Adults 1948–52	7	3
Juveniles 1942–52	10	1
Matrimonial Cases 1948–52	0	3
Employment (of chief male of house-hold) of those graded:		
Miner	11	9
Factory skilled	4	1
„ unskilled or labourer	5	3
Transport	2	2
Clerical	2	0
Self-employed	0	0
Miscellaneous	3	3
No information	1	3

114 *Introduction to the 5-Point Scale*

The above table gives the essential facts about the two streets chosen for comparative purposes in Area D.

The Knoll Estate is situated to the west of the town, and is about two miles from the Market Place. The Estate was started in the inter-war period, most of the houses in the Drive and Road being constructed in the mid-1930s. These two roads form the core of the Estate, and were the first to be constructed. Lilac Grove, which forms a stretch of 8 houses in the middle of one side of Knoll Road, and several houses adjoining the Grove, were not constructed until 1946. As Lilac Grove constitutes a continuous road with Knoll Road, the street will hereafter be referred to simply as Knoll Road. Many more houses have been built (and are in the process of being built) on the Estate, and these constitute roads leading off from Knoll Drive. The Estate is situated on higher ground than most of the town of Radby, and is at some distance from the collieries, so that the area is one of the more healthy and open parts of the town. The Estate is surrounded on three sides by open country, farms and allotment holdings, and is connected with the rest of the town in the east by Farm Lane, one of the few "residential" or "higher class" areas of Radby. The Estate is thus comparatively isolated from the rest of the town, though a 'bus service operates from the town as far as Farm Lane. This service is made the more necessary by the fact that there are only four shops on the Estate, and also because, apart from employment on the building sites, there is none at Knoll itself, so that most of the men work in Radby or in the City, There is a Community Centre, which is not widely supported, although it holds functions for people of all ages. Apart from this, there are no social amenities on the Estate. The nearest public house, the "Eight Bells", is about ten minutes walk distant.

The first occupants of the two roads to be compared (and therefore of the Estate) moved up to the Knoll in 1936, when only a few houses existed. Building continued at a fairly rapid pace, and the two roads were complete in 1939 when the war broke out except for about 16 houses in Knoll Road which were not built until after the War. The Estate did not prove to be a popular place to live in at first, because of its relative isolation and lack of amenities, and because also of the high rents as compared with those for the older houses in the town.[1] But with the outbreak of War, and the influx of people who came to work in the Radby factories and pits, the houses became occupied. Some of the

---

1 Rents range between 13s. and 15s. A house may be bought for about £1400, but a sitting tenant may obtain one for about £1000.

Introduction to the 5-Point Scale 115

people moving into them were of foreign extraction - especially Poles, of whom there continue to be a fair number in Radby. There were also people from various parts of this country, including evacuee families from London. These two groups added to the Radby families who had moved to the Knoll from other parts of the town. There does not appear to have been much control over many of the tenants, and some of the (new) houses quickly deteriorated through maltreatment and insufficient care (although the houses are said to be "jerry-built"). There was an appreciable number of cases of "moonlight-flitting" - i.e., occupants would not pay the rent, and when some action was taken by the landlord to obtain arrears, tenants would leave the house overnight and thereby avoid the necessity for payment. A consequence was that there was a lack of stability of some of the population of the roads, and much "coming and going". It was during this time that the Estate obtained what some of its residents "call a bad name" - because of a certain number of "irresponsible" tenants who gained the reputation not only because of the treatment to which they subjected the houses, but also because of their general "rowdyness", drunkenness, "free-living" (on the part of women whose husbands were in the Forces), lack of control of children, and alleged tendency to criminal activity, Such was the reputation gained. But towards the end of the War the population became more settled - some tenants of a better type are said to have moved onto the Estate. The result is that many of the present residents consider that the Estate no longer justifies the bad reputation that it has, whilst they recognise that it has a bad name to live down. Nevertheless, of the twelve families from the two roads involved in cases of juvenile delinquency during the period 1942–1952, seven are still living in the same houses. And there were ten adult delinquents resident in the roads during the years 1948–52.

The Estate is essentially working class in character, and a large number of the working men are in the pits. The employment figures for the chief male of each household in the two streets were not obtained, but constant visits to the Estate served to emphasise its working class character. The many heaps of coal piled outside the houses (representing the monthly coal allowance) revealed that in these houses at least one member was employed at a colliery. And quite frequently such comments as "it's like a mining village up here", prompted by the large number of colliers resident in the two streets, were made. In addition to the miners, it is known that a large number of men work in factories, and others work as postmen, milk-roundsmen, etc. The occupations of the chief males of the households which were graded are thought to reflect fairly closely the general employment picture for the two streets.

116 *Introduction to the 5-Point Scale*

The houses, with the exception of one or two detached ones, are of the Council house type. They have three bedrooms one of which is very small, and large enough only to contain a single bed. Downstairs there is a living room and a kitchen. Some of the houses have very small bathrooms. The toilet is situated in the back porch, outside the back door. All of the houses have front and back gardens, and since the roads form two sides of a triangle, the back gardens on one side at the lower end of both streets are large.

The Community Centre on the Estate to which reference has already been made is accommodated in two large Nissen-hut halls. The activities at this centre have been referred to in an earlier section. Here only a brief "historical" outline of the Centre will be given. The Centre arose out of a few people meeting together in a fish and chip shop for whist drives, etc. twice weekly in the evenings. This was just after the end of the Second World War. The Estate was comparatively new, and the Centre became quite popular. Various fund-raising activities provided the large premises, and a grant from the County authority secured a full-time Warden. From that time on the history of the Centre is similar to that which appears to be true for many such places.[1] The small group who worked hard to initiate its activities began to feel that their efforts were not sufficiently appreciated, and that they were being driven out by a rougher element, who gossiped and "canted". Interest in the Centre waned, and today it may be said that the most popular activities are dances and socials, which are organised by one or two stalwarts. Activities of a more serious nature, such as the Ladies Guild, are less actively supported: but it is these activities which are organised by the new elite – the up-and-coming, younger families - who have taken over the role of those who initiated the Centre. The more popular activities, including the Carnival Band, are on the whole supported by the lower grade families. The Youth Club is badly organised, and the higher level families forbid their children to attend, because of the hooliganism.

The Community Association's policy is guided by a Management Committee, which is an elected body. This committee is the focal point of the many intrigues and recriminations which surround the Centre's activities.

The figures relating to delinquency suggested that there was liable to be a contrast, such as that envisaged in the hypothesis, between the Drive and the Road. This was supported by preliminary investigation.

---

1 cf. L. Kuper, Living in Towns

Introduction to the 5-Point Scale 117

Probably such a contrast existed previously, and during part of the decade with which the delinquency figures were concerned. But subsequent research suggested that although such differences as those postulated in the hypothesis are to be found within this area, the contrast is not between the two roads, but between different sections, or different households adjoining each other, within the two roads. So that it appeared that the position was not precisely the same as the figures (relating to 1942–52) suggested. Although Knoll Drive tends to be regarded as "not as nice as the Road", and appears also to merit the description that "a lot of fuckers live down there", there is not a homogeneity about the Drive and about the Road as such, similar to that which has been described in relation to Dyke Street and Gladstone Road. This change in the situation seems to have arisen because many of the larger house holds have moved out of the area, and many of the "wartime" families have left the town. The landlord has been anxious to sell rather than rent the houses to new tenants, so that the incoming families have tended to be of a different type. The Knoll Estate thus presented a similar picture to the Research workers as the Carnation Street Area. The position was made more clear when further interviews were carried out, following the decision to adopt a 5-point scale ranking system for these two areas. This is show in Table 11 below, where it is seen that although there is a slight tendency for the higher grade households to be resident in the streets envisaged as "good" streets in the Carnation Street and Knoll Estate Areas, there is nevertheless a tendency for households of all five grades to be resident in each of the two streets in fairly equal numbers. In the Dyke Street Area, the expected contrast is clearly reflected in the large number of low grade families resident in Dyke Street, and by the large number of high grade families resident in Gladstone Road. In each of the Areas A and D, therefore, it was decided, as has been said, to grade the households interviewed in accordance with a five-point scale range. In addition to the straightforward comparison between the sub-cultures of Dyke Street and Gladstone Road, certain households in these streets were also graded, so that the analysis made below of the five-point scale range is based upon a total of 225 households.

The 5-point Scale

An account has been given above of the reasons why it was considered necessary to abandon the street comparison in the two Areas A and D, and to substitute a comparison between households within these Areas.

118   *Introduction to the 5-Point Scale*

The Research Workers had a clear picture of two main types of household. On the one hand there were those presenting characteristics comparable with the "black" sub-culture of Dyke Street, and on the other hand those which were comparable with the "white" households of Gladstone Road. It became obvious that it was necessary at this stage to make further distinctions between households within the "black" and within the "white "types respectively. Certain differences between "black" households, apparent in Dyke Street, became more obvious when the Research was extended to the other two Areas. Similarly with the "white". Thus the "black" embraced some very low-level families such as those which Public Agencies designate as "Problem Families", as well as a large number of families which could not in the strict sense of the term be regarded as "Problem Families". The former were classified as Grade I, the latter as Grade II. With regard to the "white" households, a difference was apparent between those who strove to achieve certain standards, and those who at the same time were very ambitious and consciously "on the rise". The "white" type was therefore divided into two grades, IV and V. In addition it was found necessary to distinguish another category, Grade III.

Broadly speaking, Grade III consists of those households which are content - or at any rate not seriously perturbed - to live alongside the two "black" grades, whilst maintaining a different set of standards with regard to behaviour and physical appearances, a set of standards which accords more with that of the "white" grades. Nevertheless, Grade III homes, although they may decry to some extent the standards and codes of the lower grades, do not take great pains to ensure, e.g., that their children do not mix with those of the "black" households. Nor are they contemptuous of the lower grades. Their attitude is rather that of "live and let live". They are different from the higher grades in this respect, but also in the allied fact that they have not got the aspirations which characterise the IVs and Vs. The comparatively high number of Grade III households (94 out of a total of 225) demands some comment. Firstly it must be said that the relative numbers in each of the five grades may or may not reflect the relative proportions of the working classes in Radby. If they do, it is fortuitous. Secondly the Grade IIIs represent in fact the "core" of the population investigated. They consist of those households which do not stand out as presenting features which are likely to have a particularly adverse or a particularly beneficial effect upon their children's conduct. Finally, although no household was graded unless it was considered that adequate information was obtained on it, it may be that a few households were

Introduction to the 5-Point Scale 119

graded as III which might well have been graded as either II or IV had further information been obtained. That is to say, unless some specific point(s) clearly indicated that a household was "black" or "white" it was graded as III.

In order to grade the households it was necessary to obtain a considerable amount of information about them. This was done by formal and informal interviews with members of them, by participating in group activities with them, and by hearing what other people said of them. The things in which we were interested were the training of children, leisure-time activities, etc. - in fact all those matters which were considered with reference to the Dyke Street: Gladstone Road comparison. What did they think about education? Had they any aspirations for themselves or their children with regard to employment? what determined their attitude and actions? To what extent and in what ways were their actions affected by the neighbourhood in which they lived, the people with whom they worked, and the people whom they met in their leisure-time? what effect, if any, did the Working Men's Club or Television have upon their family life, and in particular on the lives of the children? And how far were the ideas put into effect in the kitchen guided by the latest advice given in *Woman's Weekly* - a journal which in some homes would just be thumbed over and then used for fish and chips. Such were the sort of questions to which we hoped to get the answers. If it could be discovered what sort of things people from these various households considered valuable, and also what sort of things the people actually did, then it would be possible to assess the standards by which they lived their lives, and to establish whether these standards varied significantly as between different families, and whether the significant variations were pertinent to the consideration of the social background in which delinquency arises. Thus it was not sufficient to know that a man worked in a factory as a labourer: it was necessary to find out whether he was a regular attender at work or whether he frequently absented himself. Were there any particular reasons for regularity of attendance - was it in order to have sufficient money to "go on the beer", or because he liked his work, or because he wished to buy a new stair carpet and could not afford one otherwise? What did he do when he arrived home from work - was a meal ready for him, or had his wife gone to the cinema and left him to look after himself? Were his children pleased to see him arrive home from work - or were they indifferent to the fact, or antagonistic towards him? This sort of information was sought, and in 225 cases sufficient information was obtained to place the households at some point in the scale. It is not claimed that comprehensive information was obtained for each

120   *Introduction to the 5-Point Scale*

of the families graded. This was impossible in the time available, and probably some information which would have been relevant to the grading was not obtained. But it is thought that sufficient information was amassed to approach the problem of assessing the households with some confidence.

No single one criterion was sufficient to grade the families accurately. An overall picture was essential. Standards of cleanliness and tidyness, education and leisure-time pursuits, ambition, expenditure patterns, relations between the sexes - all these and many other factors were of significance. In some cases the fact of delinquency itself contributed to the decisions as to whether the family was graded for example I or II. But the fact of delinquency did not of course determine that a family be placed as a I or II. It merely served to confirm a decision made with reference to the other factors mentioned above. Discussion between the Research Workers preceded the placing of each family in the 5-point scale, and the attempt was made to "balance" the various phenomena taken into account - thus a house might be dirty, poorly furnished, the chief man in the household might be unemployed, and there might be a juvenile delinquent present. This did not imply that the household was ipso facto graded at I or II. If, for example, the parents were genuinely grieved about their child's offence, and trying, in so far as they could, to improve their home and to live according to the grade III way of life, then that family was graded as III. Table 10, below, illustrates the fact that delinquency alone did not relegate a household to grade I or II.

The problem of stating our criterion precisely is complicated. For example, no satisfactory measure of standards of cleanliness or of housekeeping has as yet been devised by the sociologist, and the standards applied in this Research were mostly those arrived at by discussion between the Research Workers. No inflexible standard was possible; but it was thought feasible to distinguish between those households were were outstandingly efficiently cared for, those most inefficiently tended, and the ones that were about middling. There was another difficulty which prohibits absolutely precise definition of each of the grades: one of the factors taken into consideration in placing a family was the Research Workers' assessment of relationships within the family and of the parents' concern for their children as reflected by the general way in which they spoke to them as well as by the actual things they said to them (e. g., whether the parent desired a Grammar School education for the child). Such matters were often assessed with reference to quite small things, e. g., the look on the mother's face when scolding her child - whether this was done

Introduction to the 5-Point Scale 121

with spur of the moment anger or calmly as part of a planned method of correction. The chance cuffing, and the loud "bloody" and "bugger", were things that played their part in the general assessment of a family. Their significance is undoubted: but there are many pitfalls to be avoided when such factors are taken into account. As Marshall[11] has said, "not only do words and phrases carry different weight for different people - one man's "blast" is another man's "damn" - but the testimony may be consciously or unconsciously falsified, as every one knows who has tried to draft a questionnaire". All that can be said is that we have endeavoured to be consistent and rigorous in our analysis of the households, and to support our decisions by cross-checking and by constant discussion of the material. Some of the households may have been wrongly placed through misinterpretation or through lack of additional information of significance. Nevertheless we think that the majority have been graded accurately according to the criteria employed. The actual distinctions made between the five grades are certainly valid, even if the placing of certain families has been inaccurate. The factors considered are objective and we think that other Research workers in the same field would agree with the distinctions made.

In placing families within the range moral judgments were avoided as far as possible, We did not think of a household in terms of "good" or "bad", but in terms of the characteristics that it presented.

So much for the general aspects associated with the adoption of the 5-point scale. It is now necessary to state more precisely the differentiations which determined that we placed a family in one grade rather than another. The scale is, in fact, a continuum, not a separation into rigid classes. But the five grades are certainly convenient sections, and help to focus attention upon the differences which undoubtedly exist. The scale falls into three main parts - the (I and II), the (III), and the (IV and V). The differences between the IVs and the Vs are less distinct, and at the same time of less significance to this Research, than are the differences between the Is and the IIs. For convenience the IVs and Vs have been considered together in the section below, whereas it was considered necessary to devote separate sections to the consideration of the Is and the IIs. The distinctions between the grades, although quite clear to the observer, are nevertheless difficult to convey briefly, Furthermore, as must be stressed, the grading was based upon

---

1 T. H. Marshall <u>Sociology at the Crossroads</u>, Inaugural lecture, delivered 21st Feb., 1946, Longmans, Green & Co., Ltd., 1947.

122 *Introduction to the 5-Point Scale*

a composite picture built up by the Research Workers of each family graded. So that it is obviously not possible to list every factor which contributed to their decisions. To give some indication, however, we may consider one or two examples of "ideal types". <u>Other things being equal</u>, a family presenting the characteristics outlined below was assigned to the corresponding grade. If some other factors <u>negatived</u> these particular factors, the family was placed differently in accordance with the overall picture.

1 Housekeeping Standards

Grade I	Permanently squalid.
II	Intermittent effort but no real interest in keeping the home clean and tidy.
III	Effort made to ensure that the appearance of the home does not fall below certain standards – but no particular concern with maintaining high standards of tidiness, etc.
IV	Obvious effort to achieve higher standards than those of the IIIs - standards which are often above those which the present parents knew in their homes as children.
V	House proud. Even more than the IVs, they put money into the house, which is the centre of their family life.

2 Husband: Wife Relationship

Grade I	Extremely unstable: often "Irregular" - i.e., co-habiting, indiscriminately. Precarious.
II	Mostly the husband and wife are living together, but the relationship is not particularly stable. If husband does go off (a fairly rare occurrence) a new man is brought in on a permanent basis and the relationship is regularised. But husband and wife could not be regarded as partners in the venture of family life.
III	"Solid" relationship. The man takes his pleasure, the woman hers. Steady and unspectacular. Duties and obligations of husband and wife clearly defined and rigidly adhered to.
IV	Husband: Wife relationship is that of a partnership within the family. Duties are not so rigidly separated, the man "does things about the house", and tasks and obligations are regarded as the pleasures of married life.
V	c.f. the IVs, but emphasised.

Introduction to the 5-Point Scale   123

3   Relationship with Children

Grade I   Complete disregard and lack of training. "Not bothered". The aim is to keep the child quiet or out of the way. Little concern for physical welfare, and none for "spiritual" or "mental".

II   Inconsistent in their dealings with the children. No common policy between husband and wife about children - need for such a policy not recognised. No concern with smartness, work, school or play. Don't put themselves out too much for the sake of the children - but are concerned re physical dangers, e. g., road accidents, and like to give them material benefits in the way of toys, etc., but not in the form of a comfortable home.

III   Concern for cleanliness, "reasonable" behaviour in the home. But no conscious attempt to maintain high standards of conduct. Concern with not doing things wrong rather than with doing things right. Strict within narrow limits.

IV   Definite and consistent training. Standards sot which the child is taught to live up to. General ambition to be "higher" than the IIIs.

V   As with the IVs but more definite ideas of achievement. Definite ambitions for the child - based upon a knowledge, e. g., that if he goes to such and such a school he will be qualified to get a better job.

4   Education

Grade I   Complete unconcern about school - Children go if they want to, don't go otherwise.

II   Child may or may not go - parent decides. If he is wanted at home to help in the house he's kept away from school, and this is not considered to be wrong.

III   Parents are particular about their children attending school - it's the proper thing to do, and there might be trouble otherwise.

IV   Unheard of for children not to go - for the child's sake it is obviously a good thing.

V   As with IV, but in addition if the child is to have a "better" job he must attend regularly to learn.

It is hoped that some indication has been given of the criteria employed for grading the households. The characteristics of each grade, and the differences between the grades will become more apparent in the following detailed descriptions. In them the differences between the types will be stressed, and although these differences are important the fact remains that all of the families are similar in that they are working class.

III F. The 5-Point Scale of Households a Detailed Account

In the following section the object is to indicate briefly certain general aspects of the 5-point Scale and of the 225 households who were ranked on it. The tables to which reference is made will be found on pages 129 to 135.

Table 7 indicates the working class character of the 225 ranked households, It shows that in 135 households the chief male was a miner, and that in only five households was the chief male a white collar worker. Mining is the chief occupation of all of the grades except V, but even in this, the highest grade, there are four unskilled workers; and the four men who are self-employed are in work of a manual nature such as house decorating, Table 16 shows that elementary education is the rule for the great majority of these households; only 25 have children who had, or are having, other than elementary education. The working-class nature of these families is also to be seen in the physical character of the houses – their smallness, proximity to each other, and general lack of space and amenities, The rents of the houses in the old areas of the town range between 8s. and 11s., whilst those of the houses on the Knoll Estate are only a little higher. Only 48 of the houses (cf. Table 12) are owned by the occupants.

It is seen from Table 5 that only 70 households take noticeably effective effort with their house. The remaining 155 households are not noticeably clean or tidy and in 25 cases the effort taken is noticeable ineffective. It would appear that attention to the appearance and comfort of the home is not a primary concern for a large majority of the families. This lack of special concern for physical standards of the home relates chiefly to the three lower grades. Table 14 shows a surprisingly large number of households-noticeably in the lower grades - with at least one member of the household who is regularly in bad health or who suffers from a major physical or mental defect. In one or two cases (of the total of 47) their disability is of the serious nature

The 5-Point Scale of Households a Detailed Account 125

of blindness or deafness. But in the majority It is of a different order – either slight mental abnormality, "nerves", or general debility.

In spite of the significantly different characteristics apparent in the five grades, and in particular of the low level of housekeeping and of personal appearance in grades I and II, there is no great difference throughout the grades in the incomes of the chief male of the household. This is indicated by the similarity of occupations pursued by the chief male. The structure of the households, and in particular the fact that the lower two grades have a large proportion of households in which there is more than one person employed full-time (Table 8), indicates, however, that the income of many of these low grade households are considerable – and certainly exceeds in many cases the total money coming into some of the higher grade households. This fact is emphasised by the larger family allowance payments which the families in most of the lower grades receive, since they have larger numbers of children of allowance age per family than have the higher grades. In connection with this, a difference in attitude may be detected between the lower grade families (receiving on the whole, larger net incomes per family) and those in the higher grades. The former tend to live for the present, spending their money as soon as they earn it on things which give immediate satisfaction. The higher grade homes tend to think ahead – to plan their expenditure in accordance with a scheme of action, "the children will need new shoes in a month's time; and after Christmas we shall have to put so much aside for the washing machine. " Although this broad distinction may be made, there is no such contrast over the children's money - whether to give the child a weekly allotment and no more; or whether to buy him roughly what he asks for, are found throughout the range. But, and this is important, the higher grades treat the children's money as a matter that calls for training rather than one of indifference or mere convenience.

Broad distinctions may be made between the grades with regard to their membership of formal organisations and in particular their attitude to education. Table 16 shows that the three highest grades hope that their children will attend a Grammar School - the figures in the table show that 33 households from these grades were met who would definitely like their children to go to such a school. On the other hand throughout the range were people who disapproved of the extra year at school (pupils now leave school at 15 instead of 14). The widespread discontent with this extra year is not reflected fully in the table. Many of the people interviewed felt that the extra year at school is a waste of time - that the children learn no more, should be out at work at the age of 14, etc. Despite the fact that there are two well-appointed modern schools

126   The 5-Point Scals of Households a Detailed Account

in Radby, it should be pointed out that the poor physical nature of certain of the Radby schools provides little inducement to parents to acclaim the regulation that children be confined within them for the extra year. Table 18 gives some indication of attendance at Sunday School and Youth Organisations. In the five grades there are 137 households with children aged 0–14. Exact information was obtained from 80 of these with regard to Sunday School attendance, and from 85 with regard to attendance at Youth Organisations. Thirty-seven households have children who attend Sunday School regularly for 43 who do not; and 33 have children who attend Youth Organisations regularly for 52 who do not. The figures obtained are thought to reflect the general position, and it seems fair to say that there is in general little interest in such institutions, and hardly any interest at all displayed by grades I and II.

Comment has been made earlier on the popularity of gardening in Radby, and of such leisure-time activities as the informal groups at the pub, the Carnival Band at the Community Centre and so on. With regard to Television, Table 6 shows that 58 out of 225 households have sots. the majority of these are in the top three grades. However nearly 3 in 10 of the households graded possess television sets, and in view of the speculation as to the effect on Children of T.V., and in view, also, of the low educational standard of the Radby children as a whole, the following points are thought to be relevant. There may be no inducement for the children to make the effort to read, since they can get entertainment by turning the switch. Many children stay up until the evening's programmes conclude at about 10.30 p.m. according to information supplied by a Radby headteacher. He is conducting a private survey on the effect of T.V., as reading difficulties are a major problem in his school. It is also thought that the children become so used to the noise from the TV or wireless set at home, so that when at school the teacher's voice tends to be regulated, like TV or radio, to a drone in the background.

Table 6 also shows the keeping of pets is fairly general throughout the five grades – 100/225 households are known to have either pets or livestock. But the pets of grades I and II include mangy dogs and thin cats, which contrast with the wellkept dogs and canaries of the higher grades.

As will be elaborated below, the 5 grades show some contrast between the relationships between men and women and in particular between that of husband and wife. In general it may be said that the men and women in the lower grades lead far more separate lives than those in the higher grades - they take their pleasures apart, the men going to the pubs or clubs and the women to the cinema or a dance, and perhaps just meeting the husband for "the last hour" in the pub. At the same time the relationship is more precarious (Table 13). In the higher grades, husband and wife share many of their leisure-time activities - their weekly

The 5-Point Scale of Households a Detailed Account   127

visit to the cinema and so on. To the IVs and Vs the family is much more of an enterprise than it is to the lower grades - and it is considered as a joint enterprise, to be discussed and planned together.

In the account of the Dyke Street community, given in Section IIID above, some attention was given to the fact that the families in this street had considerable numbers of relations living nearby. It was pointed out that this led to much gossiping, and visiting of an informal nature. The same position obtains with regard to the present households, 61 of which have relations living within a few houses. And in particular does it obtain with regard to the two lower grades, where 14 out of 25 and 17 out of 47 households respectively have close relations living within a few houses (Table 4)· In addition to the relations living nearby, 49 households have grandparent(s), or grandchild(ren), or married child(ren) living at home (Table 3). This again is a phenomenon which is more apparent in grades I (10 out of 25) and II (12 out of 47) than in the higher grades. It is fair to say that the kin-group plays a much larger part in the lives of the grade I and II families than in the others, reinforcing and perpetuating the way of life of these families through constant contact. Even where there are relations living nearby, in the higher grades (particularly in the IVs and Vs), it seems that there is much less continuous contact between them - e.g., meetings are likely to take the form of a pre-arranged cup of tea once a week, rather than informal meetings throughout the 24 hours. To the IV or V families an Aunt or Uncle is an accepted social role in a more formal sense than is an Aunt or Uncle in the I and II homes. Here the uncle's role is rather that of someone who lives down the street, is seen fairly frequently, and whose exact relationship to the children may never be clearly established in their minds.

The phenomenon of neighbouring has been referred to previously. In the grade I and II families, and indeed in the IIIs, this is an important and accepted part of the daily life, especially in the old part of the town. Certainly it serves to establish and reinforce the accepted codes of conduct in these grades. But the IVs and Vs do not on the whole "agree" with it – it is not part of their way of life to gossip indiscriminately. It interferes with the privacy which is valued so much, and with meals to prepare and new jerseys to knit for the school children; time really does not permit of neighbouring. Thus the external contacts made by the IVs and Vs tend to be more selective – the chosen Community Centre as opposed to the casual pub, the Wednesday night "Bright Hour" as opposed to the Working Men's Club, the organised Scouts as opposed to the (very) informal Knoll Youth Club, Friends are more likely to be made by selection rather than to grow out of mere geographical proximity.

128   *The 5-Point Scals of Households a Detailed Account*

In a mining town it is accepted that a high proportion of the men will be miners. In Radby there is no evidence to suggest that there is any particular prestige value attached to being a mineworker – at any rate within the town. There is a grievance amongst some of the non-miners (in all grades) about the comparatively high wages of the miners, and about their coal allowances, and there is an associated philosophy, wishful thinking perhaps, that the good time for the miners "won't last for ever". But these are practical grievances, and do not reflect any dissatisfaction with the relative status of minor and non-miner.

In concluding this summary, attention should be drawn to Table 10. In the Introduction reference was made to the fact that the picture of delinquency presented by the official statistics does not give sufficient indication of the extent of undetected crime, and "anti-social" behaviour. During the course of this Research, the Enquirers were able to discover facts which enabled them to classify some of those households which had committed misdemeanors that were not officially recorded. In addition, information was obtained about such matters as irregular sex relations (e.g., within a family, incest, adultery, etc.) and matrimonial troubles other than those recorded in the official statistics. It was thought that at least 47 out of 225 households had at least one "irregularity" of such a nature. Table 10 also shows that "official" delinquency is concentrated in grades I and II - as are the "irregularity" cases just referred to. The fact that no juvenile or adult delinquents come from households in the IV and V grades must not be taken to imply that it is considered that all delinquency results from living in a household - or sub-culture - of the type of grades I, II, and to a lesser extent, III. The matter was discussed more fully in the Introduction. Although no delinquents do, in fact, occur in grades IV and V, this is thought to be to some extent fortuitous. It would be quite possible of course for a boy from the higher grade household to be a delinquent because of some psychological maladjustment (assuming that some delinquency does arise from such a condition). A boy may become a delinquent through sociological factors, other than those analysed in this Research which relate to the lower grade type of home. Or it would be possible (though unlikely) for a boy from a higher household to become so influenced by a delinquent or gang of delinquent from a lower grade that he himself commits an offence of the same order. However it is considered significant that the delinquents are almost confined to the two lower grades. Taking the Is and IIs together, 5 out of 72 house-holds have had at least one case of adult delinquency, compared with 1 out of 94 in grade III. The corresponding figures for juvenile delinquency and for the general factor of "irregularity" are 15

The 5-Point Scale of Households a Detailed Account   129

out of 72 and 37 out of 72; as compared with 5 out of 94, and 9 out of 94 respectively. These figures are supported by those in Table 13, which relate to households in which husband and wife are living apart, or where the man and woman are not legally husband and wife.

Table 1 Total number of households graded 225

Graded		
	I	25
	II	47
	III	94
	IV	43
	V	16

Table 2 Size of Household

Persons	1	2	3	4	5	6	6 plus
I	–	2	–	3	2	3	15
II	2	7	4	10	11	7	6
III	4	23	20	18	22	2	5
IV	1	5	6	23	8	–	–
V	–	3	4	5	2	1	1

Table 3 Number of Known Households with Grandparent(s) or Grandchild(ren), or both, or Married Child(ren) or <u>all three living at home</u>

I	10
II	12
III	20
IV	6
V	1

Table 4 Husband or wife with relatives living <u>within a few houses of their own</u>

I	14
II	17
III	23
IV	5
V	2

130 *The 5-Point Scals of Households a Detailed Account*

Table 5 Does the Housewife make
noticeably effective/ ineffective
effort with the house?

	Noticeably effective	*Noticeably ineffective*
I	1	11
II	2	12
III	32	2
IV	25	–
V	10	–

Table 6 Known Households with TV
and Pets or Livestock

	TV	*Pets or Livestock*
I	2	12
II	5	25
III	21	42
IV	23	13
V	7	8

Table 7 Employment of Chief Male of Household

	1	*2*	*3*	*4*	*5*	*6*	*7*	*8*
I	21	2	–	–	–	2	–	–
II	29	6	–	4	–	1	5	2
III	61	8	4	4	–	4	11	2
IV	23	6	2	2	1	2	5	2
V	1	–	3	1	4	4	3	–

Key: 1 Miner
2 Unskilled Factory or General Labourer
3 Skilled Factory or Craftsman
4 Transport
5 Clerical
6 Self–employed
7 Miscellaneous
8 No information

The 5-Point Scale of Households a Detailed Account 131

Table 8 Persons other than Husband in Household
employed full time

	1	2	3 or over
I	5	3	7
II	9	6	3
III	24	16	3
IV	10	4	–
V	3	2	–

Table 9 Women's Employment

	Chief Woman of Household Employed out of the House	Of Whom, Employed Full Time
I	2	2
II	9	7
III	17	10
IV	8	3
V	3	–

Table 10 Delinquency, etc.

Households (see Key)	1	2	3	4	5
I	4	9	2	2	17
II	1	6	4	–	20
III	1	5	–	2	9
IV	–	–	–	–	–
V	–	–	1	–	1

Key: 1 Any member before Adult Court 1943–52
2 Juvenile Court 1942–1952
3 Matrimonial Court 1948–52
4 Divorce Court
5 Any reference to: delinquency, matrimonial trouble, irregular sex relations, Court case, in addition to official cases.

132 *The 5-Point Scals of Households a Detailed Account*

Table 11 Distribution of Grades by Streets

	Dyke Street	Gladstone Road	Carnation Street	Charlotte Street	Knoll Road	Knoll Drive
I	19	–	4	–	1	1
II	27	2	4	5	4	5
III	35	27	7	7	6	12
IV	3	22	1	4	8	5
V	–	7	–	1	3	5
	84	58	16	17	22	28

Table 12 Those known either to Rent or Own <u>(or are buying)</u> their House

	Rent	Own or Buying	No information
I	24	–	1
II	38	1	7
III	60	20	14
IV	21	14	8
V	3	13	–

Table 13 Matrimonial Irregularities

	Known Households with Chief Woman living apart from Husband	Man (not her husband) living with Chief Woman
I	7	6
II	2	2
III	–	4
IV	–	–
V	1	–

Table 14 Known Households contains anyone in Permanent Bad Health, or Major mental or physical Defect

I	10
II	14
III	19
IV	3
V	1

The 5-Point Scale of Households a Detailed Account   133

Table 15 Households known in
which anyone was married
at age 20 or under

I	7
II	15
III	7
IV	4
V	3

Table 16 Education

(See Key)	1	2	3	4	5	6
I	2	–	–	5	–	11
II	1	–	2	8	–	11
III	9	5	8	18	4	4
IV	10	3	16	10	4	–
V	3	2	9	1	1	–

Key : 1 Known households with children who have had education other than elementary·
2 Children attending Evening Classes or Day Release Classes.
3 Would definitely like children to attend Grammar School or Technical School.
4 Thinks extra year at school undesirable.
5 Desirable for some and not for all.
6 Education records showing bad attendance and/or I.Q. below 80.

Table 17 Attitude to Nursery Schools

	Chief woman known to Approve of using Nursery Schools	Emphasised that this would allow Mother to work	Emphasised that this would benefit the child
I	6	2	–
II	7	6	1
III	4	7	2
IV	6	5	6
V	3	2	2

134   *The 5-Point Scals of Households a Detailed Account*

Table 18 Children's attendance at Sunday School and Youth Organisations

See Key	1	2	3	4	5	6	7
I	21	5	13	3	2	15	4
II	28	3	14	11	4	16	8
III	46	11	12	23	15	12	19
IV	31	15	2	14	8	8	15
V	11	3	2	6	4	1	6

Key: 1 Households with children aged 0–14.
2 At least one child who goes regularly to Sunday School.
3 Child(ren) who do not go regularly to Sunday School.
4 No information about children's Sunday School attendance.
5 At least one child who goes regularly to a Youth Organisation.
6 Child(ren) who do not go regularly to a Youth Organisation.
7 No information about children's Youth Organisation attendance.

Table 19 Age of chief woman of household

	18–34	35–49	50–64	65 plus	No information
I	1	3	14	6	1
II	2	10	18	12	5
III	4	12	37	28	13
IV	3	13	21	5	1
V	–	5	8	2	1

Table 20 Households sharing house with another family (i.e.. the families eat and live separately)

I	3
II	8
III	9
IV	–
V	–

Table 21 Remarriage

Known	Chief woman of household married more than once	Husband married more than once
I	2	1
II	3	1
III	4	1
IV	1	1
V	–	–

The 5-Point Scale of Households a Detailed Account 135

Table 22 Length of Residence

Years	−2	3–19	20 plus	No information
I	2	7	2	14
II	3	19	4	21
III	5	40	19	30
IV	4	26	6	7
V	2	10	4	–

Table 23 Intelligence Quotients of Children coming from 63 graded households who sat School Entrance Examination during 1949–53

I.Q.	76 & under	77–90	91–100	101–110	111 & over
I	3	3	4	1	–
II	6	9	3	2	–
III	–	7	6	4	3
IV	–	1	2	1	4
V	–	1	–	1	2

Grade I Factual Information

The following section relates to the twenty-five families who were graded as Is, i.e., placed at the bottom end of the 5-point scale. While the families in question are not necessarily ones which school attendance officers, health visitors and so on, would class as Problem Families, they are sufficiently below the average to call attention to themselves. Even those neighbors, graded as IIs, e.g., tended to mention them, at an early stage, in any casual talk with the interviewers. Pretty well every one of the twenty-five families is regarded by most of its neighbours as a household that is below the speaker's own and as one that is shiftless, to say the least of it. The families themselves do not seem to worry about their dubious reputation. They seldom attempted to make any excuse to the interviewers for such things as a baby who was extremely dirty, or a child who was being very disobedient, or a husband who was in gaol.

The Home: Physical Character

The physical appearance of the homes is squalid in the extreme· The front door of one house, for example, has lost its top and bottom

136 *The 5-Point Scals of Households a Detailed Account*

panels. A piece of unpainted plywood has been substituted for the top panel, and someone has splintered a large hole even in this. The bottom panel is replaced by two old boards propped up on the inside of the door. They have to be shifted every time the latter is opened.

Nothing is whole in these homes. Tools are few and what there are don't work. Plaster is breaking away, handles are missing, table legs uneven, window panes are out and stay so indefinitely. Furniture is of very poor quality and there is no attempt at comfort. Even in the relatively new homes of Knoll, the walls may be filthy. One such house has nothing on its walls but a few coloured prints of film stars, stuck on haphazardly. Pride in household goods is noticeably lacking, although perhaps the exception may be made of the odd one or two which have a TV set or a framed photograph of a wedding (a man comes around to the door taking orders for these and they cost up to £3 a pair).

At some of the houses meals are never set. The necessary furniture may not be available, even if the family is in the habit of sitting down together. According to one of the local Headmasters, some of the children cannot use a knife and fork. "We have them at home but we keep them for best", was the excuse of the child who was thought to be ashamed to admit that his home did not possess enough cutlery for everyone to have a meal together. This lack of a set meal time means that food stands about on the living room table all day long. And since this table is generally the only available space, food lies alongside things like the basin in which one of the girls is washing her hair and the herring that are being gutted. One house keeps all its shoes under the table at which the food is being prepared the meals are eaten, and round which the life of the six people of the house gravitates.

Another characteristic of the Is is that they do not recognise the deficiencies in their own way of life. The I home just does not seem to see that anything is wrong - e.g., a neglected child - whereas the II home would recognize that the child ought not to look like that: and the higher grades would not merely recognize the situation but try to alleviate it. Mrs. Y's thirteen-year old boy goes around in all weathers and all day long in old plimsoles. He has had bad "sweaty" feet for years apparently, and gets blisters and his feet hurt him. But Mrs. Y makes no effort to help him. she seems to accept the fact that he always has painful feet as she accepts the fact that the walls of her scullery are incredibly black and greasy. If the house does seem to

The 5-Point Scale of Households a Detailed Account   137

have got a bit out of hand, even in her eyes, she may produce a bit of an excuse but she doesn't <u>do</u> anything about it. One woman did excuse the bucket of urine that was standing in the middle of the living room. The lavatory door key wasn't handy or was lost or something. In other words, many of these women have given up the struggle of trying to present a fair face to the world. No one seems able to suggest to these women any reason that holds good, in their eyes, as to why they should make the effort necessary to keep up with the "average" homes of the street. Some homes do not even "trim up" at Christmas, i.e., put up the paper streamers with which every self-respecting Radby house and factory reckons to ornament the place. It must be a final admission of failure.

The women's own appearance at home is very slatternly. Mrs., G (45) is as untidy and dull-looking as the house. She "hasn't been out of the yard for weeks". She looks ill and it is probably true that she hasn't the energy to do more than try to cope with her own three children plus a grandchild. Her life has been hard and she was one of those who married at 17 because I had to". Mrs. I (40) with an able bodied girl lodger in the house to help her, can be found any time of the day, wearing nothing but a dirty dress. She has no underclothes on, nor her teeth in. Mrs. I is one who probably never does tidy herself up, but some of the women can, when they choose, look quite smart. They will dress up to go to the pub of course. Mrs. H, going down the street at 9 p.m. to the "Bull", in her green coat and stylish shoes, might be a tidy housewife from the best road in Radby. At 9 a.m., standing on her doorstep in her ordinary clothes and swearing at her 6-year old son, she is a positive virago. Decent neighbours throw it at the women of the I houses, at Mrs. B, e.g., that "she looked twenty-five when dressed". They regard this as a scandal and it adds to the growing disapproval of Mrs. B who is "living tally"[1] anyhow. Smartness, or indeed normal cleanliness and tidyness, is only put on for the occasion. As in the case of Mrs. G quoted above a good deal of the low physical standards of so many of these women is due in part to bad health. The obesity of some of the older women and their bad feet; the slovenly carriage of some of the older schoolgirls; and the sores and peaky faces of some of the toddlers, certainly suggest that there is a good deal of minor physical trouble amongst these I homes. Indeed 10/25 homes were known to contain at least one person who had a major physical or mental defect

---

1 Co-habiting more or less permanently.

138 *The 5-Point Scals of Households a Detailed Account*

or was in permanent bad health. It is likely to be connected with the 11/25 homes where the housewife made noticeably ineffective effort with the house.

Structure of household : Length of Residence: Related Families

Almost without exception the I households are crowded ones. This crowding is accepted by them as "normal" – it is not a condition to be ameliorated. Indeed, over-crowding is added to in the 12/25 households which keep pets. The slatternly habits of the occupants make the houses seem more full of occupants than they really are: but they do, in fact, contain more people per home than do most of the homes. Of the 25 homes, 15 have seven or more people living in them. Mrs. D, e.g., in her four-roomed house and yard of eight houses, has herself and her (second) husband, her married sister (who lives apart from her husband) and the sister's baby. Then she has her own two girls (19 and 17) by her first husband, and the two children (5 and 4) by her present husband. This D household, though not officially a shared house, thus contains two sets of people, the D's and their children: and Mrs. D's sister and her family. This is typical of the I homes where 10/25 have some variation of the above "unofficial" sharing. Added to this many of the I homes have one or more related families living nearby. This is the case with at least 14 of the 25 homes. It is a situation which tends to perpetuate itself. A daughter who marries is often encouraged to "stay on in the front". This is cheap since it saves buying furniture; it enables the girl to go on working; it saves her bothering about the difficulties of cooking and housekeeping; and it is nice not to have to leave your mother. The question of leaving home is a real trouble to some of the adolescents. They are very dependent on their mothers, and will put up with lower physical standards than they would like in order to stay near her. All told, marriage, for the I homes, is not only less of a physical break with the old way of life but is less of a new and joint enterprise altogether. Even after several years of married life, a couple may refuse the chance of a new home because one or other will not go any distance from the parents' home and the known locality.

All this means that many of the households lead a kind of tribal life among their own kind. Young Mrs. Dean's house is a case in point. She married at 18 and is now 26, She lives in a house which her husband took exactly opposite his father's home. His grandfather, too, lived in Dyke Street, and there are still at least four sets of Deans at the top of the street. Mrs. Dean is an anemic woman,

The 5-Point Scale of Households a Detailed Account   139

with little energy. She has no pride in the home, scamps through the housework, and is in and out of the neighbours' and her relatives' houses all day long: or she just sits about in her kitchen smoking, shouting at her own kids and having a bit of talk with the various children who mill in and out of her home. Two of them (aged 7 and 4) are her own, three are nieces and nephews who live opposite. Then she can go into the house of her mother-in-law, who also lives opposite, and into two households of sisters-in-law who live a few doors further down. The people who live in the houses above and below Mrs. Dean (7 people in one house and 9 in the other) also move in and out of the Dean's all day long; as do the members of the Dean family into the houses of their two neighbours.

Mrs. Ince, in contrast with the Deans, lives a life that is relatively self-centred. She was born, in a house in this street, of a family that has had a bad reputation for years. She has five children and is pregnant. Her sister, who lives just opposite, has four. Mrs. Ince herself is the woman referred to earlier who has a lodger, a girl of 20 who married an American soldier at 16, but whose husband has been away in America for some time. This girl, apparently, has never had a job and she seems just to sit about all day with Mrs. Ince, smoking and chatting, Mrs. Ince does not associate with her next door neighbours. The lodger and she think that one neighbour has "men in and out of the house" and that "the meister bumps his wife" (i.e., hits her about). According to this same neighbour, the lodger herself is supposed to be "five months gone", an idea that the lodger treats as a good joke. It shows how soft the neighbour is. Mrs. Ince is likewise at loggerheads with a woman a little higher up the street who has a mentally deficient boy. This child is "wide and crafty, shits all over, will steal, bites", in fact does all the things Mrs. Ince makes an unsuccessful attempt to keep her own children from doing. Mrs. Ince also runs down another neighbour, Mrs. V. The latter's husband is in gaol "and Mrs. V knows what he does (i.e., to get gaoled) all right". Mrs. Ince is likewise at loggerheads with the schools, "why should the children have to go all that way and cross the big road?" She thinks the Park is kept disgracefully: and she has no use for any of the various youth organisations that her children have been urged into by a series of social workers. In any case she equates youth organisations with bad behaviour, "a lot <u>have</u> to go so you don't fancy them for your own kids do you!" All told, she, and perhaps half a dozen of the I households live a relatively self-centred and hostile sort of existence that is a marked contrast with the tribal existence of people like the Deans.

140   *The 5-Point Scals of Households a Detailed Account*

Employment, Earning and Spending

All the chief wage earners are in manual work (Table 7): and 21 are miners. The two self-employed are in normally disparaged jobs like that of a very small scale wood and coal dealer. In only two cases does the chief woman of the house go out to work. The fact that more of them do not take even a part-time job (to the extent that the women of the IIs do), is said, by some of the neighbours, to be due to their general laziness and fecklessness.

Table 8 points to an interesting feature of the I households, viz., how many of them have more than one wage-earner. Nearly a third, 7/25, have three or more people besides the chief male working full-time; and another third, 8/25, have at least one other full-time earner. Only 10 households have one full-time worker. The big wage families tend to put their children "on board" early (which is thought to be generous by the mothers); but on the other hand the family allowances are relatively more satisfactory than is the case in the smaller-sized families of the IVs and Vs, Where clothing, shoes, etc., cannot always be handed down to such a long succession of younger children. All told it is thought that the weekly income of some of the I homes may well be in the £40 range. Most are much less and some may be as low as that of the following home. The husband "never goes out for a drink, as he can't afford it". His maximum wage is £6 per week, of which he retains about 30s. With this he buys his own shoes, and ties, cigarettes, and admission to football on Saturdays. His wife receives an allowance from her father, with whom they live, but says that she cannot get through the week without credit because of the high price of food. This household consists of three adults and a baby. The father of course gets through his money quickly at weekends by drinking and treating.

The spending habits of the Is are uneconomical. Cheapness is all in things like pots and pans, while money goes extravagantly on cream cakes and tinned peaches. New clothes are not put away in cupboards (they don't possess them), so the children handle them, they get dirty and shabby and are quickly thrown out. One girl of fourteen points to her (fairly new) shoes and says they will not be worth mending. They will just be put on the fire when the soles have gone. The same girl says that her family buy most of their clothes through a club. A Knoll woman was said to have had three homes (i.e., bought and returned on hire purchase) in the fifteen years she had been there. Two tradesmen also had refused to serve her.

It is not so much a struggle against the housewife's poverty, or even the home's lack of money through inefficient spending, that is the chief

The 5-Point Scale of Households a Detailed Account   141

characteristic of the I households. What stands out is their continued acceptance of the old low standards that were necessitated by the real poverty of former days. "Acceptance" is too strong a word. They seem to have no conception of anything better than the discomfort, squalid habits and inadequate housekeeping allowance of earlier days. They counter this by bursts of spending. But this has not the dash or novelty of real extravagance. It is just a rather more extensive edition of what they spend on their day-in-day-out pleasures. The spending of a little party of five adolescent girls when they went on an outing to the City was typical. They had 2s. to 3s. each, and it went on just the same kind of ices and sweets that they would have bought if they had been shopping in Dyke Street.

Education

Certain of the children are noticeably below average. This is born out by their I.Q. records (Table 23). Three of the children tested at school (of all for whom information is available) had an I.Q. of 76 or under; and only one was over the 100, average, figure. The children tend not to like school (they are bad scholars anyhow) and some parents are ready to keep them away. Maureen (12), e.g., has an official school record which reads, "badly dressed and not very clean". Asked by another child why she had not been to school all the week, Maureen said "I just didn't want to go" The 15-year old girl of another home, who (an exception in the Is) had got to a Technical School, was allowed by her mother to leave at 15, "she wanted some money to spend, didn't she?" And anyhow "they look that big" (i.e., it's hardly nice for girls who are so developed physically to be still at school). This latter argument was brought up repeatedly. Mrs. D is another who is impatient with education. Her boy, Mike, now in his last year at school, "would be much better down the pits". Mike, incidently, is the boy referred to earlier who has sweaty feet that blister.

Delinquency

The official delinquency figures for the I households is high (Table 10). Four households have had at least one member appear before the adult courts since 1948: and nine appear before a juvenile court, since 1942. Two households have had a member appearing before a Divorce, and two before a Matrimonial Court, since 1948. In addition 17 households were thought by the interviewers to have been involved in some "trouble" - matrimonial, irregular sex relations, etc. These include such

142   *The 5-Point Scals of Households a Detailed Account*

things as the woman who used to lie in bed "reading and eating chocolates till 12 o'clock, get the three children up for their dinner and put them back to bed again for the rest of the day". The result, according to the neighbours, is that one child, who is now three years old, still cannot walk. This woman even used to neglect to feed the baby. Her career as a Dyke Street wife ended when she left the home and the children, taking two week's money with her. Another kind of trouble in a I home concerns a half-daft woman who is a menace to the yard. She "can't understand why my husband won't live with me", but argues that "five minutes of my son (who, like his mother, is simple) is better than a life time with me husband", Or again, there is the family where the father has recently served 6 months for indecent assault: or there is Mrs. M who is husbandless, and the mother of three children; she says defiantly, "No man in this house" but is alleged by the street to get her pleasures elsewhere. Mrs. M's is one of the several homes where the interviewers could never make contact with the children, but, as the neighbours explained, the children would probably have been taught "you don't want to go there (to the Play Room): nor to talk to her". According to the neighbours "this is the sort of home you'd best not talk about",

How do the I families react to these "troubles"? Some of them seem to be resigned to "trouble", others not to recognise it as such, or others again just disregard it. One or two definitely worry that their children will get involved in "trouble". Mrs. D, e.g., whose husband is in gaol, has a constant preying fear that something bad is liable to happen to her children, The "bad" may be physical harm or a police court case and one is as worrying as the other. In other words "trouble" is always just round the corner for the I homes; and if they do slip into it it is no shock but only what they expected,

Personal Relationships

The relationship between the husband and wife in the I homes is seldom a "normal" and constant one. Husbands don't live at home, wives go off, another man is brought in, and so on. If it is not the chief couple who have an irregular relationship, then someone else in the home has. "My sister who don't live with her man" is there: or "this boy Dennis, he's not mine of course", though whose child he is is not explained. Relationships are extremely involved. The Vicar, e.g., called in to christen what he thought was Mrs. C's sickly baby, found out that the child was not Mrs. C's; but whose it was (of the various adults living in the house) he never did discover. A classic example of some of these households

The 5-Point Scale of Households a Detailed Account   143

is the N family, whose two children (10 and 12) were regular patrons of the Play Room. "Grandpa" was Mr., Jones, whose wife died years ago in a mental home. He now co-habits with "Grandma" who was parted from her husband years ago. Mr. Jones has two sons (27 and 26) by his wife, one of whom perhaps lives in the N house – or possibly he lives up the street, The present "Mrs." Jones (oddly enough she always refers to Mr. J as "my man", never "my husband") has an illegitimate daughter (35) who co-habits: another illegitimate daughter (33) is an epileptic. The illegitimate child of this latter woman is the Play Room boy. His father is thought to be "Grandpa". Mrs. Jones likewise has a much younger illegitimate daughter who is the other Play Room child. From time to time there are also at the home a woman of 28 and a man of 25 (the latter has been had up for a sex offence against a girl of 17). Both these adults are called Jones, but the relationship to Grandma and Grandpa has never been discovered. Six adults and two children were living in the house at the time of the Enquiry.

Some of the co-habiting is very temporary: in others it is said that the relationship has improved with the years. Mr. Jones, e.g., used to chase Grandma round the yard and give her a good hiding but he never does it now. The same with Mrs. R. Her first husband kicked her about shamefully: but nowadays she and her man come home arm in arm from the "Newcastle". Actual blows between men and women are less frequent than they were thirty years ago, and everyone agrees that Saturday night is quieter in Dyke Street than it used to be. A great deal is forgiven: or not reckoned of less account as it would be in other types of home. One man, e.g., who came on leave from the Army, suspected (rightly) that his wife had been having sexual intercourse with other men. He smashed most of the furniture, set light to it, and then turned his wife and children into the street. It was possible to condone even this behaviour for the couple were reconciled subsequently.

"Trouble" that arises from irregular sex relationship is not hidden, not even from the children. In a way this is logical since it is not regarded as anything that brings moral disgrace. Mrs. G, e.g., pointing to Sarah (an illegitimate grandchild) whom she brings up, and who is older than her own youngsters, says that she had Sarah's mother two years before her own marriage. She says this to a comparative stranger and before a girl of thirteen. Mrs. W has a sister and the sister's child living with her. The sister "got let down". In both the above cases the matter is treated as a grievance. There is no suggestion of a moral issue, nor much antipathy towards the man. It's a bit of bad luck, really, and might happen to anyone.

144 *The 5-Point Scals of Households a Detailed Account*

In the I homes the relationship between parents and children seems, in some sense, to be a closer one than that between man and woman. There is some affection, rough and ready as it is, in most of the homes, and some sacrifice, anyhow on the part of many of the mothers. A girl of 16, e.g., out at work, is always willing to give her mother 2s. on a Thursday if the latter is spent out. It is a sign of real affection. One of the roughest, most foul-tongued women said that she "always feels badly (i.e., she missed the children and worried about them) all the day when my kids are at a school outing". Another mother says "If I refuse them anything it upsets me"; and she means it. Mrs. W, who has very little to spend on her own pleasures, tries to give her children "all they want". She spent £20 on Christmas presents for three toddlers, all but a bit for a pair of shoes and a necklace for herself. "I try to let 'em have what I didn't", says a fourth, and, in the interviewer's eyes, she speaks for the majority of the mothers even in the I homes. This genuine affection docs not necessarily mean that the children are wisely treated. Parental control is noticeably weak, and so much emphasis is placed on satisfying the child's immediate wishes and so on, that the long distance welfare of the children is neglected. The matter is only touched on here as it is equally characteristic of the II families and is discussed in the section on them.

A good many of the I home don't look after the children adequately however fond they think they are of them. They don't even see adequately to their physical safety although this is the first duty which they acknowledge. Toddlers are allowed to hang on to a crowd of school children and go off to a colliery dump, twenty minutes' walk away, and no one bothers about them. Some grown-ups don't begin to worry about quite small children being away from the house until one of them fails to come in for his meal. Then it is serious. Nor do some parents ever talk to their children beyond a "Don't do that you" – or "Have your dinner then" or "Get that 6d. and go on out". The children of course retaliate by regarding the adults (but seldom their mother) chiefly as providers of <u>things</u>. The W kids (6) (4) (4) besiege their grandmother every time she has been down the street with "What have you got for us?" She produces bits of toys (1/6 worth) and complains bitterly "I always have to do this". Certain parents who are not actually unkind to their children, trade on them. They set them to do endless jobs at home; make them entirely responsible for the younger ones for hours on end; or allow them (for a few shillings) to take on unsuitable work. Ellie, e.g., is a white, delicate looking thing of twelve, but she has to be up at 6 o'clock every morning to do a paper round from 7 to 7.30 a.m. As soon as school is over, from 4.15 to 4.45

The 5-Point Scale of Households a Detailed Account 145

p.m. she does another round and then, as likely as not, her mother puts the two toddlers in her charge for the rest of the evening. It is not until a child. like Ellie gets out to work that she, or especially he, can make a stand. Then the parent rapidly begins to disclaim responsibility "I don't know where she goes at night, I'm sure" says a mother of a fifteen-year old. "I don't know and I don't care" is implied. The cane gets used still, at school and at home. one father who used the strap, to no avail, on his boy who had truanted, did so, not because he thought it bad for his boy to be a truant, but because he had a summons for the boy's non-attendance. This family has two children in the care of the Local Authority but is not sufficiently interested to know their whereabouts. Several times these parents expressed a wish that their other boys should be taken away to a home – so as to relieve the parents of the responsibility.

Some of the harsh treatment that parents meet out probably represents less ill-will than might be thought, because it is customary usage to most of the children. But certain parents, as reported by neighbours, are definitely cruel, as in the case of the child (8) whose parents got her up from bed, when they came in from the pub, and threatened to turn her out of the house. More often the parents' ill-treatment consists of continual ill-usage, but not of the kind for which they could be prosecuted. Two cases of the kind may be quoted. Mrs. Williams, who has had three court cases with a neighbour and a stand-up fight, has her sister-in-law and the latter's illegitimate child, Dickie, living with her and her two children. Dickie is the black sheep. The mother and the aunt both neglect him, nag at him perpetually, and beat him constantly. He has two weeks now, Mrs. Williams says, but her own father used to cut her back open so she thinks little of it she has come to the conclusion that Dickie's wretchedness is due to his blood "his father was a bad 'un" (and is thought to be in gaol now). So she has given up any hope of reforming the child, and is not going to bother herself any more with him. He is six. Mrs. Dean, referred to earlier, is another who, though not actually cruel, is utterly out of sympathy with her children. She is very bad tempered with her two, Norris (5) and Lucille (7). She never sees they are properly dressed, they wander the streets and are in and out of other people's houses all day long. She shouts at them, cuffs them, gives them 6d., and tells them they are bloody nuisances all in one breath. One or other child is for ever in tears, or is knocking the other one about. When Mrs. Dean was in hospital for some months, Norris turned into a reasonable, cheerful little boy, much like the other children he plays with. He was asked, the day Mrs. Dean was due back, whether he was glad his Mum would be home today.

146 *The 5-Point Scals of Households a Detailed Account*

He didn't answer, and his cousin (10) explained the silence – "She's always hitting him. He don't want her to come home".

Grade II Factual Information

The Grade II families associated with the Is in public, but felt themselves superior and ran them down in conversation with the interviewers. The bad behaviour of the I households was a frequent topic of conversation among the II homes, whose bad behaviour, nevertheless often verged on it. The demands which the children of the I homes made upon the IIs were a constant source of irritation; and their children were often regarded as a potential danger, but not to the extent of the IIs forbidding their off-spring to associate with those of the I homes. This apprehension about the I families was tempered by the fact that their family history was generally well known. People in the IIs often took sides with either the husband, wife, or children of a I home, and would say, e.g., that "Mrs. T would rule that boy of hers but her husband don't back her up". The fact that they take sides in this way suggests that they realise how near they are to being in the same position themselves. Moreover, while conscious that they were "superior" to the Is, the IIs recognised their own limitations. When visiting the University a group of mothers explained to the interviewer with some pleasure, "that bus conductress, she didn't think that you'd be one of our lot". Or again, when they had been behaving in what they felt the interviewer might think was not the correct way, they said, half seriously, "we're only Dyke Street". But they didn't bother. The Is would not have noticed the above situation: and the higher grades would have worried about it. It should be pointed out that many parallels can be drawn between the Is and the IIs. The latter, however, constitute a distinct grade since they embody the "adverse" features of the I home to a much lesser degree.

The Home ; Physical Character

As with the Is the external looks of the home are depressing, but to a rather less degree. In most cases the house is a "yard" one, and the yard may, as in the following case, have such embellishments as an ancient and large heap of potato peelings just by one of the back doors; a broken down wall between this yard and the next; an old sofa and go-cart lying on their sides waiting for next year' s Bonfire Night; and four open and broken lavatory doors at the opposite end of the yard. If the house is on the new Knoll Estate, and therefore has a garden, this

The 5-Point Scale of Households a Detailed Account 147

is uncultivated even if it has once been roughly dug over. A squalid collection of buckets, brushes, rags, wheelbarrow, etc., lie about.

Inside the home many objects are broken. There is little attempt at comfort and none at all at smartness. Few houses have a chair that is easy. Mrs. P, e.g, lets Janet (her married daughter), Janet's husband, and their two children have Mrs. P's front room as well as one of her two bedrooms. But Janet, who goes out to work, takes no care of this front room, which is about uninhabitable, piled up with old wooden boxes. It is dirty too, and, like the rest of the house, smells. Even in the comparatively new houses of the Knoll Estate there may be no attempt to make the living room "nice" with flowers and so on, far less to keep it clean.

A quarter, 12/47, of the grade II homes are inefficiently run to a noticeable degree (Table 5). While not excusing the inefficiencies of the households which arise from their lack of concern about standards, the difficulties they have to face must not be overlooked. The task of keeping these houses in a reasonably tidy manner is not easy. In the first place they are overfull of occupants, since half, 24/47, (Table 2) of these two-down-two-up-and-perhaps-an-attic houses have five or more people living in them. Moreover the rooms are small (approximately 12 feet square) and low and dark. If the housewife is naturally slow-witted, or lazy, or in poor health, or indifferent, the house can so easily slip into slovenliness. It can happen if she is out of it for just a few hours. Mrs. D's husband is a low-paid Council labourer, so, for the sake of her three children, she goes out to work from 9–12 and 2–4 p.m. The house-keeping is then liable to get on top of her. One dinner time, e.g., she came home as usual and what she calls "tidied up"; but she left the greyhound chained to the fireguard. When she came in at 4 o'clock the room was wet and reeking. The D's, as so many of the II households, like to keep a pet or to have some livestock, and if such pets complicate the housekeeping they don't bother about this any more than the D's bother about the coal which they store loose on the scullery floor where everyone has to walk over it to get to the sink. In any case Mrs. D (who is a relatively "good" mother) has given up trying to keep herself "nice". She wears rags, literally, and has dirty hair and skin. She has Just had a miscarriage, too, which has not helped her half-hearted fight to keep a relatively comfortable home.

There is no clear cut distinction about what should be used for what. Implements are used indiscriminately, e.g., the saucepan that does for any kind of cooking is the bowl in which Mrs. W washes the blood off her child's bleeding lip; or the baby's bottom is cleaned with any bit of rag or paper that happens to be within her reach. Nor is anything

148   *The 5-Point Scals of Households a Detailed Account*

planned ahead. At the above-mentioned Mrs. D's, e.g., a child is sent off post-haste, as Mrs. D gets in, to buy something to fry for Mr. D's tea. She knows this always has to be ready by 5 o'clock but her shopping, as all her housekeeping, is a last minute affair. She never has any stock of food. When "a snack to take with me" was wanted by her child for an impromptu little picnic, Mrs., D had nothing in the house but bread and some marg. - no jam, paste, cake, fruit or biscuits. Fish and chips for a meal is so popular partly because it can be got at the last minute, partly because it obviates the need of plates and cutlery, Any housekeeper has to meet an emergency on occasion; but these mothers live in a perpetual state of emergency.

In these low-level families poor health may have some connection with inefficient housekeeping. Ten out of twenty-five (I), and 14/47 (II) households have someone in the house who is regularity in bad health or has a serious mental or physical defect. Mrs. R, e.g., (35) is always ailing. She is found sitting on the sofa, her head in her hands. "It's me nerves", she explains, This is a recognised disease that covers depression and lack of energy. Her husband also has some vague malady (a couple of neighbours say it is drink) that keeps him off work periodically. Another woman, Mrs. Y (35) has actually been in hospital for "nerves". She gets "fed up with the house" and the mucky yard, "No one about, except just when they come in for their dinners". Ill-health connected with pregnancy was often mentioned, Mrs. C's sister, aged 28, has already had six "misses", i.e., miscarriages. Two women who were obviously pregnant when first seen, apparently never gave birth to the baby. Their figures came back to normal and no mention was made of the subject. To be really ill, and especially to go to Hospital, is, of course, a dramatic, status-giving situation, Whatever the explanation, ill-health was much more often mentioned in the "black" streets, where the lower grade homes were mostly found, than in the "white" ones,

Structure of household: Length of Residence; Related Families

Half (24/47) of the houses have five or more occupants (Table 2) a figure which sounds reasonable enough, until one realises the very small size of the rooms in all the houses except those on the Knoll Estate. Even there, in, e.g., Mrs. C's relatively ample home, there are Mr. C, two other men, two other women, three schoolchildren and three babies. Mrs. J, who lives in Dyke Street and has only two bedrooms, has herself (a widow), her son Ted (20), Ted's wife (21) and their baby (6 months), Then

The 5-Point Scale of Households a Detailed Account   149

there are her two elder sons (25 and 19) and her two school boys (13 and 11). She lives in a yard of four houses, and has a half-simple woman next door who is a menace to the children, "three a lot of ashes on the baby one day, in the pram". Another time this woman gave Mrs. J two black eyes. Mrs. J got her summonsed, but the woman got off with a caution. Mrs. J thinks the police useless, they don't help law-abiding citizens. A neighbour, however, says that Mrs. J deliberately aggravates the daft woman. It all shows what difficulties can arise where too many people have to live at too close quarters, even if the house itself may not be technically overcrowded. A divided house (i.e., one where the families live and eat separately) may be more harmonious than a single household one, but only 20 out of all the 225 households graded occupy a shared house, of these 8 are in the II homes (Table 20). Unofficial sharing is, however, common, A quarter, 12/47, II households (Table 3) contain at least one person outside the husband-wife-child group.

The tension that arises in such circumstances is relieved to some extent by getting away from the house. Though absolute privacy (in the sense of being entirely alone) may be unwelcomes, the people from these packed homes escape from them; and in particular from certain annoying individuals whom it is physically impossible to ignore if you are in the same house. This almost certainly helps to account for some of the men's pub-going, the adolescents' intensive cinema-going, and town walking, and the children's day and night street life.

It is not only those who actually sleep in the house or who live in the same yard who may get on each other's nerves. In a third, 17/47 of the II households the husband or wife has a related family living within a few doors, Charlotte Street, e.g., has six families of Hesters or in-laws of Hesters. Old Mrs. E in Carnation Street, has four married children living within ear-shot: and the street has six Rodneys (or Rodney-related) households. These related families tend to have similar standards. If the standard of one home should be markedly different, there is much less coming and going between the non-conforming household and the rest of the related families than is the case with the similar type of homes.

Table 22 shows that only 3 of 26 families for whom information was available, had moved into their house as recently as the last two years, Mostly the people have lived in the house (or at any rate in the street) for so long, or have had relations there for so many years, that they know each other's history and habits intimately: so it is only reasonable for them to "neighbour". In any case it would be impossible for most of the homes to stop their small children from crawling in and out of the practically contiguous, and ever-open doors of the next-door

150 *The 5-Point Scals of Households a Detailed Account*

houses, yards, and lavatories. A woman with only one child might do it, like a grade III woman, Mrs. B, who has always kept her Maureen from playing with the other children. But the Is and IIs regard her not only as a snob but as inhuman to the child,

Employment, Earning and Spending

The chief man (for all the households) is in manual work (Table 7); and 29/47 are miners. None of them is in a position of responsibility, At least seven of the chief women are in fulltime employment. The girls are in routine factory jobs. Work is in Radby itself, and the non-miners (except those who live at Knoll) try to get home to their mid-day dinner.

It was found very difficult to get information about house-hold incomes and the way in which these were built up: and what information was obtained did not lend itself to classification. Some single examples of facts relating to specific households (in various grades) are as follows :-

EARNING AND SPENDING - SOME ISOLATED EXAMPLES
(figures approximate)

<u>Children</u>
<u>Age</u> (age for girls in a bracket, thus ().)

(10)		2/6d. week plus 3d. from father.
(12)		1/6d. ” ” treat (pictures) about once a week from mother.
(10)		2/6d. ” ” odd 3d.s
11		weekly pocket money plus "bonus".
7		” ” ” ” savings money.
8		no regular pocket money. Money box.
12		weekly pocket money plus 9s. from job (gives mother part, saves part, has rest to spend).
At age	(10)	weekly pocket money 2s. (saved 1s.)
	(13–14)	” ” ” 2/6d. (” 2s.)
	(15)	” ” ” 12/6d. (” 2/6d.)
Sisters	(5) (7) (9)	no regular pocket money. "2d. each If good".
Sisters	(13)	about 4s. weekly from mother and 6s. from job.
	(16½)	earns £3. 10. 0. to £5. Has 30s. pocket money in a good week. Mother buys clothes.
(14)		no pocket money. Earns 5/- to 6/- week for doing Grandmother's work.
At age	(14)	earns 6/6d. doing a paper round plus 2/6d. tips plus 10/- "bits and pieces".
	(15)	at work. Earns ? Gets 10s. pocket money. "worse off than when at school".

The 5-Point Scale of Households a Detailed Account   151

Adolescents (age 15–21)

Age	job	Earning	Pocket money or Board
(16)	Machinist	88/-	15/- "mother buys clothes, shoes, etc.
(17)	?	?	30/- "mother buys everything".
(18)	?	100/-	40/- "mother buys clothes, etc."
(19)	Factory	112/-	"60/- pocket money this week"·
(19)	Overlocker	114/-	40/-
(18–21)	?	110/-	Pays 40/- board.
(18–21)	?	110/-	Pays 35/- board.

Adults (figures in brackets = total number in household)

Approx. Age·	Job	Pocket money or Board
25	Coal Delivery £6.	Housekeeping allowance to wife 90s. Wife also receives allowance for one adult. (4)
45	Painter £10.	Housekeeping allowance to wife and, occasionally, "£9. for yourself". (4)
35	Miner-Deputy	Housekeeping allowance. Husband pays for all clothes. (4)
40	Miner	Housekeeping allowance 120/- (plus money from two children earning. (8)
50	Miner	Housekeeping allowance 75/- (plus board from two children earning). (5)
50	Miner's widow	Pension 53/6d. (plus board from two children earning). (5)
50	Miner's wife separated from Husband Husband	Allowance 80/-. (2)
35	Milkman 112/-	Housekeeping allowance 100/-. (4)
?	Colliery Electrician	Housekeeping allowance to wife. Also buys things for house and will buy her a dress.
35	Miner - Face worker	Pays board to mother. This has not Increased since he was 18. (3)
24	?	Pays whole wage to mother. Is allowed money for clothes.
?	Miner ?	Paid whole wage to mother till week he married. Used to get £1. week pocket money plus more when courting "because 'his girl's' mother pawned everything· . Mother bought his wedding suit.

152   *The 5-Point Scals of Households a Detailed Account*

One Family

Approx. date		
1910	Mrs. X's father = Miner	Housekeeping allowance 24/-, 2/- for self.
	" first husband (tradesman)	Housekeeping allowance 60/- "for years".
1944	" second husband (miner)	Housekeeping allowance (? amount).
	" married children	Paid whole of wage to mother till married.
1954	" unmarried daughters Ages (16)(17) Factory.	Pay whole of wage to mother. Receive pocket money.

There was no evidence of acute poverty, or of low housekeeping standards caused chiefly by poverty. Non-mining homes, or homes with a miner on part-time work through an accident, might be poor compared to the average household, There was, e.g. the miner on a disability pension for the last five years whose total income, apart from his two children's allowances, was £6 odd, old age pensioners, living alone, were "the poor"; and their plight was recognised by the attention they got from their neighbors at the Coronation Festivities, at pub outings, etc.

Certain mothers who go out to work say they do this because of the financial difficulty; others say (of them) that it is for pin money for cigarettes, the pub, etc. The precarious nature of their husband's contribution is alleviated by having some money of their own to spend, and it may be to ease this situation that they go to work, as much as the fact that what their man allows them for housekeeping is too low. The wife's basic housekeeping expenses do not vary greatly; while her allowance may depend on his betting luck, or his readiness to put in a full week's work, or just his whim that Friday. It is probably true to say that when wages rise above £7–8, most of the men in these families keep at least as much for themselves as they give to the housewives for food, rent and clothing. This generalisation is supported by two facts: (a) although wages are adequate, a comparatively small amount is spent on food, clothing and the house, (b) many men spend considerable amounts of money on cigarettes, pools and drinks during the course of a week. The frequency and extent of the men's drinking habits were referred to in Section II. While the miners, by reason of their comparatively high wages, are able to keep the pace up throughout the week, other workers are liable to be "broke" by Monday.

Table 8 shows that the IIs have not so large a proportion as the Is of additional wage earners: but nevertheless 9/47 have two or more

The 5-Point Scale of Households a Detailed Account   153

people working full time besides the chief earner. The adolescent children of the lower level homes are in the non-apprentice type of job where even first wages are good. For some years they are expected to "tip in", i.e., to give all their wages to mother. This is a regular sum (in the 25s.–35s. range) at least until the youngster is about eighteen, and often much later. The big income homes are said to be those where the youngsters are allowed to go on to board early, i.e., at eighteen or so.

Education

In the entrance examination to secondary schools, the children of the IIs show up badly. The I.Q. figures (Table 23) suggest that, like the Is, they even started life with a handicap, since 6 out of 47 have an I.Q. below 76: and only 2 are above the 100, average, mark. Their schooling itself (Table 16) reflects their low abilities. Only one of the 47 is believed to have been to a more advanced type of school than a secondary modern one: and none, at the time of the survey, were attending evening classes or day release classes. Equal opportunity in education may have been achieved in theory; but the children in the low-level homes can't or don't benefit from the new facilities as much as do those in the better working class homes. Perhaps "don't" is the more accurate word to use in this case, since their parents have little ambition for them to go to grammar or technical schools, and would strongly prefer the leaving age not to have been raised to 15. The latter point was discussed with at least 17 families of various grades. Fifteen of them had similar views to those of a Mrs. Bird who has watched four children pass through school and has strong views on what she wants for her youngest child, a boy of five. What she would like is for him to have started at four, and to leave at fourteen. "They are a problem at four, don't know what to do with their selves. And that last year they don't do a deal". Mrs. G is another who says that "they can't learn them anything that year. They are that big they can't even get into the desks. The Grammar Schools perhaps have bigger desks. They don't have enough to do. Bert (14) comes home miserable. The teachers don't seem to bother much, do they? Lads come out of school smoking". She sympathizes with her three children's dislike of school and sends them off with "Now go along me ducks and get the shift over". Mrs. Young, who has seen three of her youngsters pass through school (and whose Clarice got a scholarship to the Art School in O. but did not take it up) argues with a neighbour on the following lines. Children are little devils at four. They would be better at school. The extra year would be all right if they did something to benefit their job. It is expensive too. And

154   *The 5-Point Scals of Households a Detailed Account*

the girls are that big looking to be at school that it is really disgusting. The above views are typical of the expressed attitudes of the lower grade families. In general they do not recognise that education is of much value, whereas to earn is of prime importance. Such an outlook may well be a rationalisation of the parents' own lack of education.

Leisure

It was found difficult to get accurate information on the membership of organisations, and any figures obtained were not felt to be sufficiently accurate to quote. Few of the women belong to any kind of formal group, except that one or two attend the Salvation Army, and the social and religious meetings of the Free Churches. Any societies that the men mentioned, a Produce Association, e.g., or a Darts Team, were connected with a pub or a Working Men's Club. Shift work cuts across regular use of any leisure-time organisation by miners or their wives and mothers; but other things also hinder it. They have very limited interests and few skills apart from that of their job. They were likely to have been bad scholars at school, and they still rank too low socially, among Radby people, to take on any position of importance in a club. The one responsibility they can (but do not always) accept is the domestic one - to their wife and children or, in some cases, to their mother. Beyond that they do not aspire to go. Old Mr. W, e.g., a widower, is very conscious of his own old-fashioned clothes and ways compared with the smartness of those who live in the Council houses. In Knoll, the adults of the socially low-grade families do not, as a whole go to the Community Centre. The children from the lower grade Knoll homes are less self-conscious about their deficiencies, and a "couldn't care less" attitude is not so developed as it is in the case of older people, so that many do attend the local Youth Club. The fact that the low-level home youngsters use the Centre's youth club doubtless accounts for the continual hooliganism for which the club is ill-famed. The Knoll youngsters, too, have no other roof on the Estate under which they can congregate. Whatever the reason, they certainly differ from the youngsters of the I and II grades in the older Radby areas, among whom non-membership of youth organisations is typical. Table 18 shows that three only of the families with children of 0–14 and ranked as IIs are known to have at least one child who goes regularly to Sunday School; the opposite holds for 14 families (no information on 11 households). Youth Organisation membership is as follows – four households have a child attending regularly as opposed to 16 who have no child attenders (no information on 8 households). The figures

The 5-Point Scale of Households a Detailed Account   155

are less revealing than the general attitude. Mothers explain that "it's up to them", Johnnie (6), Leena (8) and Sam (4), whether they go to Sunday School or not. Mostly they don't. The children spend their non-school hours in small, fluctuating, sets of friends. These sets seen to be formed on the basis of living near each other, rather than of definite selection. The chief meeting place is the bit of street opposite one's own home. The grown-ups use the pubs nearest their home, and to go to the "Bull" or to the "Newcastle" is about the only bit of pleasure that some of the women ever seem to look forward to. Inside their home, they have the wireless on of course, and some have the TV (which may come and go if the payments fail). As with the Is, relatively few, only 5/47 homes, have a television set. Reading, except for just one or two women who like love–tales, is confined to the local papers, the Sunday papers, and comics. All the family, in one house, has a read of the comics before going to bed. Not many adults or children have hobbies. Adults, when they are inside the house, lie about a lot, go to sleep on the sofa, or, in the case of the woman, go round to the neighbours for half an hour's gossip. People ranked as III look down their noses at this – "You must be calling (becalling) someone if you sit talking together for as long as half an hour".

Attitude to Delinquency

What is the official record of delinquency among the II families? Six out of 47 households had a juvenile who was known to have been convicted before a court in the 1942–52 period. Only one home had someone who had been convicted before an adult court: four who had someone who came before a Matrimonial Court. More significant than this, however, was the large proportion who, in addition to the above, and to the best of the interviewers' belief, was involved in such things as delinquency, matrimonial trouble, irregular sex relations or excessive drinking. Nearly half of the families, 20 out of 47, had one or more members who was involved in some such "troubles" as these. General talk, even with a comparative stranger, gave the impression that trouble, in the sense used above, was a common feature of their lives. But "trouble" may well be a nuisance to them rather than a disgrace. A theft may be a worry because it involves going to court rather than because it is "wrong". Mrs. W, e.g., is always frightened that Tom will pick up with the bad ways of the Hetherington boys opposite, one of whom is now in an approved school. It is never one's own child who is to blame, of course, "He may be a bit weak, but he is good-hearted" – or it's a case of "the Masons, they shielded their George; we didn't

156   *The 5-Point Scals of Households a Detailed Account*

with our Jim". At the same time one has not the confidence noticeable in the higher grade homes, that one's own children will stand up to temptation.

Personal Relationships

Husband : Wife

Marriage tends to take place at an earlier age (under 20) than is the case in the average artisan household. Of 36/225 families who were believed to have some member who had married at 20 or under, 15 were in the II homes. A wedding that occasioned no surprise or any hint of adverse comment was that of a girl who married when she was just 18. She had been courting since she was 14, and had had no other boy. One of her sisters had married at the same age; and her brother's wife was also 18. The only criticism of early marriage is that it stops a girl from having a good time for as long as she might. Early marriage is so normal as to be regarded as inevitable, and is desired for such various reasons as that of sex, status, security and financial gain. It is romantic, of course, at the moment, but that it is likely to be a source of long-distance happiness, is hardly hinted at.

Courting, brief or otherwise, is the proper leisure-time occupation of adolescents. If the youngster chooses to start half-serious courting before the normal age of about 16, that is his own concern. The relationship becomes official when "she" is asked to "his" home. Courting takes place almost entirely outside the homes. The back row of the pictures is one of the proper spots. The behaviour there – "deep" kissing, etc. – is quite open and it is taken as a matter of course that those seats are to be used for love making rather than for seeing the film. The girl, of one couple of 16–year olds, hardly looked up at the screen during the whole programme.

No evidence was forthcoming as to how far pregnancy speeds up the date of marriage; or is regarded as something that demands marriage. As with the Is, the subject is certainly not kept dark, anyhow among women who have been married for some years. As with the Is, too, an illegitimate child, or the prospect of one, is treated as a grievance, a bit of bad luck. That it is not recognised as a moral issue was suggested by the fact that no attempt was made to keep the topic from the interviewers, whereas an apology was sometimes made for such a thing as swearing.

There does not seem to be much knowledge, or anyhow effective use, of contraceptives among the married women. This statement is

The 5-Point Scale of Households a Detailed Account   157

made from the fact that these families are large, are not Catholics, and are not the kind who (as in certain of the IVs and Vs) are classed as couples who "go in for children", i.e., deliberately choose to have several. Chance bits of talk also suggested that contraception is not widely practised. Mrs. C's sister "is only 25 and she's had six pregnancies in four years". Mrs. S, with five youngsters, "didn't really want this one that's coming". Mrs. T, asked if she intended to have more children replied, "You never know, do you".

The wife appears to consider it proper to give her husband intercourse when he wishes. It may be a matter of custom, or duty, or a method of keeping him. Adolescent girls in other parts of England, but who come from homes similar to the Is and IIs, sometimes point out that, to hold your boy, it is good policy to let him do more or less what he likes with you. The general tone of the Radby women's talk does not suggest that sexual intercourse is a particular pleasure to them. There were a few who spoke lovingly and stressed their <u>general</u> content – "My husband is ever so good to me" – which may well cover physical satisfaction as well as generosity in money matters. But this attitude was much less common than in the IVs and Vs; while the following one was not untypical. The woman, Mrs. J, was about forty, had been in service as a girl, had a shockingly dirty sister-in-law next door, and three troublesome children aged five to fourteen, She had a sister who was reputed to have had a baby in the back kitchen, At the first meeting with the interviewer, Mrs. J made no direct reference to her husband, but said that men have a better life than women. The call up takes them all over. Men just work and they think they have done all they should. The woman works too, at home, don't she? The home wears you down. You worry so. You keep on thinking. You never see any new faces, even at the local, you don't. The children get you down. Husbands used to share in looking after the kids. Now they leave it all to you. Families are getting bigger too.

The stories that the Play Room children wrote (Appendix A) made many references to rows between husband and wife, husband leaving the wife. etc. It is clear that domestic troubles were not, indeed how could they be, hidden from the children. These adult rows and the threats were an obvious anxiety to them.

When the husband has been drinking all evening he is often inebriated, and his conviviality in the public house is transferred, on arriving home, to a wife if, e.g., she starts to complain about her lack of money. If the house is overcrowded, and the children not in bed, the general atmosphere is such as to raise a man's temper. He works hard all the week, and hands over some of his earnings to a wife for whom he no

158   *The 5-Point Scals of Households a Detailed Account*

longer has any particular affection for the upkeep of the children he never really wanted. And yet his wife expects more from him than he is prepared to give. It has been stated that the standards of housekeeping are often low. This reflects a "couldn't care less" attitude by the wife. But she is in a difficult position. She has got to tolerate a lot in order to prevent her husband from reducing her housekeeping allowance, or from being unfaithful. On the other hand, some of the wives do not trouble to make themselves even reasonably attractive-looking for their husbands.

They don't begin to approximate to the glamour girls of the men's weekly papers. It may be noted, too, that most of the men get so dirty at work that they are accustomed to have a good clean-up when they get home (or at pit baths). Their wives tend to confine their personal smartening up to the occasions when they go out to the pub. The problem of unfaithfulness is not peculiar to the women of course. In wartime, and with the call-up, many opportunities occur when the husband is away from home. Though the IIs probably don't come to physical blows to the extent that the Is do, the relationship can be very inharmonious. Mr. and Mrs. Vine (45) are probably typical of the couple who don't actually come to blows but live in constant warfare. Their rowing wakes up the Hanson's next door at 2 a.m. The Vines, interviewer in the room or not, bawl at each other the whole time. "He always wants the wireless on – I don't"; "You heard me, didn't yer?" It never stops. These rows, even blows, may not be taken too badly. But for one of the partners actually to leave for good is a dreadful threat and is more typical of the Is than the IIs. Young Mrs. Lily Dean, e.g., was bitterly condemned by the street for the following action. She had helped the woman next door (of a I home) to leave her husband and her three children, and had had the neighbour's suitcase packed in the Dean home, all ready, for several weeks.

Adults : Children

If the expected baby is the incidental result of an experience disliked by the mother, maternal love may well be damped down at the prospect of yet another child to be fed and washed and worried over, and another body to fill up the beds and the living space that is already crowded. It is not only the mother who has to carry the new bit of trouble. Her husband will have the nuisance of housekeeping and will have the other kids on his hands when she goes to hospital: he will have to make journeys to go and see her; and the baby itself will turn into a restless, poking, dirty, accidentprone toddler who will make yet another fourteen-year-long

The 5-Point Scale of Households a Detailed Account   159

series of calls on the man's purse and patience. Some fathers don't hesitate to show their feelings. The above-mentioned Mr. Vine bites out at his six-year old son "What did we have you for?" Which is not to suggest that the children, generally, are unloved when they do come. Most of the mothers met had genuine if often misguided affection for their family. An aspect of the low-level homes which should not be forgotten, the close emotional relationship even mother and children, does not necessarily cease as the children grow up. Some of the eighteen-year old girls are so closely tied to their mother that they will not leave her to live away when they marry, a fact which probably helps to account for the number of those who "live in" with their parents. It is noticeably the others, not the fathers, nor even the parents as such, who control the children. "I would cheek me Dad all right – not my Mum, not much I wouldn't" I says a fourteen-year old girl.

All but an odd one or two mothers are concerned for the physical safety of their children. It is their major worry. How the children occupy themselves is a different matter. Mrs. B says that she does not know what her children (7 and 5) do. "They come in from school, say what they want for their tea, and go off out". Mrs. T's girl (8), and a friend of the same age, go regularly to the last house of the pictures at the other end of Radby. Some are sent to the first house and told not to come home till the end of the second so as to give the parents a good night at the pub. Children often go to sleep in the pictures: Eva (6) regularly goes sound asleep in the "Olympia", so her sister says.

There is a strong feeling that the children should be allowed to do what they want, provided they don't get into physical danger. Mrs. B will sit and watch her children break up a piece of furniture rather than spoil their fun. A child will scalp a new doll, and no one protests. As distinct from the Is, some of the mothers do question the wisdom of always trying to do what the children themselves want. "I cannot be mean with them", says Mrs. D, but adds, doubtfully, that "It's not always best for them perhaps". She is thinking of her Sallie (7) who only wastes the 3d's and 6d's she is continually worming out of Mrs. D, who is very badly off.

The ineffectiveness of some of the grade II mothers, as far as controlling the children go, is nevertheless, often a kindly one. Mrs. C, e.g., is at the beck and call of her three children but she takes care to be at home when they come home from school, "It's nice for them". Another ineffective mother is Mrs. A. She isn't even able to go out to work because of the line her ten-year old takes, "I'm not stopping at school for my dinner". It is the same with Mrs. E, where this kind of conversation takes place. Ned (13) rushes in from school with "I

160　*The 5-Point Scals of Households a Detailed Account*

want 6d., Ma". "What for?" "The Baths". "No you don't then – you got a cold". Ned sulks, and tries again. Mrs. E reinforces her case with "Your father said you weren't to". The boy sniffs, puts on an aggrieved air, and is plainly going to get his 6d. the minute the interviewer has been got rid of.

Some of the children are not only disobedient, but cheeky with it. "Shut yer big gob", says a child of five to a shop-keeper who sends him packing for drawing on the window. Since, to their child's mind, any distasteful order is open to argument, there is constant nagging on both sides. This possibly helps to account for the rowing that is so common a feature of adult life in the lower grades. The one or two mothers who will not have their children question an order, are regarded as "very hard". These same mothers, if they bother a good deal about what the children are up to, are regarded as "harassers", and are foolish in most eyes. Under such upbringing, to make the children obey essential orders, or to get a bit of peace, it is necessary to resort to a species of "Childgeld". Mrs. A, e.g., tries to tempt Gladys with 2s. on a Friday if she will wash the pots, but Gladys won't take it, She probably gets the money whether the pots are washed or not. Inconsistent treatment on the part of the grown–ups of course means that the children never know how far they dare go. It all depends on what kind of favour they are in at the moment,

There is another side to their upbringing. "Easy" as this may appear to be, a great many of them patently do not get the shielding that their years demand. The only good night tenderness which one child is accustomed to, according to a neighbour, is to be sworn at - "get up them bloody alps". These children see and hear all that goes on in the grown-up world. Peter, who is seven and bright, listens to adults discussing which couples in the street, all of whom are known to him, are "living tally". How much the quarrels, the meannesses, and the cruelties of the grown-up world do frighten some of the children is suggested by their little Play Room writings. In spite of this, there is often, as has been said, real affection between parents and children. More pertinent, perhaps, is that the children are half expected to be a worry rather than a source of happiness.

Grade III Factual Information

The following description of the 94 households that were ranked as IIIs is based on four families only, three in Dyke, and one in Carnation Street. They are all well known to the interviewer and have been in regular contact with her for about twelve months. The children from two

The 5-Point Scale of Households a Detailed Account 161

of these families came to the Play Room, and an adolescent girl from another of the families was at the School Camp referred to in Section III A. All four are families to which the interviewer goes for factual information (e.g., what type of job certain men in their street do): or to discuss a particular topic (e.g., why the boys they know do not join a specific youth organisation). All four homes contain children, and three of them have a child aged 12, 13, 14 or 15. Living in the type of street they do, therefore, juvenile delinquency (though they themselves have no idea that this is the subject of the Enquiry) is not just an academic issue. It is very much of a live one, and one that relates to a current generation of children in their own and neighboring homes. Another point that caused the interviewer to select these particular families was that three of them had several families of relations living nearby. Also these particular households are on good terms with their street as a whole. Moreover the interviewer had seen various members of these particular families in a variety of circumstances and on many occasions. What they had said on one occasion (e.g., about the extra year at school) could be checked on a second. On the above grounds, therefore, it was decided to give a rounded picture of these four households rather than, as in the case of the analysis of the I and II, and IV and V grades, to rely on isolated examples of behaviour and attitudes drawn from a number of families.

The basic facts about the above four households are as follows :-

List A. The Household : Size and Structure[1]

The Freemans	Mr. (40); Mrs. (38); son (17) miner; nephew (15); daughter (15) machinist; d. (13); s. (12). Terrace house. Rent 7/–· "2 up and attic, 2 down". Ash yard of four houses.
The Marks	Mr. (48); Mrs. (48); d. (15) tailoring. Terrace house. Rent 8/11 plus 1/6 for new grate. Paved yard of six houses.
The Bonningtons	Mr. Daneham (56); Mrs. Bonnington (45) black-smith's striker, widow; d. (18) factory;[x] d. (15) factory;[x] s. (13);[x] s. (9);[xx] s. (6);[xx] x = Mrs. B's children by first husband. xx = Mrs. B's children by Mr. Daneham.
The Waters	Mr. W. (34); Mrs. W (28); s (7); d. (4) (delicate and retarded); Mrs. W sen. (65)· Terrace house, rent 7/9· "2 up and attic, 2 down".

---

1 In the interest of anonymity the occupation of the chief male has been omitted. All are manual workers.

162   *The 5-Point Scals of Households a Detailed Account*

The Home. Physical Character

"Mrs. Waters. A tidy looking house. Front room used.

Mrs. W tidily dressed". "Freemans. Tidy house, medium poor furniture". "The Bonnington's. A tidy superior household, Mrs. B always tidy looking, so are the children. Look well fed". "Mrs. Marks. A paved, tidy yard. Mr. Marks likes his wife to stay at home and see to the house". The above notes were among those that the interviewer happened to write down after her first encounter with each of the four "selected" families.

They are typical of the physical character of these households. As the constant use of the word "tidy" in the notes suggests, each aspires to a reasonably "nice" house. The elder Bonnington girl, e.g., was genuinely shocked at something she noticed about Buckingham Palace when she went to London on the works' trip. The front curtains at the Palace did not match: and it was a sign of pretty sluttish housekeeping in her opinion. It should be stressed that these families have coped relatively effectively with an environment that is no different from that of the squalidly kept homes. Mrs. Waters, e.g., has no larder, and has to manage with her sink in the front room. The back room has to be used as a bedroom for old Mrs. W and Peter (7) since the back bedroom and attic are unusable. What she most minds, however, is that to get to the lavatory they have to go down nine steps from the living room, through a cellar, and up into the yard. She mentions, incidentally, that this lavatory has been out of order for nine weeks. All four of the housewives are in fairly good health, and Mrs. Bonnington in particular, is a very hard worker. She was left a widow with three children and had to keep the four of them on 30s. a week. To eke this out she let her front room to a lodger. He is now the accepted head of the household, and the father of the two youngest boys. She works full time except one day a week when she has a day off and is up at 5 a.m. to do the washing. Mrs. Freeman is another hard worker. Her first husband treated her so badly that she just looked after the house and the children and had no pleasures whatever. He went to the pub, of course, and he had another woman. A week before Pat was born he kicked Mrs. Freeman down the stairs. Finally she left him, parked her three children with her mother and went out to work (at £3.5.0 per week). She did so for several years – until she had saved up £84 for a divorce. She married again, happily, five years ago. But these four women are more than hard workers, they are efficient ones, and so have time and heart to add a few frills to the house, like a pretty electric light bracket. Mrs. Bonnington, for all her packed room, sees

The 5-Point Scale of Households a Detailed Account 163

that the children look after their clothes and toys. Michael's miniature TV set works; and Paul's books are carefully handled. If a visitor goes to Mrs. Bonnington's she gets a good tea, cleanly served, the children, though they eat roughly are obviously accustomed to sit down to their meals. Shoes are properly cleaned. Mr. Daneham gets his done by the 17–year old girl. Attention is paid to birthdays and a great thing is made of Christmas Eve. Mrs. B is not swamped by the preparations but looks forward to them.

Employment, Earning and Spending

The employment of the head of the household, and of the adolescents of the four families is much like that of their neighbours, in the Grade III families as a whole, where 61 out of 94 of the chief earners is a miner. The men are not in any position of responsibility, and three of the four adolescent girls are in routine factory jobs. The women have a thoughtout policy about going out to work. Mrs., Marks could take on an outside job easily, but she prefers to make £2 a week at home by looking after two children of neighbours. She does this most conscientiously. Mrs. Bonnington is such a good manager (she really rules her children although she does it in a kindly way), so that they are probably not really neglected although she is at work all day. Part of the secret of the efficiency of these mothers is that they spend sensibly. The Bonnington boys get really good presents – a ventriloquist doll and a conjuring set that keep Michael happy for hours. And for Bob, who will be sitting the scholarship exam. next year, a book chosen to help him with his reading. The Bonnington's regard an annual holiday as a good investment. The Waters spend on holidays too, and so do the Marks, though in the latter case the parents were prepared to save about £40 to send their one girl on a school trip to Germany. They think about their children's spending habits, too. Mrs. Marks says that most children today get too much money. It teaches them to look down on those whose parents cannot afford to give them much; and "if they are kept a bit strict they learn the value of money". She has seen what happens in the case of her friend, Mrs. Kelly, a widow, who only gets her husband's pension, £2.13.6 and her two older boys' board money. Her two schoolboy sons get despised and are very discontented, because she just can't let them have the half-crowns and so on that others give the kids to get shut of them. It's not fair on Mrs. K is it? At twelve Mary Marks got regular, but not too much, pocket money - just 2/6. Young Johnnie Waters (7) gets only a small sum ("6d. off his Dad, 6d. off his Mum") and he is taught to save a bit of that. He took £1 from his

164   *The 5-Point Scals of Households a Detailed Account*

money box and gave it to his mother for the holidays. His father didn't give it back to him, on principle.

Education

The above notes rather suggest that the four families are a consciously "superior" set of households. This is far from the case, They have, e.g., no intellectual pretensions. Mary Marks, who has just left school, apparently never reads anything whatever, while the Bonnington's is the only one of the homes that has any books in evidence, and those belong to the children. Nor are the parents particularly keen on their children getting to a Grammar School. The Freemans certainly would not bother about it. Mrs. Bonnington was disappointed that one of her girls who passed the scholarship could not take it up, but the family really needed her wage. The Waters would quite like young Johnnie to go to a Grammar School, "if he's good enough". They really are more interested in whether they can get him into the new Secondary Modern School instead of the old Church one where "there's too much religion and not enough good teaching". In other words, educational ambitions are strictly within the familiar range and similar to those which are characteristic of the IIIs as a whole. As Table 16 shows, only 9 out of 94 III households had a child who had had other than elementary education: and only 8 were known to have definite ambitions about getting their children to a Grammar or Technical School.

Leisure

The attitude of these four families to other media which might help on the children is more apparent in what they do and say about youth organisations than in their views on formal education. The same is true of their attitude to the local Churches (with which most of the Radby youth groups are connected). All four families have some effective link with a church, though only one set of adults (the Waters) are regular Churchgoers. Mrs. Marks is typical of many of the all homes, was brought up Church but doesn't go now. But she always goes (to Peak Street Chapel) for the Anniversary and for special occasions, and she saw that Mary went to Sunday School regularly, and is glad that Mary is now a Sunday School teacher. The Freemans are an old Salvation Army family - back to a great-grandmother who must have been a contemporary of William Booth. The Freeman adolescents, as well as those of school age, frequent the Salvation Army organisations weekday and Sunday. Mrs. Freeman often thinks about religion

The 5-Point Scale of Households a Detailed Account   165

and the non-material world. Her mother used to read the tea cups and Mrs. Freeman herself quotes instances of second sight in her own life that sound convincing, Religion in some form or other means a lot to her, as is not infrequent with old "Army" families. She sums up her outlook when she says that, for all her Army background, she "does not mind the pub if you still remember God". The Bonnington's too are staunch Sunday School and Youth Club supporters. Margaret (15), according to her mother, "lives for" the Peak Street Chapel Youth Club. Mrs. Bonnington used to go herself but some there "wouldn't acknowledge me when in me muck", so she gave it up, but she sees that the two younger boys go faithfully to Sunday School. She is careful to go herself to their prize-giving. The prayers, the choruses, and so on evidently mean a good deal to her, This is not just pride in Michael and Bob, though they do win a gratifyingly expensive armful of prizes. Mr. and Mrs. Waters, are actual Chapel members, They take Communion, teach the little girl (4) to say the Lord's Prayer, and see that both the children go to Sunday School. At the moment Mr. and Mrs. Waters are much taken up with a new youth club the chapel has started, a club that any child can join. The Waters think this a good idea because with most of the clubs, Scouts, etc., you have to go to the church as well as the society and this stops lots from joining. They say that children don't go to church and Sunday School as they did because "parents find it too much trouble to get them ready on Sunday after a bellyful of ale on Saturday night". Their neighbour, Mrs. Robson, wants the Waters to take her two along to Sunday School, but, says Mrs.Waters, "why should we be bothered with taking other folks' children?", a sentiment that suggests certain limitations in the Waters' own church-going,

It so happens that each of these four households is linked with a church, but they should not be taken as representative of the III households in this respect. No reliable figures were obtained on the Church affiliations among the adults of the III households as a whole, but it was certainly less extensive than was the case with these four homes. The youth organisation membership (Table 18) was certainly lower for the IIIs as a whole.

Apart from church-linked activities, the leisure of these four families seems to be spent much as is that of their neighbours. The Waters are unusual in that they are Labour Party members. The men go to the pub, and none of the wives expressed any anti-pub views. Mrs. Freeman regards it as a step towards a reasonably pleasurable life that Mr. Freeman goes with her to the Bull. Indeed, if she is not up there by a certain time, he will come and fetch her. This is indeed affection.

166 The 5-Point Scals of Households a Detailed Account

Mr. Freeman tends to stay off work, "beer–ill", after a Bank Holiday, which Mrs. Freeman regards as quite normal. Mrs. Marks has stricter views and supports her particular friend, Mrs. J on the subject of drink. They agree that Sunday afternoon boozing (as distinct from that of Saturday and Sunday nights) is now common. On the other hand, perhaps because the beer is less strong, the regular Saturday night bloody fights they used to see in the street, have ceased. More women go to the pub nowadays, with their husbands, but they go partly "to keep him off bad women – a lot of them about". The children's and adolescents' leisure seems to be similar to, and is intermingled with, that of any of nearby children, except that it is rather more subject to control from their parents in regard to cost, and to calling-in time off the street, The matter is discussed in the section below on adult : children relationships.

Attitude to Delinquency

Officially the four families are delinquent free (i.e., no one connected with them appears in the adult and juvenile delinquency figures for 1942–52 quoted on page 72). Except for the Marks, however, all the families in question are known to have been concerned in some type of "irregularity" (if such it may be called). Mrs. Freeman's own unhappy experiences with her first husband have already been referred to. He is a shocking payer and has been in gaol for non-payment of her allowance. Indeed, she still has to go to the local court at times to get her money. Her sister has had an equally unfortunate marriage. She "had to lower myself" and say she had committed adultery to get her divorce though "her husband he got off with it by saying 'she' (the other woman) was his housekeeper"· All this was reported to the interviewer before Sallie (14) and two younger children (6) and (4). Mrs. Bonnington's relations with her man are probably "irregular" though she is so respected herself that the interviewer heard no disparaging reference to this household in her twelve months' connection with Dyke Street. On the other hand, Mrs. Bonnington's brother in Gladstone Road on more than one occasion was a little reluctant to acknowledge that Mrs. Bonnington was his sister, a typical example of the different outlook of the two streets towards the situation in question. With the Bonnington's, too, the interviewer heard some vague story that Hugh Bonnington (13) had had a summons or a warning from the police for stealing or damaging a telephone post. Unfortunately the interviewer could find no way of checking this without direct interrogation of the family which she was anxious to avoid.

The 5-Point Scale of Households a Detailed Account   167

All four of the families move in circles, and intimate circles, in which delinquency, official or otherwise, is relatively common. Mrs. Marks' particular friend, Mrs. J, is the woman who comes to blows with her neighbour and rather boasts of it. One of her boys (13), seen dragging a large piece of sawn wood he had got from the pit heap, was asked deliberately, "Isn't that stealing". His reply was "Coo, it's only a £5 fine". This was boy's swank, of course, (What's £5 to me?") but it certainly suggested that the theft, as such, was no issue with him – nothing to worry about there. The Waters are surrounded by delinquent households. The people who live next door have a long and involved record of court cases - indecent assault, illegitimacy, etc., and their children run in and out of the Waters', borrowing milk, asking to be looked after at 11 p.m. because "me mums at the Newcastle", etc., etc. During the last six years a twelve-year old boy at the next house has been concerned in a breaking and entering case, and a fourteen-year old girl opposite in a shop-lifting affair.

What views do the four families hold on all this? Mrs. Marks (as always, in conjunction with her friend Mrs. J) thinks that as a child she herself was brought up too strictly. She likes her children to have an easier time. Her own one-child family is perhaps an outcome of this aim. Today's children "like its Jim Francis opposite", are not a bit scared of the police. Jim Francis, the boy who lives opposite, is now in an Approved School. Mrs. Freeman mixes freely with a very undisciplined family next door where the housewife's particular friend is alleged to be the accomplice of a husband who is now in gaol. But Mrs. Freeman does draw the line at a really notorious family (the Davis's) when it comes to a thing like this. The Davis boy hit Gloria Freeman with a rope that had a knot in it, fixed to a stick. Gloria hit back and Mrs. Davis had the nerve to come down to Mrs. Freeman and complain. The two women Waters (mother–in–law and daughter) had thought–out views on children who "get into trouble". They warned the interviewer to keep a watchful eye on the Play Room plasticine, "Look after them things. Some will take 'em off". They went on to say that if a child brings in something that is not his you should make him take it back. If you take it, he is not "embarrassed". Lots don't make their children do this and the kids take it for granted that it's O.K and it just becomes the usual thing. There's "that Duncan lad (13) who stole lots of pencils and things off Woolworth's and his parents gave them away as presents to other children. I told our Peter (8) not to take any and not to go with those boys. If the big ones do it the little ones will copy". The younger Mrs. Waters, as distinct from her mother–in–law, is glad that children are less scared of the police

168   *The 5-Point Scals of Households a Detailed Account*

than they used to be. The police can help them really, if they get lost for example. Children are definitely more destructive than they were – the war excused this perhaps. Also they are more high-spirited, not so repressed. Mrs. H, a neighbour (55) then approached and joined in the talk about former days. "How gormless I was then", she said, and recalled that even when she was as old as 17 she was not expected to sit and talk at table with her parents. She would not have dared to. If anyone talked of babies it was "you go out and play". Today anything is talked of with the children except very bad subjects. And the children argue, too. Young Mrs. Waters would never have confided in <u>her</u> Dad; but she wants Peter to be willing to talk to her.

Personal Relationships

Husband : Wife

The "Meister" is definitely the master in three of the four households. Mrs. Bonnington and the whole house wait on Mr. Daneham. The 18-year old girl, e.g., cleans his shoes on a Saturday morning. Mrs. Bonnington must have his tea ready the minute he comes in. Mrs. Freeman, too, expects to make the house revolve round her husband, as far as meals go anyhow. She has no illusions about men but is grateful that he gives her the pleasure of going up to the Bull with him. <u>His</u> only pleasure is beer and cigarettes, she says. She is careful to keep her husband ignorant of the fact that Gloria Freeman (15) is courting, though she approves of this herself on the principle that you should enjoy life "for a bit anyhow"., i.e., before the toils of matrimony fall on a girl. Mrs. Marks, too, though less obviously subservient to her man, respects his wishes in that she does not go out to work. Mrs. Waters' relationship with her husband is less easy to establish: but, anyhow, she, he, and his mother seem on good terms even after living together for nine years under most trying physical conditions. Husband and wife go to their Chapel societies together and both belong to the Labour Party. Their views on other people in the street roughly coincide, as do those on the up-bringing of their two children, They are a "close" family, too, in that they take note of family anniversaries. On their wedding day, Mrs. Waters takes a bunch of bought flowers to the Chapel. Some of these are then given to an ill person, and the others come back to their packed little room in Dyke Street. Mary Marks often gives her mother a nice present, and actions such as these seem typical of all four households.

An outstanding feature of these families is that they seem to be less flummoxed (if one may use the word) by sex than are the adults of the

The 5-Point Scale of Households a Detailed Account   169

I and II homes. The Waters, or anyhow Mrs. Waters, believes in sex talks at school. When Peter asked her "What is adultery" she told him "If I left Dad and went to live at a man's house, I'd be an adultery". She had such difficulties herself ("my mother never told me anything") and such worrying experiences as a girl - "lot's learn the wrong road especially in the factory"- that she is all for frankness, Old Mrs. Waters does not hold with it. She was scandalized when some child remarked that his mum "don't lay eggs like a hen. She carries the baby in her belly", What so shocked old Mrs. Waters was that it was a teacher who had told the child this. A teacher! As regards the Bonnington–Daneham relationship, the following analysis is guesswork, but is included as a possible explanation of the situation. Mrs. Bonnington has so strong a character that she has lived down any suggestion of scandal about her relationship with Mr. Daneham. Everyone regards them as a Mr. and Mrs. and respects them. The chances are that he has a wife somewhere and is unable to marry; and that Mrs. Bonnington and he don't try to hush things up but prefer to keep their own surnames knowing that the street will accept them in any case. Mothers expect their girls to be masters of sex, so to speak, Mrs. Freeman and Mrs. Marks both gave their girls "a good talking to" about sex when, at 14, the girls started to go with a boy. After that they were content, and probably with good reason, to let the girl have a boy so long as the proper rules are observed, viz., that both the boy's and the girl's family approve, and that the girl goes to "his" home before he comes to hers.

Adults : Children

The children in the four families, like their parents, show rather more commonsense than those of the I and II households. Fred Bonnington (9) was a most efficient guide when directing the interviewer to a house in another part of the town. The same child set his mind, months ahead, in winning a Sunday School prize for regular attendance – and did so. They also seem better tempered, not quite so ready to attack one of their contemporaries, or to give bad-tempered slaps on the sly to a younger one. This does not mean that they differ noticeably from the I and II children with regard to personal appearance or habits. The Bonnington boys are among the roughest looking in Dyke Street, and the Freeman girl was one of the least smartly dressed and least well–spoken of the thirty girls at camp. They get shouted at by their parents much as the other children do. But it is a reasonable shouting and a consistent one so that the youngsters take notice and are relatively obedient. Mrs. Bonnington is said by the "kinder" mothers to

170 *The 5-Point Scals of Households a Detailed Account*

control hers very strictly – too strictly they mean, "It's not kind to the kids". All the same she talks to her children which is more than some do. For example, she will listen patiently while Michael tells the tale of Jack and the Beanstalk, illustrated by his toy TV.

None of these households, except perhaps that of Mrs. Marks, put the following views into words: but what they did about their children's upbringing suggested that they recognised that children are not just small-sized adults who will grow up all right if fed and watered. They recognise that children have specific needs and needs that are not confined to physical ones.

Relationship with Neighbours

All four households are in good repute with their street. This is not the stand-offish superiority of the woman who will not let her child play out: but it is reflected in such a fact as that Mrs. Marks is one of the two women who always go to every house in the street if there is a collection for a wreath.

"Esther" (i.e., Mrs. Bonnington), "we think a lot of her", say a couple of women who live right at the far end of the street from the Bonnington's. It is not really surprising that such families don't want to leave the street, for all the physical shortcomings of their houses, or even the low repute of the street itself. To them, too, the delinquency record of their neighbours (which was always at the back of the interviewer's mind) was not an abnormal thing. They disapproved of bad behaviour and warned their children against it, but their family and the delinquent families were mingling, at a certain level, all day long. Under such conditions juvenile delinquency is not a matter about which one takes a rigidly censorious attitude.

Summary

Three things stand out about these four families who have been ranked as typical IIIs. The first is this – that both the grown-ups and the children seem to be more sensible than those of the I and II households. The attitude to children's pocket money e.g., is both practical and, in the truest sense, kind to the child. Secondly, they take advantage of opportunities. Mrs. Bonnington, as soon as she heard about the Play Room being started, decided that her children should be encouraged to use it – "Here's a chance to help Michael get on". And thirdly, they try to make a stand on certain matters, provided these are within their own territory: though they would not go so far as to do what one

The 5-Point Scale of Households a Detailed Account   171

woman (ranked as a IV) did. She took the extreme step of going round to the woman next door whom she heard late at night threatening to turn her child (8) out of the home. Within their own homes these families fight for what they think is important. "My Dolly and my Brian are <u>not</u> going to steal. I won't have it". Unlike the I and II parents, their's is a long–distance policy and not just an occasional, flash in the pan, effort.

Grades IV and V Factual Information

The households in Grades IV and V are very different in many respects from those in Grades I and II, in particular, and also from those in Grade III. In general it may be said that the Vs, as compared with the IVs, are more ambitious for themselves and their children, achieve higher standards of living from the point of view of such things as home comforts and leisure–time activities, and strive more consciously to maintain the standards which they set themselves. The contrast between the higher grades and the lower ones will become more apparent in the text. It may be noted that the higher grades are on the whole at once more consistent and more sensible than the less vocal lower ones in their comments and views upon the subjects discussed.

The Home

Physical, Character

Most of the houses are clean and neat, both externally and internally, and in a good state of repair. The doors and walls are well painted and papered, and the interviewer often made such comments as "spotlessly clean", or "a very pretty, spotless, expensive room, new tiled grate, pretty loose covers, flowers in bowl" In several cases the husband does all the house decorating – working on it at weekends and evenings for several months. Furniture is sufficient, of a reasonable standard, and well cared for. In one house the interviewer was shown the kitchen, which was a particular matter of pride to the household. The husband had constructed a range of stove, sink, cupboards, etc., in his spare time, and it was pointed out as a contrast to the "pig sty "conditions of some of the households in the street. Table 5 shows that 10 out of 16 Vs, and 25 out of 43 IVs, take noticeably effective effort with their houses, and none make noticeably ineffective effort. Their homes play an important part in these people's scheme of values - the bare minimum of furniture is not enough for them. If possible, e.g., a piano is

172 *The 5-Point Scals of Households a Detailed Account*

bought, and the walls are decorated with photographs, pictures, horse brasses, etc. They set up their homes with the intention of improving them as it become economically possible. Thus one woman remarked that she had been "building her home up ever since she was married". Seven out of 16 Grade V households and 23 out of 43 Grade IVs have Television sets, and others are saving in order to purchase them. Thirteen out of 16 Grade V, and 14 out of 43 Grade IV homes, are buying their houses, or already own them, believing that it is a good plan to expend a little more at the moment in order to provide for the future.

Housekeeping

Keeping the home pleasant and "spic and span" is a matter of principle. At one house the woman was busy cleaning when the interviewer called. He was invited back on another day, but the house-cleaning could not be interrupted for him. A contrast is evident here with the lower grades, where in many cases no set time is allotted for housekeeping, and a visitor provides a welcome excuse for breaking off from work. The higher grades "do the place out thoroughly once a week". And if a visitor is coming, then a special interim clean-up is the order of the day. Housework is an important part of the daily life, and is considered both necessary and a valuable contribution to the family life – that is, in helping to make a pleasant home. Thus some of the housewives have a fairly rigid timetable. Meals are served at set these during the day: in one house the occupants apologized for still eating their dinner at such a late time, 3 o'clock. This was obviously an unusual phenomenon, caused through the husband's visit to the hospital that morning. Another woman "cannot tolerate children eating scraps between meal times". She goes to town regularly each morning, and early, in order to get the provisions for the day – then she can "settle down to the housework for the rest of the day". Another typical example is that of the woman dressed in old trousers, and with a cloth round her head ("it's no use wearing decent clothes for working"). She "likes to get washed and changed before her husband arrives home at 4 p.m., and have the baby's nappies dried and put away, for it is not nice for your husband to arrive home and find things in a mess". Ironing and washing, cleaning the carpet, preparing the meal – all these things receive priority: so the hope is expressed that the interviewer "will not mind if they carry on cleaning the shoes whilst talking to him". The women have an interest in their cooking. They are pleased to attend cake making demonstrations at the Community Centre for example. They are supported in their

The 5-Point Scale of Households a Detailed Account 173

efforts by their husbands, who do odd jobs about the house, help with the dishes, etc. Often, however, the husband's specific task is the tending of the garden – not only digging, but laying concrete paths to prevent the children bringing mud into the house, fixing up fences and so on. As has been said, the women are houseproud – but this is not just a mania about having a speck of dust in the house. It is an integral part of their lives. Deep satisfaction is gained from having a "good" home, and from conforming with the standards which they set themselves.

Size and Structure

The sizes of the households are shown in Table 2, where it is seen that only two households in Grade V have more than 5 persons, and none in Grade IV. At Knoll the houses are of the same type and size as those of the lower three grades, so that there is more space per person available in the higher grade homes. In some homes it is proudly declared that they are able to provide the two children with separate bedrooms. Not only is there less crowding within the home, but for purposes of sleeping segregation of the sexes is possible in these homes, whereas in many of the lower grade houses it is not. As will be discussed later, the smaller size of these households is usually a matter of choice: it is decided that the parents can afford so many children and no more, and that it is convenient from the point of view of space and facilities to have a certain number. It is not usual for near relations - or indeed anyone other than direct relations (father, mother, and children) to live in the same household, Table 3 shows that in only 7 households out of the 59 are there grandparents, grandchildren or married children living in the same household as the informants.

Related Families

Nor is the tendency to have relations living nearby, a tendency prominent in the lower grades, very apparent in these higher ones. Only 5/43 and 2/16 respectively have relations living within a few houses, With regard to the Knoll Estate, of course, the fact that people could only have lived there for a maximum of about 17 years adds to the chance of not having relations living nearby. Nevertheless these facts are in keeping with the stress which is laid in these higher grades upon families "keeping to themselves", "not mixing", and in general leading "private lives". Their dealings with other people are a matter of choice and selection: constant coming and going between relatives and friends is not

174 *The 5-Point Scals of Households a Detailed Account*

desired, whereas privacy is. But the fact that few relatives live nearby also reflects another allied factor, namely the independence of these families. They desire to tend for themselves, they have their own lives to lead: and they do not wish to be dependent on a mother living next door, or a sister down the road. Nor do they wish to be bothered continually by them. They are pleased to see them from time to time, by mutual arrangement, but that is all.

Length of Residence

Table 22 shows that the majority of the grade IV and V families seem to be settled fairly permanently in their present house. Only 6/59 have been resident for less than 2 years, and half of these are newcomers to the Knoll Estate, who are buying their houses. The remainder are satisfied with their houses, or if they would prefer, as some would, "a better house", "more space", or a "better neighbourhood", they are nevertheless resigned to living in their present homes until they have saved enough to move, or "until the Pools come up", Meanwhile they set about improving their home, painting and decorating it, making cupboards, etc.

Employment

Type

Table 7 shows that the pattern of employment for these grades corresponds to that of the others, except that there is only one miner in Grade V. The clerical workers are in low-level clerical work, certainly not in an executive or administrative position. Similarly with the miscellaneous workers, an example of which is that of the Radby librarian, who served a long period in the pits, became caretaker of the library, and was offered the post of librarian on the outbreak of war in 1939. It is seen that there are five skilled factory workers in these grades, whereas none were encountered in the two lowest grades. The self-employed men work in a small way as house decorators, tailors, etc. The pattern of employment of other persons in the household employed full time is similar to that of the chief men in the household (of. Table 8). It is not usual for the chief women in the household to be employed out of the house. This is especially so in Grade V. Only 3 women in grade IV are employed out of the house full-time, and none at all in grade V (Table 9).

The 5-Point Scale of Households a Detailed Account 175

Conditions and Social Standing

The comments made earlier, in Section II, are relevant to the conditions of employment of the men in these higher grades as to those in the other grades. But one or two points peculiar to these higher grades may be made. The five skilled men are employed at a local engineering works, and it seems to be recognised by the people themselves that to work at this place carries a certain prestige – compared with the job of the ordinary labourer. On the other hand, these men are not necessarily to be considered as a "class apart" from the other workers by virtue merely of their occupation.

Generally speaking it may be said that the attitude of the IV and V grade men to their work is good. Work is not regarded merely as an evil, made necessary by the desire for "beer money". Work is the means to an end – that of building up a pleasant home – but it is also something about which to plan ahead to some extent. Some of the men had been apprenticed and had attended evening classes in order to learn more about their jobs. Their interest in their work is reflected also by their willingness to do jobs of a similar nature about the house. There may also be a pride in the job. One (retired) miner, e.g., is very proud of his service in the pits, for which he has several long service certificates which were displayed to the interviewer. Then there is the chauffeur, who had "been used to mixing with the gentry and the higher classes" – a fact which provides satisfaction for him and for his wife. Two other miners are keen First Aid men, feel they are more useful employee at the pits because of this, and, at the same time, gain greater satisfaction from their work. Similarly, a skilled engineer was said by his wife to "have worked his way up from being a garage-hand", whilst a policeman was studying for his sergeant's examination. The self-employed men, too, are obviously anxious to make a success of their efforts. For all this it must not be thought that all these men had established themselves in secure jobs from the time they left school. Some men had suffered long periods of unemployment (7 years in one case).

Intelligent comments were made about conditions of employment, e.g., about such things as danger in the pits being accentuated to an extent by modern machinery which sets a higher production pace. One miner considered that the new mining trainees are "hopeless" - they don't work nearly so hard as he had to work when he was only 11: and he thought that many unsuitable lads went down the pits solely because of the "big money" offered. Nevertheless, the principle of a training scheme for lads entering the industry was applauded by most of those with whom the matter was discussed. Some deplored

176　*The 5-Point Scals of Households a Detailed Account*

unnecessary strikes, and two men were very specific on this point. It was a "pet subject" with one Grade V man, who criticized unnecessary strikes. He referred also to workers who left their jobs because a higher official corrected them. He thought that the more experienced man is entitled to do this, because of his experience and position. A few weeks later these same men return to the job, and are taken on because they are trained men and there is a shortage of employees. He said that "full employment has cost this country a lot of money". because of this sort of irresponsibility.

As has been seen, few of the women in these grades work full time. The part time women workers are mostly in work of a clerical nature, or they are shop assistants. Some are employed at factories. One grade IV woman declared that she would like to work, not because of the extra money but because "It keeps you young and it's a pleasant way of passing the time". But this is an exception, and the primary reason for those who are employed out of the house is to get money in order to improve the position of the household and family by purchasing new furniture or clothes, or by saving for a holiday. The more general. view is that the woman's place is in the home, where there is plenty of work for her to do, especially if she makes dresses for the children, etc. The extreme form of this was expressed by one grade V woman who declared that her husband would kill her if she suggested going out to work.

These grades, in particular the Vs, are anxious that their children should "get on". In some cases their children are employed as nurses, or in a clerical job. They want them to get "clean jobs" – one mother wants her child to become a doctor, and another would like her son to be a surveyor, "or something like that". The latter woman referred to two relations, one a schoolteacher, the other an architect. "We seem to be the only ones who haven't got on", she said, her husband being a bricklayer.

Income

Wages

An account was given in Section II of the wages of the miners and factory employees. The clerical workers in the higher grades are not on high rates of pay. Having regard to the fact that few of the wives are employed (at any rate full time), and also the fact that fewer members of the household other than the chief men are employed full time, it is fair to say that the net income of these households is less – often considerably less - than that of households in the lower grades. In a few cases the

The 5-Point Scale of Households a Detailed Account   177

wife went out to work immediately after her marriage, in order to save for the home. Those women who do not go out to work stay at home of deliberate choice, not merely as is so often the case in grades I and II, because young children have to be looked after. It is the opinion of several of the higher grade households that those women, especially in the Is and IIs, who do go to work nowadays, do so not because the extra money is essential to the economic well-being of the family, but because of a desire for personal luxuries, cigarettes and "boozing money".

Supplementary

Some of the families "do the Pools": but the view of Mrs. R, a grade IV woman is typical of her grade. She and her husband "would not like to win such a lot of money that there is no need for Mr. R to go out to work, but we'd just like a bit more to do the things that we plan". Those households with children of the appropriate ages receive, of course, family allowance payments. Under the heading of supplementary income may be considered the product of constant attention to the garden, the growing of fruit and vegetables, etc., in an effort to maintain a certain standard of living not possible on the bare income of the household. The fact that some men do their own house decorating can in a sense be considered as a supplement to income.

Expenditure

Expenditure and saving is planned carefully and in accordance with chosen standards and criteria. Such a question is asked as "can I afford to go out for the evening, or will it mean a delay in purchasing a new coat for the children, or an electric washing machine for the wife", The adults smoke and drink little as compared with the lower grades. Thus one husband and wife "used to go for a drink before they were married, but can't afford it now", and they smoke little, because they can't afford it and at the same time maintain the standards at home and for the children which they wish. Such items as cigarettes are considered as luxuries which are only to be indulged in after the essential expenditure – on good food, clothing and the home – has been met, and after provision has been made in savings for next year's holiday, for Christmas, for some special purchase, or for the future, In some cases the families are satisfied with their present reasonable standard of living, and therefore spend more on leisure–time activities than others who are aiming at further improvements. But, in any case, it is recognised that a choice has to be made – and the choice is made in favour

178   *The 5-Point Scals of Households a Detailed Account*

of the home first and foremost. A grade V woman saved up to "buy some nice gloves for the children", although "this meant going short of some things" herself, Another grade V woman said that she "could not afford to let her children ill–treat their clothes", as "some do". She has a raincoat discarded by an older child, pressed and packed away upstairs ready for her younger child when he is big enough.

Another family goes away on holiday each year – but this would not be possible unless the husband worked overtime in the evenings and at weekends especially for this purpose. In one case it was stated that the husband did not get a high wage, and although he receives a bonus each year they "could not afford to go on the spree with it". They have to spread it out over the year. A grade IV family installed a new fireplace in their rented house· The justification was that "even if we move in a few years we shall have had the use of it" The people in these grades often contrasted their own attitudes with those of people in the same area who "spend a lot of money on drink" in preference to paying the food bill; or who "spend a £1 in one evening on beer and a coach trip" even though they are in arrears of payment with the rent. Indeed, to some, it was a source of amazement how the lower grade families got through so much money without improving their homes or personal appearance and with "nothing to show for it except arrears". One mother does not draw her family allowance weekly, but lets them accumulate until there is sufficient money to purchase new clothes for the children. This sort of thing is typical. The delayed earning caused by letting a child go to a Grammar School is not a source of discontent. As one mother put it, "we are not bothered about getting a return from our children as some people are".

The people in these grades know how to enjoy themselves without spending a lot of money. Much of their leisure time is spent with their children in the home, and they spend on the home itself to make this a pleasant place in which to pass their spare time. For them a visit to the countryside is not so expensive as a visit might be for one of the lower grade families. In the latter the licensing hours are likely considerably to curtail the actual time spent "in the country".

The housewife knows roughly what is her weekly expenditure, and plans her money in such a way as to avoid getting into arrears or debt. To be "spent out on Monday" is unthinkable, and reflects bad planning, If hard times do befall the family – one household "got right down" through the illness of the husband – then there is no holiday this year. Savings are drawn upon regretfully, but "it's a good job you've got something behind you". As a grade IV housewife said, "you've got to take the rough with the smooth".

The 5-Point Scale of Households a Detailed Account   179

The attitude towards Hire Purchase of, e.g., TV and washing machines, varies, though the "package" man who supplies clothes in return for weekly payments is generally disparaged. The aim in general is to "pay your way" each week. Families in which wages are "poured down the throat" instead of into the home are criticised. It is considered essential to "have a good table" - that is, food must be plentiful and of good quality. The second priority is clothing for the children, and the third a comfortable home. The mother recognises the need for careful expenditure, and the husband appreciates the financial requirements of his wife in order to eater for the home ("My husband does not keep much, he gives me most of his wages"). Doubtless there is at times some dissention about the appropriate amount of "housekeeping" to be allotted – but in general the household is considered as a joint enterprise to be approached co–operatively.

Note on Expenditure and Children

There is no agreement in these grades as to whether children should be given a fixed amount of pocket money weekly. Some think that a child should receive a certain amount regularly, but should be taught to save some. The children must learn how to spend money, and the parents like to know where they stand as regards supplying the children's minor needs. They argue that it is an advantage to the child in later life if he is taught how to spend money properly. Such are some of the views held. Others "always keep sweets in the house, and try to buy the children what they want". They take the children out sometimes and this is an expense. when one little girl attends Guides each week she is given her "bus fares and 3d. for chips", and this is a "special. treat which the child looks forward to". It is thought by these grades that the lower grade families give their children money just to "save the parents from bother, and the kids are not taught the value of it".

Similarly with regard to toys and presents – the emphasis is more on the worth on the present as such and upon the educational value of it to the child. Thus, one child at Christmas was given a good quality stamp album –"he'll be taught to use it properly" – and an instructive book on birds. One grade IV woman stressed the importance of giving children enough money, and said that "leaving school and getting spending money often does a 'bad' boy good". He becomes "somebody", and "if a lad has no money he will go to any lengths to be on equal terms with his mates". This kind of argument reflects a conscious effort by the parents to prevent delinquency – they recognise the dangers and attempt to ward them off in good time.

180   *The 5-Point Scals of Households a Detailed Account*

Education

It is thought that the vast majority of the chief men and women in the households in these grades left elementary school and started work at the age of 13–14 years, with the exception of two women in Grade V who stayed at school until they were sixteen at which age one became a nurse and the other had a baby. Some men, in particular the clerical workers and the skilled factory workers, continued some kind of formal training in order to qualify for their work.

As in the case of the lower grades, there was some difference of opinion about the extra year at school brought about by the Education Act, 1944, which raised the school-leaving age from 14 years to 15. Table 16 shows that 10/43 and 1/16 respectively thought the extra year undesirable, whilst 4/43 and 1/16 thought it desirable for some but not for all. The sort of reasons that were put forward in support of the various views are all based upon a conception of the well-being of the children. One woman said that "fourteen is too young to start work, isn't it?". Another said that a child could "take things a little easier in the extra year", and get adjusted to the prospect of work as well as getting "a sounder approach" to life. Others thought that the extra year "gives more confidence", and regret that they themselves had not had the opportunity to further their education. Another view was that unless a child was at a Grammar School he should leave at 14, especially the girls who should be helping at home: whilst one person who condemned the extra year felt that although it was "alright for those who are that way inclined" (meaning those who have the ability) the extra year at the moment merely provided the opportunity for children to "get accustomed to idling – which is bad when they start to work".

A total of 9 out of 59 would approve of using a Nursery School, and several more thought that children should start school at 4 years of age when "the child is old enough and would be in company" – although one person pointed out that this eventuality was unlikely to occur because of the shortage of school accommodation. And 4 to 14 is a receptive age, and at the age of 14 a child is "not learning anything and would rather be at work".

The I.Qs of children from these households are not available in their entirety, but Table 23 suggests that the tendency is for children from grades IV and V to be more intelligent than those from the lower grades. This is supported by Table 16 which shows that children from 10/43 and 3/16 households respectively have had other than elementary education. An associated factor is that none of the children from grades IV and V appear in the Education Records for bad attendance.

The 5-Point Scale of Households a Detailed Account   181

16/43 and 9/16 of the households would definitely like their children to have a Grammar School education. One woman (grade V) considered it especially beneficial for a boy, who will have ultimately to "keep a home going" and who will require employment for which "his education will suit him". And as another woman said, referring to the associated delayed earning of schoolchildren, "some say you get nothing back from them, but we don't look at it that way". This woman kept her son at school until he was 16 even though her husband was unemployed at the time. Many were most anxious for their children to pass the Grammar School Entrance Examination. A grade IV woman said that "it was a shame" for children to pass a scholarship and then not be allowed to go to Grammar School by their parents. She and her husband were "overjoyed" when their son passed, and they determined to give him the chance. If he did not succeed then it was his fault and they would have done as much as they could for him.

The achievement of having a child at a Grammar School is some cause for pride in itself to these people: but it is also regarded as a means to an end. These grades are very ambitious for their children – they want their sons to be doctors, architects, etc., and their daughters to be school-teachers, dress designers, or at any rate to "grow into ladies". Also, a Grammar School education is felt to lead to a broadening of interests which is considered of value. And one mother pointed out to her child that she would appreciate it later in life when she went to apply for a job, if she worked hard now. There is a keen sense of education as a means of "getting on", and as a vehicle for the children to "do good" (i.e., to themselves). Those whose children are not good scholars are concerned about the fact – about Peter "being backward at reading and writing" – and seek to remedy this situation by teaching them to apply themselves to reading and to instructive hobbies.

Towards this end, there is conscious co-operation with the school authorities through such means as the Parent-Teacher Association. And there is also a knowledge of and interest in the schools and in the general education of their children. A grade V woman referred to the pleasant new school in the neighbourhood, and said that although many people in the district thought that the Head-teacher was too strict, she supported the teacher. For discipline is essential, especially having regard to "some of the children and their homes". One or two parents displayed a sound knowledge of their children's school careers – what subjects they are studying, what examinations they would sit, etc. Their general approval is given to a Grammar School education, not only because "it stays with you all your life", but more particularly from the practical point of view – it is a means of rising socially.

182   *The 5-Point Scals of Households a Detailed Account*

On the other hand, one parent (grade IV) thought that teachers in the ordinary school were not competent to deal with 14-year old boys – they had had insufficient training themselves, and at the age of 14 boys can recognise a bad teacher. The wider value of a Grammar School education was remarked upon by one woman, who considered it beneficial because "you see Grammar School girls going about with Grammar School boys", whereas "the girls from the elementary schools go about with men" – i.e., the "better" education also acts to prevent "dangerous" situations of such a character from developing.

Day-release from work for extra education was favoured by some. Table 16 shows that only 3/43 and 2/16 households had members attending day-release or evening classes at the time of the survey.

Leisure

Organised

It has been said that grade IV and V families value the privacy of their homes, and spend much of their leisure-time in them. Nevertheless a few participate in organised activities – in particular those from the Knoll Estate who are active at the Community Centre. Some of the women, especially in grade IV, attend the Ladies Guild, and one of these was previously secretary of the Guild. But she "gave it up because of lack of support" – when she had arranged for a visiting speaker, for example, and few people turned up, so that she "felt awkward" and had to apologise. Several of the women of the grade V families previously worked hard to form the Community Association, but they dropped out when intrigues developed and gossip took the place of discussion. Now, only one person from the grade V families is a member of the Management Committee: and one couple, a husband and wife (grade IV), act as instructors at the Dancing Classes and Sewing Classes held at the centre. Two men are active members of a First Aid Team. One man is a keen member of the Colliery Sports Club, and another attends Workers Educational Association Classes and is a Trade Union official. But on the whole the adults in these grades are not particularly anxious to participate in organised activities of a permanent nature (though one or two acted as officials in the temporary organisations set up to organise street Coronation festivities). One exception is that of a grade IV family, where the mother declared that if she "won the pools" she would purchase the Community Centre buildings and thus relieve the Association of financial difficulties. For the Centre is "an excellent idea", and she "never thought she would dance again" until

The 5-Point Scale of Households a Detailed Account   183

the Centre began to function. Regular participation in formal organisations is made difficult for the parents in these grades with young children, They like to spend their leisure-time together, and it is difficult to do so and at the same time attend organisation's activities. They "would not think of going out and leaving the children". Also, there is a widely held view, particularly amongst the grade V people, that the Community Association has "got into the wrong hands", and a suspicion about the motives of those in control. It is alleged that they are there for their own glory rather than for the benefit of the community. It is true to say, nevertheless, that those who do participate in formal organisations recognise their value and think out constructive methods by which the objects aimed at may be achieved. Those who don't join often enough have analysed the various merits and demerits of the society and found them lacking. In other words non-membership is not just a question of "couldn't care less".

With regard to children's organised leisure-time activities, much thought is given to this matter by the parents in these grades. The figures given in Table 18 do not fully reflect this interest. Table 18 shows that of 11 grade V households who have children aged 0–14, 3 are known to have at least one child who goes regularly to Sunday School whilst 2 are known to have children who do not go regularly (no information 6 households). With regard to Youth Organisation attendance, 4 have at least one child who attends regularly and the children of one household do not attend regularly (no information 6 households). In grade IV, of 31 households with children aged 0–14, 15 have at least one child attending Sunday School regularly and 2 have children who do not attend regularly (no information 14 households). Eight households have a child who attends a Youth Organisation regularly and 8 have children who do not attend regularly (no information 15 households). In spite of the large number of households on which insufficient information on this point was available for tabulation, it is believed that the relative numbers in each of the "regular attender" and "non–regular attender" classes give a fair indication of the position for the grades as a whole. Most of the households from grades IV and V with children of the appropriate ages encourage them to attend Sunday School. But there is less encouragement for them to attend Youth Organisations, particularly amongst the grade IV households. Furthermore, on the Knoll Estate, several parents in these grades discourage their children from attending the local Youth Club because of hooliganism and its bad reputation. "What you need", said one person, reflecting the opinion of many, "is a full-time Youth Leader from out of the area, so that he will be treated with respect." Parents in these grades also tend to favour organisations such

184　*The 5-Point Scals of Households a Detailed Account*

as Cubs and Scouts and Guides, rather than Youth Clubs. For it is felt that these organisations have capable leaders, and also that they attract the "well-behaved boy", and "children from the good homes", These views are unconnected with social snobbery, but reflect a conception of desirable standards to maintain, and to be instilled into the children.

Informal Leisure

Leisure time is spent decorating the house, cultivating the garden, watching TV, listening to the wireless, and so on. In these grades leisure time seems to be considered in terms of activity on the part of the children as well. as the adults – playing with a meccano set, reading, learning to do carpentry, and so on. The family spends much of its leisure together – children are taken into the country, or to see the "Ideal Homes Exhibition", or "his father takes him to the cinema when there is a jungle film on", etc. Some men attend Clubs, and go to the pub for a drink "when they can afford it". Three households were met where the family are keen readers. One woman (grade V) reads one book a week regularly. Another, a grade IV woman, is a little anxious because her son reads such a lot – she wonders if it will affect his eyes. Nevertheless, she is pleased, because he is learning and at the same time he is quiet, and "we do like it quiet in the home". Children are taught to use their recreation time usefully and in an orderly fashion – "I always make him tidy up before he goes to bed", It is noticeable that in those households in which there are a large number of books (in several cases stacked neatly in a home-made bookcase) the majority belong to the children. The adults "don't get much time for reading".

The general lack of interest in formal organisations, and the concentration of interest upon the home and upon the children, implies that the adults have few hobbies or leisure-time activities which are unconnected with the home, which is for most of the people in these grades the one great interest in life. when the children grow up something of a void is created in the adults' lives. Recourse is made to further improvements about the house ("which we couldn't afford before"), and sometimes to an extension of activities outside the home, mostly of an informal nature. Sometimes, of course, it leads a woman to go out to work, generally on a part-time basis.

Attitude to Delinquency

It is seen from Table 10 that none of the households in grades IV and V have any delinquency cases officially recorded against them. And,

The 5-Point Scale of Households a Detailed Account 185

indeed, several mentioned that they are "very thankful that we've had nothing of that sort". But this does not mean that the parents are not conscious of the problem. It constantly receives publicity in the popular press, and they encounter it in their daily lives – the men at work, and the women through conversation with their friends. Even though they "do not mix", they nevertheless hear about "so and so who was up in Court last week", and are duly shocked. This is particularly true for the people who are living in the Carnation Street Area and the Knoll Estate – especially the latter. For as was pointed out above, in these areas the "good" and the "black" families live in close proximity to each other. They must accordingly take steps "not to let their children out in the street", for they "don't like them playing with those Smith children who live down the road". As a result of these things, the problem of delinquency is known to many of these people, and in particular it is considered by them in relation to their own children: how can they ensure that their children do not get into trouble with the police? But not only do the people from these grades have opinions – and indeed associated politics – about juvenile delinquency, they were also prepared to discuss them openly with the interviewers, The following account consists of a discussion of the views put forward by the people from these grades. They see the problem as a contrast to the standards which they have set for their children.

One woman – who obviously is interested in children as such, in addition to being very fond of her own – thinks that delinquency arises because of the "bad homes", and she instanced families from Dyke Street. The attitude of the lower grade parents arises, she thinks, partly because children are unplanned. They come "willy nilly" and are accepted as small editions of adults – that is to say, there is no conception of treating them as different from adults. The babies it is true receive special treatment because "everyone loves a baby": but as they grow older – and more tiresome – they get little special treatment. One man from the Knoll Estate remarked upon the bad state of their house when they moved into it – the window sills carved, dart marks in the walls, and so on. The man "couldn't understand people being destructive like that". If people behave like that in their homes, and allow their children to behave similarly, small wonder, he said, that other people's property is treated with similar disregard.

The parents of one grade **V** household relate delinquency to age. At 9–10 years of age children begin to think that they are grown up, and copy adults as seen in the cinema and in comics. Some children go to the cinema far too much – fourteen is quite old enough to start going to the cinema regularly, and not before. At 13–14 children get "silly" but pass through a phase which most "get over": this is nevertheless

186 *The 5-Point Scals of Households a Detailed Account*

a difficult age, when parents must be specially alert to prevent their children from "getting into trouble". The boys get into gangs and dare each other – "I'll go one better, the boys say". Girls' wickedness is different *from* boys' – "you can't see it so easily". Some dislike "a lot of the stuff that's put in the newspapers" – children read the crime and sex reports and get ideas. Such sensational items need to be "hushed up". All this is a very different outlook from that in some of the lower grade families where jokes about "homos" and "sex changes" keep pace with the current reports in the daily press. In the IV and V households, too, children must be taught to respect the law, The policeman must be accorded the respect which is appropriate to his position. In the low level grades, the "bobby" is often regarded with contempt even by the very young children. The higher grades in some cases deliberately instruct their children from an early age important things like "never to take something that belongs to someone else", and minor ones like "always say good morning nicely", It is necessary to resist temptation: as a result of teaching, one woman's son "would never swear – he would count ten instead", To other households the very idea of delinquent conduct is foreign – "it would never occur to me to steal anything, and my children are the same". Boys get into trouble because they are "more on the loose". Adults "keep an eye on the girls", for girls can come to more obvious harm (i.e., sex). A distinction is made between the well-behaved boy and the bad boy. Of course, all children are "naughty" in some ways, and all misbehave at times: but there is a difference between those who are "plain cheeky" and those who are "really insolent".

It is widely held in these higher grades that parental unconcern is the major factor in juvenile delinquency. The parents, they say, go out to the cinema and the pub, and "as long as the children don't bother them they can do as they like". Personal enjoyment comes first, and everything else, including the children, last. Also, parents don't stop their children doing little things that are "wrong", and "it leads on" until the children are the slaves of their inclinations. If a child demands money or a toy, the parents often say "oh let him have it, we can afford it" – regardless of whether the child deserves it. One man described how he caught a neighbour's boy throwing tomatoes through his bed room window, and thrashed him. The child's parents threatened him with a summons, but they did not even come and see him about it. If it had been his child who was involved, he would have straightened the matter out by apologising to the people concerned and by remonstrating with the boy himself. Parents are "not strict enough" – and if others chastise children, "you get a mouthful back". In a place like

The 5-Point Scale of Households a Detailed Account 187

Dyke Street, one woman said, "adults dare not and will not chastise other people's children" (even if they thought it necessary). In Gladstone Road, on the other hand, they will, and "the children are better for it". "What you do at home you do outside" sums up the opinion of one woman. She and her sister "would not have dreamed of answering back their mother", and would not have their children doing it today. It is wrong for mothers to go out to work, some people state, for young children are left to get even younger children off to school, to do the shopping and to prepare meals: for the rest of the time they are left to themselves.

Although punishment is necessary at times, the best way of dealing with the problem, it is generally believed, is to prevent trouble from arising, and, if it does arise, to deal. with it through reasoning rather than "spanking".

Personal Relationships

Husband : Wife

In general it seems that the husband : wife relationship of people in these higher grades is at least reasonably pleasant, and in the case of families which are making a great effort to "better" their homes and conditions for the children, the relationship is based upon mutual regard and coperation. This is reflected in such matters as the manner in which a wife speaks of her husband – "She talks very pleasantly of her husband", and, "she speaks very proudly of her husband as a good, wise man who has done well at his work through his own efforts". A widow spoke of missing her husband a lot – "we were so happy together", whilst the Warden of the Knoll Community Centre said of a grade IV husband that he "treats his wife very well, and is unusually tender for this district". Such comments as the following were made : "I like to have a good meal ready for him when he arrives home", and "he helps me with the housework when I am busy". One woman said that she always waits up for her husband when he is on evening shift at the pit, no matter how late he is arriving home. Efforts are made to understand the "ways" and requirements of the husband or wife and their special needs are catered for. The man works hard for the money, and the wife spends it in a way which will give satisfaction to him. The interests of each other are allowed for. If one likes dancing and the other does not, then father will look after the children whilst mother goes out. Often when there are children which cannot be left, neither of the parents goes out in the evening ("We have not been to

188   *The 5-Point Scals of Households a Detailed Account*

the cinema for two years because of the baby"). Usually, if they do go out at all, it will be together and when possible they take the children with them. An exception is made each year by one couple with three children. "On our wedding anniversary my sister comes to look after the children and my husband and I go out for the evening". This woman confessed that the following day she usually thinks how they could have put the money they had spent "into the house". It is obvious that the parents of children in these grades not only discuss their children constantly, but also talk over other things of interest to them. Several women informed their husbands of the interviewer's calls, and sub sequent discussed the topics with him. Other parents argued over the topics in a friendly way while the interviewer was there. Unlike in the I and II homes, there seemed to be little hesitation on the part of the women about discussing matters in their husband's presence.

With regard to sexual matters, one woman indicated that, unlike some men in the district, her husband would "never put her down" – that is, he would never enforce intercourse against her wishes. Upon enquiring whether the parents would like more children, the interviewers were frequently told, "well you never know, do you?" Such comments suggest that there is little knowledge of effective contraceptive methods. At the same time, the fact of these families being smaller on the average than those of the lower grades, and the preoccupation in the higher grades with maintaining certain standards of living (thus another child will be considered in terms of "can we afford it?") indicates that limitation of families is practised in some way, probably by an appropriate amount of abstention from sexual intercourse. This presumably involves self-control in order to abide by pre-determined standards. It is seen from Table 15 that few households in grades IV and V have members who were known to be married at 20 years of age and under (4/43 and 3/16). Certainly such matters as the "good" age for marrying, how many children to have, and when to have them are seriously considered. One woman thinks it is a good idea to have all the children that you intend having when you are still young, so that you can "enjoy life together". Another said that she had hoped not to have a baby until at least two years after her marriage, so that she and her husband would have time to save. As it happened, a baby was born one year after her marriage, and now she is hoping for another. It is considered good for the husband : wife relationship to have children. And childless couples are referred to with sympathy – e.g., "the woman next door has no children, and cries every Christmas about it". The parents must set a good example to the children – "me and my

The 5-Point Scale of Households a Detailed Account   189

husband never disagree before Peter" either on how he is to be treated or about other matters.

The one matrimonial case which occurs in grade V (there are none in grade IV – see Table 10) concerns a woman living apart from her husband (Table 13). The woman gave birth to a child when she was 17 years of age, and her parents made her marry the man who was the father of the child. Two more children were born and then the husband ("a bad lot") left his wife. The latter now lives with her children and her parents. They are a united house hold, as the mother and the grandparents are very fond of the children. Even taking into account this household which has experienced matrimonial trouble, it may be said that the emphasis in grades IV and V is upon the family as a unit, based upon reasonable relationship between man and woman.

Adults : Children

The parents are obviously interested in their children and concerned for their welfare. The emphasis is upon training the children "properly". They recognise that there are special problems of parenthood and apply themselves to them. A child should be punished for doing something wrong, but should be punished in a reasonable and consistent way. One lad who "cheeked his father" was sent to bed without his tea, although an egg had been cooked for him. similar consistency is reflected in the case of a lad who wanted to go to camp, and whose mother had said that it was too cold for him to go at that time. The boy persisted, and the father finally said to the mother that the child could go, and find out how cold it was for himself. But the mother said that she did not let him go, as it would have been wrong for her to change her mind because the child kept pestering her. Punishment is prescribed, then, for corrective purposes: but it is "no good shouting at a boy", for he will take no notice if he becomes used to being shouted at (a truth which is not yet recognised in the lower grade households). The parents think about the family and make plans for it. They also want the children to "do well", a fact which was considered in the section above on education. One man states that he wants his son to have an education which was denied to him in his youth. Another mother considers that she was "too anxious" for her son to do well at school, and that this had an adverse effect upon the child. There is a conception which has just been referred to, of the "right" size for a family, determined by such things as "how many children can we afford?" The usual decision is that "we can't manage more than two or three".

190 *The 5-Point Scals of Households a Detailed Account*

One mother with an only child says that she would have liked another, but was unwell. And now that the child has grown up she realises that they could not have done all those things which they have done for the child and which they wished to do, if they had had more children. It is considered wise not to have too big an age gap between the children. One mother, for instance, refers to the difficulty she had with her oldest child who was aged five when her second child was born. The older child could not appreciate why less attention was paid to him.

The parents never go out and leave young children by themselves, unlike "some people you hear about". If they do go out, they ensure that there is a competent baby-sitter available. It is ensured that children are "indoors before it gets dark", and in bed at a certain time, depending upon age. Some parents read to the children who are in bed each evening. The children are taken to the cinema rather than sent there. One mother accompanies her ten-year-old daughter to Sunday School, and her husband fetches the child home afterwards. Children's friends are selected (in so far as it is possible) – "I don't let my child play in the street, as I don't like him to mix with some of the children who live round here – I prefer him to play in the back garden with the little girl next door", The Youth Club at the Knoll Estate is regarded as a place to protect the children from. It is "a bad influence, and the children who attend it are hooligans". These families ensure that their children attend school regularity – for they recognize the benefits of this – and that they look smart and are reasonably clean and well-behaved. In particular they are taught to behave at the meal-table, "one think I do like to see". A grade V woman "likes the three children to come home from school for their midday meal", rather than have their meal at school. She likes the family to be together and apparently considers it one of the functions of family life to prepare a meal for the family which they partake of together, This attitude is in marked contrast with that of some of the lower grade mothers who are only too pleased for their children to have their meals at school, thus saving the mother time and trouble.

Some parents feel that perhaps they do too much for their children – denying themselves things which they might otherwise enjoy. Some women go to work with the express purpose of "doing a little more for the kids". Some express the opinion that their sacrifices are not sufficiently appreciated by the children, who tend to accept as normal what would have appeared to the parents as something more than extraordinary in their own childhood, This attitude was expressed by a woman who said that her aim was for the children to have the discipline and respect for elders she had as a child, and yet

The 5-Point Scale of Households a Detailed Account 191

for them to have the home advantages – material and otherwise – which she did not have, but which she was trying to give them. Others felt that they were not quite as strict with their children as was good for them. One woman with an only child dwelt on this point, and said that her child tends to "take things for granted". If he sees a new toy he knows immediately that it is for him – who else could it be for? Because of this she would like to be able to send him to a nursery school, so that he would be mixing with other children, and would not always "have his own way".

Relationships between the Sexes

Several people spoke of the need for sex instruction for children, preferably at school. They are conscious of the need to take special care with their children about sex matters – especially with the girls, who are said to be "very sex-conscious" nowadays. It is widely believed that children "know a bit more nowadays" about sex matters than they did a generation or so ago, and on the whole this fact is applauded. Reference is frequently made by the parents to "their younger days". They were "taught nothing about sex" and were closely guarded from sex dangers ("I always had to be in at 9.30 p.m. until I was married").

Mixed youth clubs are approved of provided there is adequate and sensible supervision, although one person feels that "if a girl is going to get into trouble she will do anyhow" – that is, whether she attends a mixed youth club or not. One or two parents are worried because their children – boys and girls – are "having affairs" with other adolescents. One mother was "infuriated" to find a "love letter" in the pocket of her thirteen-year old son. Another mother says that she dislikes the tendency, apparent in some of the lower grade families, for young girls – still at school or only just left – to take home their "boyfriends". She hopes not to have this problem when her children are older, and is therefore endeavoring to give them a wide range of interests. It is thought desirable that the older girls especially should "see the world" a bit before "settling down". even so, nineteen is thought to be a sensible age for people to start serious "courting". The period of courting is not usually long, however – perhaps 1-2 years. But in a few cases even in these grades, girls have started courting at 14–15, and have eventually married their boy friend. But it causes no little concern to their parents. A typical father, in grade V, will not allow his 17-year-old daughter to marry the young fellow who has been courting her for several years until he is financially in a position to provide her with at least as good a home as that of her parents.

192   *The 5-Point Scals of Households a Detailed Account*

A final significant point raised by a grade IV woman differentiates the attitudes between the high and low grade households. The woman states that "people like us don't have children after about the age of 44, unlike the 'uneducated' people of Dyke Street".

Relationships with neighbours and with the district

The people in these grades state that they "have some good friends in the district, but that they do not mix a lot" – they keep themselves to themselves, and do not neighbour. They perhaps have a few selected friends who happen to live nearby, and they are not unfriendly with the neighbours, say "good morning", and so on. But they do not want to neighbour and to be "constantly in and out of each other's houses" at all times of day and night. The fact that they say their husbands wouldn't allow it shows that a high premium is put upon the privacy of the home and family life. And in any case the woman is too busy, she has not time to keep on "popping in next door". They help if anyone nearby is in need of course, but that is all. One man in particular is very concerned to have "as little to do with the neighbours as possible", a desire accentuated by the persistency with which one neighbour permits his dustbin to overflow into this man's garden. The intrusive neighbour may not be bothered about having a tidy – and productive – garden, but he is. Those friends whom these people do make are of course, people with similar ideas and ways as themselves. They discuss each others' children, the problems of the Community Centre, the coming school examinations, and the new vicar, etc. But they do not participate in the "canting" or "gossiping" which characterizes "neighbouring"; and they welcome the independence and close family life which neighboring denies. Constructive steps to avoid persistent contact between neighbors were taken by the adults in a group of three houses on the Knoll Estate. The woman in the middle house (from a grade IV household) complained that if she opened her front door she was right alongside one neighbour's front door: whereas if she opened her back door she was alongside her other neighbour's back door. So they set about improving the position. Fortunately one neighbour bought her house and decided to lay a new front path: so that now the households have separate gate entrances. By mutual agreement, the other neighbour and she are constructing an aluminum barrier between their two back doors, and the stated policy is to train roses over this welcome barrier. Henceforth all three households will have materially reinforced their desire to have contact only when desired

The 5-Point Scale of Households a Detailed Account   193

Quite the opposite situation has been witnessed in the lower grade families, where an intervening fence has been broken down to permit of easier access. A grade V woman from the Knoll Estate speaks of "two classes of people" in the district. She deplores the habits of those who drink a lot, neglect their children, etc. The "lower" class does much neighbouring, she says, and works up strong alliances which often end in argument and a breaking of the relationship. But after a short time, visiting will probably be resumed. She says there is much borrowing and lending amongst these people. The woman herself is "very friendly" with some people across the road, but they are not constantly "in and out of each other's houses" though they sometimes meet in the street and have a discussion about their children and so on. To illustrate some traits of the inveterate "neighbourers", the woman showed the interviewer a scribbled note which had been put through her letter box. It was from a woman who lived nearby, and asked if the sender could borrow 4s. until Friday (this was the Tuesday, i.e., four days after the previous pay day), and also, could she borrow a pair of shoes in order that she could go to work? And yet, the informant said, the household was in receipt of "good money". The same informant was asked to lend some knives and forks once: but there is no certainty that a loan will be returned. Her husband blames such situations as the above on the "packet man", the man who collects weekly subscriptions for clothing clubs – so that "the money is spent before it is earned". He quotes cases of women who pretend that they are out when the man comes to collect the payment due from them. With reference to clothing clubs, the informant said that the clothes are maltreated, and then the mothers ask such as her for clothes because their own children's are worn out: whereas she teaches her children to look after their clothes, so that they always look clean and tidy.

The majority of the people in these higher grades are content to live in their present houses, because, although the Carnation Street and Knoll areas have some "bad" families living there, there are "always good and bad everywhere", and in any case they "don't mix" and only talk with those whom they want to associate with. Several of the Knoll Estate households in these grades consider that the Estate is improving steadily anyhow ("don't think me snobbish, but it's better now that the people moving in are buying their houses"). But one or two of the grade V families would like to move to a "better" area – or, if they win the pools, to a better house: perhaps they might buy a little plot of land in a "nice" area, and build themselves a bungalow.

It is plain that the people in these grades set themselves certain standards which they strive to maintain. They do not mix much with

194 *The 5-Point Scals of Households a Detailed Account*

the people in the neighbourhood, because they value privacy and also because they fear contamination of their children by the of the less desirable households. Those people with whom they elect to be friendly are of their own way of thinking, so that the contacts which they make reinforce their own way of life.

The five-point scale range has now been considered in detail, and a sketch has been attempted of the kind of life which the people in the various grades lead, of the things which they consider important and of the principles which govern their actions. It remains to analyses these grades with reference to the problem of juvenile delinquency itself, a matter which is discussed in the following section.

Section IV
Conclusions

The hypothesis for this research is that "within working class areas different standards are upheld, and the differences between the norms of behaviour contribute to the differential rates of delinquency distribution". In the case of the Dyke Street : Gladstone Road comparison, it has been shown that although both streets are situated in a working class area, two different sets of standards are upheld. Dyke Street and Gladstone Road, in fact, constitute two well-defined sub-cultures, exhibiting in many directions contrasting ways of life. In the analysis of the 5-point scale of households, it was shown that the contrasting ways of life are also apparent within the two other working class areas chosen for the research, although in these particular areas there is no marked geographical grouping, It remains to assess how far, and in what ways these contrasting social backgrounds and norms of behaviour appear to contribute to the differential rates of delinquency distribution, It has been seen (p. 87) that there is a concentration in the black street of cases of adult and juvenile delinquency, and also that (Table 10) there is a similar concentration in the two lower grades. It has further been illustrated that in the black street and in the low grades there is a concentration of other phenomena, "unofficial" delinquency and "irregularity". There is also a disregard of such commonly accepted codes of conduct, not enforced by the law of the land, as moderation of language, care and training of children, provision of a comfortable home, and the maintenance of reasonable standards of housekeeping. Added to this, it appears that actual delinquency – illegal activity – is more general amongst the lower grade people than the official delinquency figures suggest. This is thought to be true of both adults and juveniles.

The ways of life of the people of the black sub-culture are reinforced and supported by their constant contact with each other. In the case of Dyke Street this is especially apparent by virtue of the fact that it

196   *Conclusions*

is a <u>community</u>, and is recognized as such by the people who live in it. The street itself reflects and upholds the codes of conduct of the people who are a part of it. And in the case of the low-grade households in general (not necessarily living in such close geographical proximity) the institution of neighbouring and the use of working men's clubs, pubs, etc., reinforce their own codes. In the higher grades, on the other hand, where independence and privacy are cherished, a reinforcement of their social codes comes from such sources as the following. In the first place, the associations (especially the children's clubs and organisations) in which they participate, serve to guide and maintain those principles which the family itself seeks to uphold. Secondly, the friends whom they select have similar opinions and attitudes to then, and are indeed selected because of this fact. And thirdly, the people in the higher grades consciously co-operate with those external authorities whose function it is to maintain specific social standards and codes of conduct. For example, they co-operate with the education authorities through parent–teacher associations, In other words, white influences white and black, black. But whereas the white family draws upon a variety of external agencies to reinforce its way of life, the black leads a more self-contained existence and hardly looks beyond its own bounds for any re-enforcement. Indeed, the larger society does not provide officially any reinforcement which would be acceptable to their way of life.

Nevertheless, the influence of the black home extends beyond the lower grades. The black code of conduct affects adversely (from the point of view of delinquency) some people in the higher grades, This is particularly true of the children, and especially those from grade III homes, who mix constantly with the children from the lower grades. The children from grades IV and V, on the other hand, are likely to have been instructed by their parents not to mix with the children of the lower grade families. The children themselves may have assimilated the wishes of their parents that they should not associate with the lower grade children. It is considered that the presence of a certain number of juvenile delinquents in grade III may be attributed to this fact.

The contrast in codes of conduct may be illustrated by quotations from the Probation Records. Of a boy (8) in a family that could be called a typical grade I family, the record reads :-

> "The parents of these children are not capable of caring for them, Mr. X is a hard drinking man, concerned only with his own pleasures. Mrs. X is a woman who seems to have no conception of the responsibilities of motherhood. She is loose living and has had associations with all and sundry. The child is harmless and in need of a secure and well-ordered home life".

Conclusions 197

A household which may be graded as an III, when faced with a similar situation in connection with their boy (12), took this line:-

> "Mr. Y feels that this offence has been adequately dealt with by himself – he punished the boy at the time – and is rather resentful that it should have been the subject of Court proceedings. He feels that he has brought up a large family without trouble and is capable of dealing with his son. Has served in a Guards Regiment and patterns his family discipline a little on these lines. However, he gave the impression that he had the family welfare at heart. Mrs. Y appears a good wife and mother".

We may now go on to consider in more detail certain aspects of the contrasting ways of life which, on the one hand, contribute to the occurrence of delinquency, and on the other, operate to restrain it or prevent its occurrence The points made below do not relate in their entirety to every family graded as "black" or "white". But, on the whole, behavior approximates to the following descriptions.

The most obvious characteristic of the black street and the lower grades is that the families live for the present. In the white street and the higher grades, the people are prepared to sacrifice the immediate pleasure for more durable satisfactions. It is in this general setting that the following more detailed aspects of their lives have their context.

As it happened, no delinquent, adult or juvenile, was met with during this Research who was a member of a high grade household. As has been said above, this obviously does not imply that it is considered that delinquents in Radby inevitably come from the low grade households· It does suggest, howover, that a considerable proportion of the juvenile offenders come from the low grades. This also holds good for the adult offenders who, it must be emphasised, were not committed for the more sophisticated types of crime, Indeed, these low grade households are unlikely to contain adults of sufficiently high intelligence to commit crimes which require special ability or an extensive knowledge of the world – large scale fraud for example. In any case the Research suggests that delinquency, as it occurs in a grade I or II family, or in a Dyke Street household, is likely to arise for different reasons from the delinquency which may occur in a Gladstone Road home or a grade IV or V household. The analysis of factors operating in the black street suggests that there is nothing extraordinary in the occurrence of delinquency in that street, Whereas delinquency occurring in the white street may well be considered as unusual since there are no factors, comparable to those in the black street, operating to

198   *Conclusions*

In the "black" street and grades	*In the "white" street and grades*
1 Family life does not revolve mainly around parents and their children, but includes relatives in older, younger, and contemporary generations. These may, or may not, be living in the family's own home: but they live sufficiently near to be constantly in and out of the family's own home. This means that a child is hourly at the mercy of the commands, moods and whims of people other than his own parents. He knows no final arbiter and is not clear as to how he should, or should not, behave. His confusion is increased by the fact that the adults of "neighbouring" prone families may have much the same authority over him as his actual relations.	Father, mother and children, and no one else, is the typical unit (e.g., for meals, outings, Sleeping in the house). The child has a consistent picture of how he is expected to behave.
2 Only the mother shows obvious concern for the child's welfare and behaviour and her concern may be spasmodic. The parents' personal relationships are often inharmonious and no attempt is made to hide this from the child. He accepts bitter words or even blows between adults as a normal occurrence. At times adults handle him roughly too. He learns, and indeed is expected, to "put No. 1 first".	Father and mother share the responsibility for the child's upbringing and have a common policy about it. Any disagreement between them is kept from the child. They try to treat him considerately, and expect him to be considerate in his turn.
3 Adults do not think of a child's needs as differing in kind from. those of a grown-up person. As far as possible the children's own wishes should be complied with ("I couldn't be mean with them: though really they only want you for what they can get out of you"). They do not think it necessary to train a child about the use of money. "I like to give my three (10, 7, 3) some money every day if I can. Eileen (7) often gets 2s. off her cousin too. She just spends it and wastes it of course". They do not give regular pocket money, nor expect a child to say how he wishes to spend any money given. Moreover, to abide by a single set of standards requires more consistent effort than these parents feel it is worth making. Intermittent effort is characteristic of their actions in other spheres. For example, if a neighbor happens to pop round while Mrs. X is nominally cleaning,	Parents believe that children as such require special treatment and definite training. They try to make this reasonably consistent. They are particularly insistent that the child shall be trained about money (e.g., "My boy earned 9s. delivering papers: but that was too much for him at 13 so I took so much, and also made him put so much in the Post Office for holidays".

Conclusions 199

4 Children are not taught to pay much attention to the police or to what they represent. The children do not get threatened with the police man. In reply to a remonstrance, "That's stealing", even a small child (7) rotorts, "Pooh: The bobby wouldn't come after me".

5 The children go to Sunday School, or not, as they choose. The parents regard youth organizations as just a way of passing the time, i.e., comparable to going to the pictures or having a game of football in the street. The children and adolescents have little use for the organizations. There is too much discipline, "I only like the nights (at the B.B.) when we do what wo like". The organisations are too superior socially, "They think they are it", or "They talk posh". In other words, the standards upheld by the organisations are associated with people different from themselves, and whom they have no wish to emulate.

6 No set code of sex behaviour appeared to be acknowledged. Broadly speaking, sex relationships develop out of convenience (husband goes off, so wife brings in another man); propinquity (e.g., incest: Mr. N. is thought to be both the grandfather and the father of one of the children in his home); immediate desire and, possibly, material reward to the woman. Disregard of the generally approved code, i.e., that which the white streets uphold, may partly arise from the fact that people live at such close quarters. Intimate relations are an extension of familiar experiences (e.g., boys and girls share a bedroom) and less of a phenomenon that demands thought and decision:

Children used to be taught to fear the police. This has stopped and they are encouraged to look on the policeman as one who will help them (e.g., If they got lost).

Parents like their children to go to Sunday School regularly, and think youth organizations a "good thing". In Radby practically all the latter are connected with a Church. Church standards of behaviour therefore (to which the parents themselves have mostly been accustomed whether they belong to a church now or not) are brought to the children's attention in their weekday as well as their Sunday life. Comment made independently by two of the teachers at a Senior Girls' School suggest the possible influence of this regular link with the Church. Both had noticed that those girls who come from Church or Chapel families do not consider the possibility of the kind of bad behaviour (stealing, sex play that is relatively common among their schoolfellows.

They appear to comply with the generally approved codes on sex behaviour as promulgated by the church and supported by the law. Whether irregular sex relationships take place or not, they are, at any rate ostensibly, disapproved of.

200 *Conclusions*

In the "black" street and grades	*In the "white" street and grades*

7 Physical force, as a method of dealing with personal problems, is accepted as correct behaviour (e.g., the small children are allowed to be very aggressive; boys (12 & 13) constantly hit girls; a woman is not ashamed to say that she has given another a black eye; a girl (14) thinks it quite in order for a boy to carry a knife provided he does it "with a good heart", i.e., as a protection if attacked). Thus, what they accept as normal and proper action may well bring them into conflict with the law.

Adults only use physical force as a last resort. The children are in disgrace at home if they come to blows too often. A mother feels vexed with herself if she so loses her temper that she slaps her child.

8 People are noticeably indifferent to the looks of their house and to the state of their possessions. Since goods and chattels are likely to be limited, and since the crowded houses make it difficult to put things away in cupboards, possessions are left lying about and are seized on and used by people other than their owner, This means that their untidy or broken condition is not necessarily a reflection on the owner himself. Children brought up in such homes may hardly distinguish between what they have a right to use and what the law says they must not. Even the adults may regard the distinction as less Important than do those who live in the "white" streets. Stealing tends only to be regarded as such if the monetary value of the article is considerable.

People are proud of the appearance of their house. They like to take good care of it whether they own it or not. They enjoy the garden which must be as cared for as the house, If the walls get shabby they must be repapered. A broken chair leg must be mended at once. Things are housed in appointed places (e.g., the children have a cupboard for their toys). People take particular care of their own tools, books, bicycles, etc. Since they look after their own possessions they are likely to accord similar respect to other people's belongings in general. "Thou shalt not steal", is a principle to which they attach importance. It is one of the recognized signs of their respectable status. Tiny children have to be taught not to steal: but once beyond the toddler stage "My children would never think of it - it really never enters their heads".

9 The pleasures of leisure are very dependent on gambling. A boy's
(8) game of cards with his father is improved even if they only play
for halfpennies: "and I once won 7s. off my father." A series of
House-Housey, which may win you "two quid for a tanner" is one
of the best parts of a night at the pub. The women's mystery coach
trip is not complete without its two, 6d. raffles. Even the little girls'
sewing class, rather than charge a subscription pays for its cottons
and gives the children a thrill, by making them pay 2d. each week
for a raffle ticket on this week's toy. The children of those homes
have never had a fixed amount of money each week, but have got
what they could by a variety of means: similarly the adults hope to
improve their finances, temporarily, by any methods they can come
across. They admire the man who can raise money by means other
than his ordinary work. He is patently a smart chap is he can "make
something on the side". at the job itself, Actual theft may come to
be regarded as just another legitimate means, parallel to gambling,
of getting something without having to pay for it by the grind of the
daily job.

People may have no scruples about gambling (though
some of the church families might question it) but
their normal pleasures do not necessarily involve
gambling in any form. If they do gamble, it is on a
small scale (e.g., at the races the colliery official who
put 2s. on a horse saw two of the workmen from his
pit put on £2 and £5 respectively).

10 The parents are very conscious of the bad old days and the hard life their own parents had. ("In service when I was 10 as a 'daily', and all for 2s. 6d. a week": or "My mother had to wash all our clothes of a Saturday night and we had to put on bits and bobs till they were dry")· They are determined to make up to the children for what they themselves suffered. Today's children are to have plenty of "things" – money, toys, etc. Parents, however, do not include a more comfortable home or a better education as matters which, in their own way, would compensate for past ills. To lot their children do just as they like ("If I refuse 'em it upsets me") reflects the parents' attempt at compensation, and excuses "bad" behaviour. It is also in line with their general preference for the immediate satisfaction. Some kinds of behaviour, justified in the parents' eye on the above grounds, night well be classed as delinquent by the larger society.

Adults are not unmindful of the old days of poverty and unemployment. For example, Mr. S. has never forgotten the phrase the deputy was accustomed to use when calling out the names of the miners who were to go on short time – "These are the men of no consequence". The adults recall the low material level of their parents' days, or of their own early married life. "I was hard put to for 2d. when my children were small". But they are proud of the way in which they, or more particularly, their parents coped with such difficulties "Mine was a poor home, but our Mother never left the children alone in the house" or, "As a lad I got 8s. a week and I was courting on it too". They want their children to have "just a little bit more than we had" and extend this to such things as education, travel, holidays, etc. (i.e., to more than passing pleasures). Furthermore the wish that their children shall have a better, happier, life does not blind them to the inadvisability of always letting the children do just as they want.

Conclusions 203

encourage delinquency, and many operating in a positive way to prevent its occurrence.

This suggests that measures designed to prevent the occurrence of delinquency should be closely related to the particular factors which give rise to any particular type of delinquency, To consider the question of theft for example. In Radby there may be distinguished:

a those who just could not consider stealing. It is "just not done", "wicked", "disgraceful", and so on,
b those who weigh up the pros and cons, consider the practical risks and abstain because of the probable consequences if they are "caught out",
c those who consider the practicability of a theft and take the risk, perhaps having insured themselves to some extent by devising a "crafty" scheme to assist them in their plans.
d those who steal on a particular occasion because it is the easiest way out of a difficulty or the quickest way of obtaining an immediate bit of pleasure.
e those for whom theft does not constitute a problem – they "see nothing wrong with it", It is a legitimate social activity, unassociated with any feeling of guilt.

No single type of treatment is likely to be effective with all these five types of person.

The Introduction (Section I) pointed out that some investigations have made the case for more attention to be paid to the sociological aspects of delinquency, The findings of the Radby study support this view, To refer again to the small Dyke Street community, The codes which Dyke Street upholds display characteristics which may be considered as worth while, viz., their extensive and continual system of mutual help, their easy flowing channels of communication, and their loyal attachment to their street, At the same time certain of these Dyke Street (or Grade I or II) codes are such that they contribute to delinquent behaviour, The codes of the white street (or of the Grade IV or V families), since they are, roughly, those which are officially approved by English society, do not breed young breakers of the law. Any attempt to reduce delinquency in general, must, to start with, concern itself with the relative bases from which these differing codes derive, It must assess what factors cause the differences between the two communities (or two types of family) to develop, and analyses how these factors operate. Finally, it must suggest how these factors can be

204 *Conclusions*

so changed that the present divergence, and the conflict between the two ways of living that the divergence produces, may no longer persist.

Clifford Shaw has stressed that "from the data available it appears that local variations in the conduct of children, as revealed in differential rates of delinquency, reflect the differences in social values, norms, and attitudes to which the children are exposed.[1] He concludes that methods designed to prevent delinquency must concern themselves with the social aspects of the problem, and not merely with the individual offenders. As a result of this analysis, supported not only by Shaw's research into delinquency in large U.S. cities but also by similar research by others, the Chicago Area Project was inaugurated in 1934. The Project was organized to "utilize the latent leadership in areas of high rates of delinquency in an effort to deal with the problem of delinquency. It was the hope of the Project that it might develop a more effective prevention and treatment method in the economically poor, physically deteriorated areas through the organized efforts of the residents themselves.[2] The project, of which Shaw was the Director, is based upon three propositions.[3] They are,

1 that the problem of delinquency in low income areas is a product of the social experiences to which children and young people are exposed,
2 that effective treatment and prevention can be achieved only in so far as constructive changes in the community life can be brought about, and
3 that in any such enterprise which is likely to be effective in bringing about these changes it is indispensable that the local residents, individually and collectively, accept the fullest possible responsibility for defining objectives, formulating policies, providing financial support, and exercising the necessary controls over budgets, personnel and programs.

These propositions, it must be emphasised, arise out of research into large U.S. cities, who are the Radby research not only was based on a small town, but concentrated upon small well defined areas within

---

1 Juvenile Delinquency and Urban Areas, C. Shaw and H. McKay, University of Chicago Press, 1942, Part V. Ch. 20.
2 Annual Report Chicago Area Project and Sociology Department, Institute for Juvenile Research, 1950–51.
3 Methods, Accomplishments and Problems of the Chicago Area Project. A Report to the Board of Directors by C. Shaw. Revised 1944.

Conclusions 205

this town. We may nevertheless consider the three propositions with reference to the Radby research.

With regard to the first proposition, it has boon shown that juvenile delinquency in the black areas of Radby tends to rise out of the social experiences to which children are subjected. There is similar agreement with the second proposition, for it seems apparent that effective treatment and prevention of delinquency in Dyke Street and in the low grade households is only likely to occur if there are large scale changes in the way of life of these people, in their accepted standards of conduct and norms of behaviour. With regard to the third proposition, there can be little doubt as to its validity, but its practicability is more open to question. Shaw has stated that the results of the C.A.P. may be regarded with some satisfaction, and presumably therefore the third proposition must be accorded a measure of practicability. However, an important point in this connection is that the Areas in which the Project operate have large populations, the West Side Community Committee being concerned with a population of 24,000, for example. The practicability of the third proposition is here being questioned in relation to a small township and to particular 'black' areas of that township. Firstly it may be said that were a large proportion of the people of the town (23,000) to be inspired with a positive aim to define objectives and formulate policies, and a willingness to accept responsibility for ensuring that the delinquent conduct of the 'black' areas would be eliminated, it seems improbable that their efforts would meet with success, since they would merely be promulgating those modes of behavior which the black areas find antipathetic. And in any case, it is unlikely that the 'white' population would be so inspired, because missionary zeal does not go with the desire "not to mix" and to "lead private lives". Having said this, we may consider whether the propositions as applied to the large areas in Chicago are applicable to a small area such as Dyke Street. Is it likely – or even a possibility – that the local citizens of such an area would assume positions of responsibility and aim at transforming that area into a community upholding those standards which the law of the land seeks to maintain?

The potentiality of the 'black' areas for collective action within certain limits is undoubted. There is a loyalty to the street, and the street Coronation celebrations in Dyke Street were an outward sign of the ability of its people to organize activities which they consider worthwhile and to their material advantage. There is a common sentiment amongst the people of Dyke Street which is remarked upon by other people in the town. They are recognized as a community, differing from other streets in the town, and regarded as a unit. Furthermore,

206 *Conclusions*

the popularity of "neighboring" consolidates this potentiality for collective action. The people live on top of each other anyway, and are in constant contact with each other. But it would be very difficult, if not impossible, to persuade the citizens of Dyke Street that they have a collective duty to restrain each other from delinquent behavior. Their whole life is tied up with such behavior in many ways, as has been shown.

The man returning to Dyke Street from goal and the boy from Approved School are not the subjects of ostracism. Our research suggests that they will be welcomed back, or at any rate just received back as if nothing untoward had happened. And they will recommence life as they left it off, in the moral climate in which they live, which presents a very different code from that by which they were convicted of an offence. How then may we expect the "local residents, individually and collectivity" to "define objectives" in keeping with those of the larger society and opposed to those of their immediate society? The Dyke Street code of conduct, and that of the lower grades, does not represent just an obstinate refusal to accept the laws of the larger society. Such factors as the following play a greater or lesser part in formulating and reinforcing the "black" code, factors which, it may be thought, are not without cogency. The people see no reason for accepting the principle that "thou shalt not steal" whether it be because they are informed that God said so or because the law of the land says so. If the delinquents and quasi-delinquents see no reason for <u>not</u> pursuing the course which they pursue, recognize no moral or practical reason for accepting the standards upheld by the law of the land, "see nothing wrong with theft", and so on, then it is of no avail to search for Dyke Street citizens who will change all this. Especially when the people themselves consider that there is abundant justification for them to lead the sort of life which they do lead, as will be suggested below.

In considering the ways in which to prevent delinquency from occurring in such an environment as Dyke Street, therefore, it is necessary to take into account the terms of Dyke Street thought. It is of little use talking to these people, for example, as if the family is the basis of society on which good social behavior is founded, when some of them do not accept the family in the sense of "father : mother : children" as providing the basis of their lives, and when they see all about them that the family as such has not the importance which it is stated to have, being in same cases only a loosely knit and transitory alliance of people who happen to sleep under the same roof for a longer or shorter time. Furthermore, they tend to base their behavior upon practical tests - does it work? - rather than upon divine pronouncement or legal

Conclusions 207

decree. And the practical test of leading an "honest" and "conventional" life does not scam to work out as it should: how about the boss working a fiddle? Is not the boss accorded status by society, and yet is not the only difference between you and he that "you steal in farthings and he steals in pounds?" Were you not constantly confronted in your Army days with men who were "in the know" about disposing of blankets to the public "on the side". The press and the radio draw attention to those status-accorded personages whose example one is supposed to follow: and draws particular attention to certain of these personages who contravene the law. Those whom one is "supposed to live up to", in fact, involve many people who do those things which the Dyke Street men and women are supposed not to do.[1] Thus there is the unending flow through the Sunday newspapers of vicars and choirboys, solicitors and frauds, majors and "drunk and disorderly" charges. Then there are the £10,000 pleasure cruises and the parties on which more is spent in one evening than you can earn in your whole working life. Such reasoning as this may be dismissed as naive: it must be remembered that the intelligence of these people is not high. But it is thought that such factors are of greater significance to them, and not, it may be thought, without some justification. They recognise inconsistencies in the world around them - the large gap between their income and that of the "nobs", a gap which is felt not to be correlated with individual effort or ability (whether or not it is in practice).

The belief derived from such facts as these linked perhaps, with previous experiences of unemployment and low incomes, is widely held. Namely, that "there is no justice in this world". Why then, abide by the laws when life is weighted against you, and when reward is not related to merit? "To hell with it all" is frequently a way of dealing with the situation - "let's have another pint". They will never have a gold plated car and will never see the south of France from a yacht - but they will have as good a time as they can with what they have got. And, since these things are not for them, what's the use of trying? Why save for the future, for there is nothing to look forward to then: they won't be millionaires and the kingdom of heaven does not suggest any immediate amelioration of their conditions.

It is of no use superimposing new agencies onto the black community - to that extent there is agreement with Shaw's third proposition. To reduce the tendency to delinquent conduct in Dyke Street, and in the lower grade households, it is necessary to substitute a scheme of values

---

1 cf. E.H. Sutherland : White Collar Criminality. Am. Soc. Review. V. 1940.

208 *Conclusions*

or a code of action which is demonstrably more efficacious than that which at present satisfies the low grade community. The maintenance of the law and order of the land must demonstrably appear as worthwhile. It would seem logical that the bases from which the 'black' code of conduct derives - the system of values and the interactions of people subscribing to it with each other and with the society as a whole, require investigation. But this is not sufficient, for it is necessary to discover also in what ways, if at all, factors present in the larger society contribute to the development of the smaller aberrant community. Shaw himself has posed the question:[1] "What are the forces which give rise to these significant differences in the organized values in different communities? Under what conditions do the conventional forces in the community become so weakened as to tolerate the development of a conflicting system of criminal values? Under what conditions is the conventional community capable of maintaining its integrity and exercising such control over the lives of its members as to check the development of the competing system? Shaw points out that any discussion of this problem is necessarily tentative.

The significant point is that the factors contributing to the development of the conflicting systems require analysis, in order to see how they operate and in what ways they may be amended. In this connection it is of interest to consider the work of R·K. Morton, in particular his essay on <u>Social Structure and Anomie.</u>[2] Morton States[3] that "the great concern of functional sociologists and anthropologists with problems of "social order" and with the "maintenance" of social systems has generally focused their scientific attention on the study of processes whereby a given social system is preserved largely intact. In general, they have not devoted much attention to the processes utilizable for determinate basic changes in social structure". Whereas the need, if the above and the following analysis is accepted, is for attention to be paid to the problem of whether or not there are factors present within a given social structure which themselves require change in order that the society may exist in relative harmony. "We have still much to learn about these processes through which social structures generate the circumstances in which infringement of social codes constitutes a 'normal' (that is to say, an expectable) response". Merton's primary aim is to discover "<u>how some social structures exert</u>

---

1 Delinquency and Urban Areas, Part V, Ch. 20
2 <u>Social Theory and Social Structure</u>, 1949, The Free Press, Second Printing, Oct. 1951, Ch. IV.
3 Introduction to Part II, p.116

Conclusions 209

a definite pressure upon certain persons in the society to engage in nonconformist rather than conformist conduct". His main hypothesis is that "aberrant behavior may be regarded sociologically as a sympton of dissociation between culturally proscribed aspirations and socially structured avenues for realizing those aspirations". As a result of the aspirations receiving undue emphasis within a given society, the society "becomes unstable, and there develops what Durkheim called 'anomie' (or normlessness)".

It is to this phenomenon of "anomie" that deviant behavior may be attributed. This is an example of the sort of way in which differing codes of conduct may develop within a society, and an indication that deviant behavior is to be attributed to a failure of the social structures as such to operate effectively rather than to an endemic failure of a small section of the society.

Merton develops his theme around contemporary American culture which "appears to approximate the polar type in which great emphasis upon certain success goals occurs without equivalent emphasis upon institutional means". It is not suggested here that Merton's analysis is unquestionably correct, nor is it suggested that his analysis relating to American society is applicable to contemporary English society, It is mentioned here mainly in order to indicate the sort of ways in which the codes and aspirations of the larger society may load to the development of codes in opposition to that society, and yet contained within it. The reader of Merton's essay may note, however, some parallels in his description of the various modes of adaption with some features, described above, of the "black" and "white" people. The mode of innovation, for example, contains some who "apply the doctrine of luck to the gulf between merit, effort and reward": there is an "orientation toward chance and risk-taking, accentuated by the strain of frustrated aspirations", that "may help explain the marked interest in gambling an institutionally proscribed or at best permissive rather than preferred or prescribed mode of activity - within certain social strata". There are others who "develop an individuated and cynical attitude toward the social structure, best exemplified in the cultural cliche that 'it's not what you know, but whom you know, that counts'". There are some similarities also between the people in the 'mode of Ritualism' and those of the 'white' grades. The "ritualistic type of adaptation can be readily identified. It involves the abandoning or scaling down of the lofty cultural goals of great pecuniary success and rapid social mobility to the point where one's aspirations can be satisfied. But though one rejects the cultural obligation to attempt 'to get ahead in the world', though one draws in one's horizons, one continues to abide almost

210   *Conclusions*

compulsively by institutional norms". There are <u>some</u> grounds for suggesting that the white grades in the Radby research, whilst exhibiting the desire to conform, yet do not appear to know for what particular reasons they wish to do so - they have no particular knowledge of any supposed advantage to their <u>society</u> as differentiated from themselves which might be thought likely to accrue by conforming. It is rather a question - at least to some extent - of (to quote from Merton's "series of cultural cliches") "I'm not sticking <u>my</u> neck out"; "I'm playing safe"; "Don't aim high and you won't be disappointed". And success to those who do aim at "getting on" is measured by material standards - getting a "better" job, etc., vicarious satisfaction being gained through their children's success.

To return to the general theme of societies generating within themselves codes of conduct opposed to those which the society ostensibly seeks to maintain, we may quote from Merton's remarks on "the strain towards anomie". He writes:

"The social structure we have examined produces a strain toward anomie and deviant behaviour. The pressure of such a social order is upon outdoing one's competitors. So long as the sentiments supporting this competitive system are distributed throughout the entire range of activities and are not confined to the final result of 'success', the choice of means will remain largely within the ambit of institutional control. When, however, the cultural emphasis shifts from the satisfactions deriving from competition itself to almost exclusive concern with the outcome, the resultant stress makes for the breakdown of the regulatory structure. With this attenuation of institutional controls, there occurs an approximation to the situation erroneously held by the utilitarian philosophers to be typical of society, a situation in which calculations of personal advantage and fear of punishment are the only regulating agencies".

Merton's analysis has been briefly outlined but it is thought that sufficient has been said to indicate the desirability of at any rate considering whether some such analysis could be applied to English society - to discover whether the Dyke Street delinquents owe their existence to any extent to a dichotomy between culturally designated aspirations and "structurally prescribed avenues". With regard to the general problem posed by Merton, his main hypothesis that "aberrant behaviour may be regarded sociologically as a symptom of dissociation between culturally prescribed aspirations and socially structured avenues for realising these aspirations", it would be of interest to consider the situation in a society which is alleged to prescribe aspirations, and to provide socially structured avenues, in contrast with those obtaining in the

Conclusions 211

United States. Unfortunately the material available on a society such as that of the Soviet Union is remarkable both for its paucity and its unreliability. Nevertheless it is worthwhile to consider in this context a discussion of Chinese Prisons by Professor W.J.H. Sprott.[1]

During the summer of 1952, Professor Sprott visited the Municipal Prison of Peking, The prison population was a little over 1, 000, of whom "some 70 per cent were in for political offences and the read for criminal offences, such as assault, keeping a brothel and theft", Two features of the prison life which stood out were the factories in which prisoners worked, and the system of discussion groups consisting of ten prisoners seated in a circular arrangement on mats. These features derive from the theory that "the origins of crime are two-fold: (1) inadequate working habits, and (2) the evil influence of the pre-liberation regime". The criminal must therefore be taught to work hard, but also to "realise what were the social factors responsible for his wicked ways. He must also learn to practise the five moral virtues: love of country; love of his fellow man; love of work; love of science; and respect for public property". The purpose of the discussion groups is that "the prisoner(s) must get a new moral outlook"... "Sometimes a text from one of Chairman Mao's works may be discussed, and they see how they measure up to the high ideals it expresses, Sometimes the discussion takes the form of criticism and self-criticism, an attempt to get to the bottom of their own and other's wrong-doing. In addition, there are cultural and political lectures of a rather more formal kind".

To understand this properly, it is necessary to consider "similar features of Chinese life", The impression gained from the visit to China was that "enormous numbers of people are experiencing a wave of moral enthusiasm. Every one I met seemed to be concerned with the part he was playing in the new society". The enthusiasm is revealed in many ways, but perhaps the most graphic example is that provided by the "neighbourhood" units:

"Peking – and Shanghai for that matter, and doubtless all other cities – is divided into administrative areas, like any other city. But each of these areas is sub-divided into relativity small units of about 1, 500 families living in about 16 alley ways.... In these small areas there are committees which deal with such problems as health, the comfort of army dependents, education, housing and the welfare of women. These committees are elected by still smaller groups, until one gets down to

---

1 The Howard Journal, Vol. VIII - No. 4, 1953 p· 267, Chinese Prisons, by W.J.H. Sport.

212   Conclusions

a quite small neighbourhood unit. These units meet and instruct their representatives to the various committees, and receive information and recommendations from him or her. Just as in factory meetings new ideas for speeding up production are discussed and passed on, so in the neighbourhood new ideas for - it may be - cleanliness are discussed... One can imagine the enormous force of social pressure that is generated by such a structure. No one goes unobserved. Everyone's deviance is brought to the notice, not merely of his next-door neighbour, but of a <u>group</u> whose goodwill he wants to ensure". As a result it is only those who are so bent on criminal activity that their neighbourhood cannot control or reform them who are sent to prison, and "with such a pressure of public opinion outside the prison it is quite on the cards that the number who have to be put inside will be kept comparatively small" in the future, assuming "the number of political prisoners to decline considerably in the course of time". Already it is stated that there is very little juvenile delinquency: children who commit minor crimes are "dealt with by the neighbourhood units, and if possible by the youth groups of their own age". There are only a few cases of persistent offenders. Professor Sprott considers that "this connection between the disciplinary techniques in prison and those in the outside world is... reinforced by the method of appointing judges and by the procedure before and after trial". The "problems of ordinary men and women" are resolved by a method something akin to what Max Weber calls "Kadijustiz" - that is to say that "each case has to be dealt with on its own merits". Professor Sprott concludes his article with the following analysis :

"Whether these methods of re-education are successful we shall not know for some time. It is, however, a remarkable experiment. Groups are being used for the twin purposes of inducing mutual commitment to do better and using mutual analysis to find out what went wrong. It is, in fact, a kind of group therapy. Great pains were taken by our informant to make clear exactly what 'criticism' means. The English-speaking Chinese were worried lest we should think that it was hostile. Perhaps, they said, you will misunderstand the nature and purpose of the process. All criticism of others must start with self-criticism and though you must show no mercy to yourself, you must approach others in a kindly and helpful spirit, otherwise the whole thing fails. They are, of course, helped enormously by having the previous regime as a scapegoat. We have gone wrong, they can say, because of the evil influence of the past - the age of 'feudalism' as they somewhat unfortunately call it. All social vice is 'feudal'; social virtues can only flourish under 'liberation'. This means that the edge of guilt

Conclusions 213

can be taken off - it is not all my fault. Doubtless this collective shifting of responsibility for past wickedness from the individual onto the social order from which he has been liberated, may make self- examination more meaningful and less painful. It may also make it easier for him to join with others to ensure the perpetuation and welfare of a less crimino-genic regime. However that may be, the Chinese assured me that prison is a last resource in criminal cases, and that only if a man cannot be dealt with by his neighbours should he go there. Furthermore, when he is there, it is for re-education and not for punishment."

The account by Professor Sprott has been quoted at length of necessity: for it describes a situation unfamiliar to the Western World, and constitutes, indeed, "a remarkable experiment". It is not possible to trace here many of the points which occur in relation to the problem of delinquency, but one or two points do seem of special relevance. The force of public opinion in consciously regulating the individual's behavior in accordance with the accepted law of the land is a force which does not operate to anything like the same extent in English society, or apparently in that of the U.S.A. The significant fact is that this force is based upon a knowledge of the fundamentals governing the life of the society, and an acceptance by the people of them. By means of discussions, self-criticism and criticism of others, the people are made aware of why a particular code of behaviour is preferable, why particular standards are worth upholding. The emphasis upon the "neighbourhood" unit in the daily life of each citizen facilitates this system of conduct based upon understanding of and support for the society as a whole. Man is recognised as an integral part of a group, not just an individual to compete with others. Nor do the groups compete with each other for the spoils of society: they are complementary to each other, and the reason for their existence is that the society may better function for the benefit of all. The contradiction between the individual's desires and those of his society are eliminated, and this factor is made plain to offenders by the demonstrably sympathetic treatment which they receive not only from their neighbourhood unit, but also from the administration of justice by the larger society through the medium of what approximates to Weber's "Kadijustiz". An offender may thus learn that "there is justice in the world" and may also learn to appreciate why it is better for himself and for the society that he should abide by the code which is not only generally accepted but is indeed actively supported. To revert to Merton's phraseology, there would seem to be in China an approximation to an everyday association between "culturally prescribed aspirations and socially structured avenues for realising these aspirations", so that everyone is capable of attaining

214 Conclusions

the status to which he is encouraged to aspire. If we want to amend the factors which cause different sets of values to arise within the same community, and in opposition to each other, so that conflict no longer presents itself, the sociologist might well examine the present Chinese society. It must be emphasised that the purpose here is not to hoist the Red Flag, but to indicate that if delinquency derives in part from maladjusted social structures the research worker must concern himself with various types of social structures in order to discover what are the significant factors in bringing about these maladjustments. Delinquency may then be found to be but one aspect (or index) of the problem of conflicts between groups, a problem to which it is the task of the sociologist to address himself.

Appendices

A Children's Painting and Writing

B Interviewer's Schedule

C Map of Radby

Appendix A
Children's Painting And Writing

Play Room Paintings

A hundred and three of the paintings, the work of 26 of the children aged 5 to 13 were examined by a psychiatrist. His comment was as follows :

"It should be made perfectly clear that my comments are based on a study of the paintings 'in vacuo'. I can suggest only some general and probable trends. In the circumstances no more specific diagnostic assessment was possible or intended.

The most striking feature is the general immaturity of emotional pattern shown by these drawings. Almost without exception, the drawings suggest an emotional age much below the actual age. One or two suggest a good deal of deep-seated emotional disturbance but, of course, such a diagnosis could not be made on single, unobserved drawings."

Play Room Writings

The writers were all volunteers. Most of their writing was done in connection with pictures, e.g., the child was given a picture (an advertisement, an illustration cut from a magazine, a T.A.T. card) and asked "Who are these people; what are they doing; what are they thinking about?" Extracts from their writings read as follows :-

Quarrels

Girl (13)

"Joan and Jim have just got engade and they are going to the flicks to selabrate Jim thinks he is a very lucky man but Joan thinks he is to good for her ... Wone night as they are going out Joan is in a bad mood and won't talk to Jim ... and Jim gets knoct over and has to be taken

Children's Painting And Writing   217

to hospital ... and Jim said I'm glad I got knoct over because now are row is over Darling".

Boy (8?)

"The man is made to the woman because she did not get his dinner ready and he is going to leave her and she is goig to repurt him and she will be on her own..."

Girl (?)

"This is Mr. and Mrs. Porter and she dropet some think on him and he was mad so he slaped his wife and she started to qerler with him and he got so mad that he pack his things and she begged him to stay ... and she coforted him and she said wood you like a cup of tea".

"... and the woman has run away becase they had a qohoc ... she desides to back to her husband" .

Boy (?)

"the woman is cring becac ure boy friend as fold out with ure and she is (shuting the door?).

Girl (13)

"Her husband his very mad and he his throwing everything about And along besace she has a nother husband.... one day she met her husband and she was a mazde to see him ... and they came back to eche other".

Love

Girl (11)

"It is a girl by herself she is crying because her husband as left her ... she is thinking of her husband and how she love him and how she kiss".

Boy (10)

"The monkey is hugging a doll and is thinking to take the doll for his wife ... the doll is thinking about meeting him again and to kiss him when the keeper is not there".

218   *Children's Painting And Writing*

Love (continued)

Girl (12)

"the thing that has frighted the lady is that she has seen a man ... and he kepted on winkig at her and she told her husband and her husband did not like it at all. And he felt like having a fiet with him".

Girl (10)

"... She has been quarraling about getting married."

Girl (13)

"John is saying to himself 'I am glad I am getting engaged ... They have been to see a romantic film and think how romantic it would be for them to go out they went out before the picture had finished ... they are likely rubbing their cheeks together thinking how romantic it would be if they had been on the back row. She is thinking of everything they are going to do after the marriage."

Girl (11)

"They are ladys they are sitting down eating chocolate. They might be thinking of men. They are going to be married ..."

Crime

Boy (10)

"That man was a crook and he had kill a wowan and he got away before the police man came."

"One nigth there was two men names George and Jack. There was a kill and they went to a house and in the home was to twin names Mary and Brenda. One of the men has a gun in his pockey and the other man is getting a gun out to shot there mother and father ... and the policeman hear the shot ... and they were put in Jaie."

Boy (10)

"... he was thinking of doing away with his wife because she was telling him off... so he didn't wait any longer... gaged her and shot her ... he buried her in the cellar."

Girl (?)

" to men called John and Harry they crept upstairs in to Jenny's room and they was just going into her draws... the police come and took them to jail for 15 months ..."

Boy (10)

"... the man was a killer and that night the man went to his siser and kill her for telling the police and he got her money all the money was gone from the safe..."

Boy (11)

"Is nam is friotuc (? Friar Tuck) And he is tide up in straps they cacht him pinching som clos and a bank ..."

Girl (10)

"This is Mrs. Smith, She has a daughter Esther and the girl has been naughty and her mother was so cross she did not know what to do with her. And at once she decided to strangle her. When her husband came in ... and heard that she was to strangle her he went straight into the girl's bedroom and he saw that she had gone ... he found her lying dead about sixty feet from her home. And her mother and father had a new baby and she done the same. And her mother went for trial and was found guilty. And her father got married again."

Appendix B
Interviewing Schedule

Household _____ Date _____

Adult( )   Child( )

House. Whole or shared ___ No. of room ____ Garden ____ Rent ___

Length of residence

Previous Home	Mr.		Mrs.	
Where born				
Nearest relatives				
Other relatives				
Education				
Membership of		x		x
societies, churches, pubs. x = how often				
Other Interests				

Children's membership of societies   Other interests

	X	
a.		
b.		
c.		
d.		
e.		
f.		
g.		
h.		
Mr.	Mrs.	

222   *Interviewr's Schedule*

INTERVIEWING SCHEDULE (PAGE 2)

G.F. _____ G.M. _____ G.F. _____ G.M. _____

( ) Husband _____ Wife ( ) _____

Name ( ) _____

School _____

Job _____

Other children living elsewhere _____

Other people living in household _____

Interviewr's Schedule 223

INTERVIEWING SCHEDULE (CONTINUED)

The original schedule included spaces for notes under the following headings : -

1 Physical character.

2 Personal Relations

    (a) with other members

    (b) with neighbours.

3 Attitude to street and town.

4 Leisure (place: equipment: interest shown by adults).

5 Societies.

6 Earning and Spending.

7 Relationship between the Sexes.

8 Attitude to Delinquency.

9 General.

Appendix C
Map of Radby

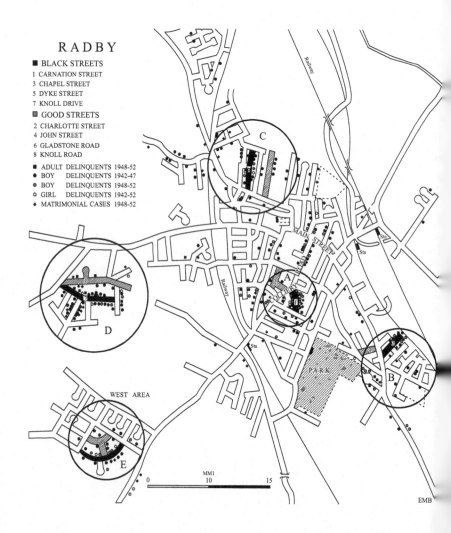